SLOW FOOD REVOLUTION

SLOW FOOD REVOLUTION

A New Culture for Eating and Living

CARLO PETRINI

IN CONVERSATION WITH
GIGI PADOVANI

TRANSLATED BY FRANCESCA SANTOVETTI

RIZZOLI
NEW YORK

Rizzoli New York

FIRST PUBLISHED IN THE UNITED STATES OF AMERICA IN 2006
BY RIZZOLI INTERNATIONAL PUBLICATIONS, INC.
300 PARK AVENUE SOUTH
NEW YORK, NY 10010
WWW.RIZZOLIUSA.COM

ORIGINALLY PUBLISHED IN ITALIAN IN 2005 AS *SLOW FOOD REVOLUTION* BY
RCS LIBRI S.P.A.

© 2005 RCS LIBRI S.P.A., MILANO

2006 2007 2008 2009 / 10 9 8 7 6 5 4 3 2 1

PRINTED IN THE UNITED STATES OF AMERICA

PRINTED ON RECYCLED PAPER WITH SOY-BASED INKS

ISBN-10: 0-8478-2873-5
ISBN-13: 978-0-8478-2873-9

LIBRARY OF CONGRESS CATALOG CONTROL NUMBER: 2006930215

To Bartolo Mascarello and Giovanni Ravinale.
And to the 4,888 farmers, fishermen, breeders, and nomads of the
Terra Madre Food Communities.

CONTENTS

CHAPTER 1	*Beginnings: 1982–1986*	1
CHAPTER 2	*The Roots: 1949–1982*	23
CHAPTER 3	*The Idea: 1986–1989*	45
CHAPTER 4	*The Sowing: 1990–1996*	77
CHAPTER 5	*The Harvest: 1997–2003*	95
CHAPTER 6	*A Snail in the World*	135
CHAPTER 7	*The University of Gastronomic Sciences*	147
CHAPTER 8	*Terra Madre*	163
CHAPTER 9	*The Future of Food*	175

APPENDIX
Twenty Stories of Presidia and Food Communities 185
Index of the Presidia
    Italian Presidia 217
    International Presidia 267
United States Ark of Taste 292
How to Contact Slow Food 295
Chronology of the Movement 297
Glossary 301
Selected Bibliography 307
Acknowledgments 311

chapter 1

BEGINNINGS: 1982–1986

THE INEDIBLE *RIBOLLITA* OF MONTALCINO
The setting is Palazzo Pieri-Nerli, an imposing fourteenth-century stone building overlooking the streets of Montalcino, a small town perched in the Tuscan hills. Behind the palazzo's heavy wooden door, the rooms are enveloped with the aroma of thrushes roasting on coals. Outside, hordes of people are carousing through the narrow, cobblestoned streets of this village, home to one of the best-known Italian wines in the world, Brunello di Montalcino. In the distance, you can hear a man singing.

His words come straight out of the *Trescone*, an ancient Tuscan song that has been associated with the Sagra del Tordo, the Festival of the Thrush. The festival's contemporary version was launched in 1957 by the inhabitants of Montalcino as a way of attracting tourists. Held on the last Sunday in October, it is a peasant feast celebrating the end of the grape harvest. Festivals like this are an Italian tradition, and it's often a good opportunity to sit down at a table and enjoy a communal meal. In Montalcino, the local delicacy is the thrush, a small bird whose migratory route passes through this area of Tuscany. After a pageantlike archery tournament held among the town's four neighborhoods, everyone's attention turns to the thrushes roasting in the coals—and the next bottle of Brunello.

The story of Slow Food and its "cultural revolution" begins here, in Montalcino, just a few miles from the cities of Siena and Florence, birthplace of the Renaissance. Fifteen travelers, among them a youngish man named Carlo Petrini, future founder of the Slow Food movement, have just stepped into the commotion of the Festival of the Thrush after a six-hour bus ride that began far to the north, in the early morning fog enveloping the town of Bra in the region of Piedmont. But we are getting ahead of ourselves.

It is October 31, 1982, and the mood in Italy is one of lethargy. The yuppie era of the Thatcher and Reagan administrations is still to come, and the country is going through a major economic crisis with inflation at about 16 percent and deficits that are running out of control. But the recent soccer World Championship has galvanized people: Italy has won the World Cup in Spain, with a goal by the legendary Paolo Rossi. After thirty-eight long years of rule by the Christian Democrats (the party affiliated with the Catholic Church), two so-called laymen—that is, non-Christian Democrats—now hold the most prestigious political posts in the country. The president is Sandro Pertini, a Socialist affectionately known as the "father of the Republic" who will go on to become one of the most beloved presidents ever to occupy the Quirinale Palace. The prime minister is Giovanni Spadolini, an intellectual of Italy's Republican Party who has been drawn into politics. The Left, strongly linked to the unions, is officially represented by the most powerful Communist party of the Western world, the Partito comunista italiano, or PCI.

But the PCI is on the defensive: with only a third of the electoral votes, it has little chance of coming to power. The revolution announced by the student movements of the late 1960s never took place; it ended instead in disillusionment, particularly for the youth of 1968. Theirs is a generation caught between utopia and tragedy, as acts of terrorism in the name of "red" ideals have turned increasingly brutal. From Turin to Rome, the kidnappings and criminal attacks have caused some to dub these the "years of lead" in reference to all the bullets spent during this period. It is almost impossible to imagine the immense political shift that will be ushered in at the end of the decade by the fall of the Berlin Wall.

By 1982, politics have already begun to move to the right, and many on the left have abandoned activism for other goals. Some have left politics entirely. Others have focused on environmentalism. And one small group has made a seemingly innocent discovery: food and wine. They explore their local wine cellars, get to know small wine producers, and end up preaching—with an almost political zeal—the cause of conviviality and its pleasures.

*

This is the group—all of them now in their thirties—that arrives today in Montalcino. Their little bus has brought them on a 500-kilometer journey down from the north, through the snarled traffic of Florence, up a road twisting through vineyards and olive groves, and into the steep streets of Montalcino. The visitors are welcomed with dances and a parade, but that scene does not seem to particularly impress them. According to the schedule of the Festival of the Thrush, they are almost two hours late, and the organizers are expecting them in Palazzo Pieri-Nerli.

The dozen or so men are all members of the Associazione ricreativa culturale italiana, known as "Arci." Arci (pronounced "AR-chee") is a strong national association supported by the Socialist and Communist parties; its branches, the Case del Popolo, are scattered across Italy. Through these "houses of the people," Arci organizes a variety of cultural events such as fairs, debates, and soccer games. The Case del Popolo centers are especially popular in central Italy, in regions like Tuscany, Emilia-Romagna, and Umbria where the administrations are "red."

These Arci members have come from Bra to Montalcino with a mission: to learn how to improve the wine culture of their region. Bra is a town of 25,000, five times bigger than Montalcino. Located south of the Turin belt of industries and factories, it represents almost a hinge linking the plain of the city with the slopes of the Langhe region. Bra is a "white" city, populated mainly by Christian Democrats and moderate political forces; Montalcino, on the other hand, is a "red" city, run by Communists and Socialists.

The Bra delegates are most familiar with the vineyards of the Langhe, the gently rolling hills that produce the intense, high-quality red wines of Barolo and Barbaresco. Now they want to savor the famous Brunello di Montalcino. In 1980, Brunello and Barolo became the first wines to receive the state seal of approval in Italy, a testament to their high quality. On each bottle of Brunello and Barolo, one can now find a small band with the inscription "DOCG," for *Denominazione di Origine Controllata e Garantita* (a guarantee of origin like the French *Appellation d'Origine Controllée*, or AOC).

One man heads the group from Bra: although only thirty-three, he is balding and has a thick, unkempt beard. To borrow the words of Catalan writer Manuel Vásquez Montalbán in his *Millennio*, he is a "solid man with the ironic eyes of the traveler." He is tall, always tieless, and wears a shirt at odds with his pants. His name is Carlo Petrini, "Carlin" for short, and he has just founded the Libera e benemerita associazione degli amici del Barolo (Free and meritorious association of the friends of Barolo), linked to Arci Langhe in Bra.

The group is thoroughly immersed in the culture of 1968 — its independent magazines, radio stations, and cultural associations — and they have now come to Montalcino to enjoy life's pleasures: good wine and food. Champions of a new healthy and "democratic" lifestyle, they count among their fans some very well-known figures in Italian life: the singer-songwriter Francesco Guccini, the actor Roberto Benigni, the singer Ornella Vanoni, and the actor David Riondino.

On the bus with Petrini are his two "lieutenants," his merry companions in some twenty years of escapades. Together, they form a trio which has been performing for some time in inns and in singing competitions, in between epic feasts and drinking sprees. The members of the "Philoridiculous" group, as they like to be called, are Petrini, Azio Citi, a city clerk who has the gifts of a standup comic, and Giovanni Ravinale, a salesman, friend, and trusted adviser of Petrini for many years until Ravinale's untimely death in 1999. Possibly the most politicized of the Bra delegates is Silvio Barbero, a factory worker of about thirty who has recently been laid off and is living on his unemployment checks. Formerly a full-time union organizer, he now coordinates social activities for tourists.

Finally in Montalcino, they all head for a building in Via Ricasoli, with a sign on the door that says: "Casa del Popolo, Circolo Arci." They enter an austere courtyard with a well in the middle and an elegant loggia. Above the loggia, one catches a glimpse of a large meeting hall with a coffered ceiling, from which are suspended the heraldic banners of Montalcino's different neighborhoods.

Although the setting meets their expectations, the luncheon, served amid a Dantesque confusion, does not: poorly cooked thrushes, a *ribollita* that is best forgotten, red wine that is served too cold, and an inedible dessert. All the while a crowd of people on the grand staircase waits to be seated.

Both disillusioned and hungry, the guests from Bra leave in a rage, headed for the Chianti area. Back in Bra, and after much thought, they decide to do something about the Montalcino experience—they will send a letter to express their disappointment. On November 3, 1982, the letter, signed by Petrini, is sent to the executives of the Casa del Popolo in Montalcino, and to the administration of Arci Toscana.

Dear Comrades,

We are just back from an excursion in Chianti where we participated in the Festival of the Thrush in Montalcino on Sunday, October 31. We are writing this letter particularly to discuss the lunch we had at your club. We are of the firm opinion that the preparation and serving of food is a serious enterprise. To be sure, at political banquets one has to be prepared to suffer a stomachache in the service of one's beliefs and perhaps to maintain a balanced budget. One can even sympathize with a chef whose true qualification is his party loyalty. These political banquets aside, however, we think we have had enough with comrades who act as cooks or as waiters; or, if that is what they want to do, at least they should specialize in one job or the other, particularly if a salary is involved. We know nothing about the budget of the Circolo Arci of Montalcino, yet undoubtedly that hideous meal on Sunday earned you something. Of course, it's fine to turn a profit, but to do so with a spread worthy only of an army barrack or a fifties diner is unacceptable. To be presented with cold pasta, inedible *ribollita*, unwashed salad greens, a dessert made inedible because of the crowd pushing from everywhere for its turn; to have to push to get ourselves out of that incredible mess; and, finally, to have to read a sign asking the members of Arci to volunteer some work for one of the many Arci outings....

If we treated our members here like that we'd be publicly lynched, we'd be considered not comrades anymore, but rather filthy reactionaries, fascists; we'd be degraded and kicked out of the association. But whatever! Apparently, there is still room for very poor taste, taste that is really no better than the taste on display in those Catholic pilgrimage hotels, which at least have the virtue of offering clean rooms. We felt the urge to tell you this because we hope that you could improve the most beautiful Casa del Popolo in Italy, and the place that makes the most prestigious wine, and so that you could also give up acting like restaurateurs before someone will finally file a claim for damages.

Stale wheat bread, white beans, oil, green cabbage, black cabbage, chard, a potato, and a pinch of *pepolino* (thyme): these are the ingredients Pellegrino Artusi recommends in his seminal 1891 book *La scienza in cucina e l'arte di mangiar bene* (Science in the kitchen and the art of eating well) to prepare the *zuppa toscana di magro alla contadina,* also known as *ribollita.* Artusi's text is known to be the first book which codifies Italian bourgeois cooking. But on that Sunday, October 31, 1982, too much haste and far too many guests definitely ruined the *ribollita.*

The reply to Petrini's strong accusations was equally harsh. Andrea Rabissi, at that time president of the Montalcino Arci (he is now the head of the city traffic police), writes in his letter:

Dear Comrades of the Arci Langhe...,
First of all I would like to thank you for saying that our office is the "most beautiful Casa del Popolo in Italy," and our town "the place that makes the most prestigious wine."

Apart from that, I have to say that your letter contained only ugly and unfair accusations about our banquet.... On October 31, eleven different tours with 530 people visited our Circolo, and I can assure you that 515 guests (i.e. everybody but you) were enthusiastic about their experience here, and our hospitality, to say the least.... I am really surprised that the sender of these public accusations is a NATIONAL EXECUTIVE DIRECTOR OF ARCI, and I would like to point out to you that it's your mistake to demand so much for these luncheons. What did you want? Table settings with dozens of pieces of silverware, waiters in white uniforms and bow ties, and the rest? If this is your (or at least your president's) new way to conduct relations and win the support of the members, I am sure you are quite mistaken. So many things in a Circolo Arci are much more deserving of attention and take precedent over eating in a refined manner....

I could go on by telling you about the activities of our Circolo, but I believe that it would be much better to discuss it openly. To this end, I am thinking about organizing a debate here in Montalcino, to compare our perspectives and experiences.

Lenin himself once said that women cooks should be part of any government. Apparently, by the 1980s, the Italian Left had forgotten the

Russian leader's idea. Taste buds are neither conservative nor liberal, and, though it may be impossible to change the world, one should at least be able to change a menu. Unwilling to let this exchange of letters be the end of the affair, Petrini accepted Rabissi's challenge with a call to arms: "Comrades, enough with these sloppy grilled chops, with this undrinkable dishwater, and this dreary and masochistic idea of political commitment." Even if, as Mao Zedong declared "a revolution is not a banquet," the men from Bra claimed their right to pleasure.

The winter went by, and on April 9, 1983, the people of Montalcino hosted a debate on a rather aseptic topic: "The Case del Popolo and their tradition of festivals and gastronomy." Barbero recalls: "We went to Montalcino hoping for a confrontation, but it was immediately clear that the people there were planning to put us and Carlin on trial. But, using his oratory gifts, Carlin managed to win over an audience at the Casa del Popolo of about one hundred people. And that's when we began to explain to the Left that the time had come to pay attention to food and not just party enrollment. It was the period when our oeno-gastronomic league, Arci Gola, was taking its first steps. It was no coincidence that the first issue of the monthly Milanese cultural magazine *La Gola* (literally, *The Throat*) had been published just a few months before, in October 1982."

Petrini made people understand that taste is a serious matter, but he also knew better than to underestimate the ideological controversy his position could arouse: he knew he was making enemies not only with the "red church"—the Italian Communist Party—but with the Catholic Church as well, since it judges gluttony to be one of the seven deadly sins. And yet, the audience in Montalcino gave him absolution.

Rabissi, the head of the Montalcino Arci, remembers that day: "After our women cooks got infuriated, after we rejected the tone of Petrini's letter, and after we explained that by giving that luncheon for five hundred people on October 31, we wanted to raise funds for our kids' sports activities, we finally got it, we understood the reasons for their criticism. I have to admit it now—and with a smile: that episode was a lesson, a fair lesson for all our cultural associations."

Mario Bindi, born in 1934, was the Communist mayor of Montalcino from 1980 to 1990. At the time of the debate, he avoided getting caught up in the ideological dispute; instead he realized—"inedible *ribollita*" or not—that something had to be done to boost the production of

Brunello. In his mind, particular attention needed to be devoted to agriculture, the health of the vineyards, and the work of farmers and winegrowers. He talked about it one day, with some pride, while sitting in the same Casa del Popolo:

> Montalcino has always been a migration place for thrushes. In the hard years of depressed agriculture, farmers caught the birds with nets and mistletoe, an irreplaceable ingredient to make the *pania* [birdlime] — a kind of glue which is now illegal. It was a ritual, involving little whistles and *vergoni* [long sticks] to shake the grove trees. With that tradition in mind, the heads of the city neighborhoods re-established the fair in the fifties; they wanted it to include a historical procession with 150 characters in fifteenth-century costumes. Arci then decided to give better use to the Casa del Popolo in Palazzo Pieri-Nerli, a noble mansion initially bought by a workers' co-op in 1918 and then adapted by the Fascist regime to become a Casa del Fascio. The palazzo was returned to us only after the end of World War II. By the beginning of the eighties, it occurred to us to invite here all the Italian *circoli* for a gastronomical tour. There is no doubt too many people visited that lounge in just one day. Furthermore, the quality of food was far from high. After we received the letter from Petrini, things got out of control. A part of Arci stayed firmly with the same convictions, while others thought the Piedmontese had a point. As a consequence, a number of Montalcino people joined Arci Gola, and some years later I became a trustee.

Between 1987 and 1989, the Casa del Popolo hosted the award ceremony for a peculiar "gastronomical competition" sponsored by the Arcigolosi (members of Arci Gola), who by then had their own page in *L'Unità*, the official newspaper of the PCI. The competition evaluated the restaurants participating in the PCI's annual fund-raising bash, the nationwide Feste dell'Unità: "inspectors" were sent out, incognito, from Bra to sample the fare in the different restaurants, with the scores and awards published in *L'Unità*. The result was a farewell to semi-burnt little chops.

Finally, the Italian Left could sit at the table and claim its right to pleasure. Today Carlin, perhaps somewhat sorry about the harsh tone used in the letter he wrote in November 1982, recalls with a faint smile:

We are now beginning to understand that rural society is an innovative element of society worldwide. It took us several years to reach this conclusion: in the beginning, we were grappling with the concept of gastronomy that originated with Anthelme Brillat-Savarin, the inventor of modern gastronomic science as we know it, who explains in his *Physiology of Taste* that real gourmets "eat slowly and savor thoughtfully." We had not yet articulated our own distinctive approach, which nowadays many refer to as "eco-gastronomy." But what our group *was* beginning to understand was a new balance between conviviality per se and a system of cultural values. After our visit to Montalcino, we too had made the first important step: for the first time, the Left and its allies laid full claim to the pleasures of wine and conviviality. Until then these pleasures had seemed suitable only for the snobbish haute-bourgeoisie—for doctors, lawyers, and journalists—and to us, they were not connoisseurs, they were gluttons.

BARTOLO MASCARELLO,
THE PATRIARCH OF BAROLO

Even before their visit to Montalcino, Petrini and the other members of the Arci Langhe had acquired a more than passing interest in wine and food. The drinking and singing sprees of the Philoridiculous group had become more serious as the participants began to deepen their knowledge of the products of their own region—especially the noble red wine made from Nebbiolo grapes: Barolo. Petrini and his friends sought their entry into the rather closed circles of Barolo wine producers through the legendary figure of Bartolo Mascarello.

The Mascarello family had a longstanding relationship with the politics of the Left. In his 1977 book, *Il mondo dei vinti* (The world of the defeated), the writer Nuto Revelli recorded these words of Giulio Casare Mascarello (generally known as Rino), a winegrower of the Langhe born in 1895—and Bartolo's father.

At Barolo, no one was ever talking about politics. If you were a Socialist, you were a subversive who had to be isolated; a Socialist was just somebody who coveted other people's belongings. I had a subscription to *Avanti!* [the newspaper of the Socialist Party] and two photographs of

Matteotti [a politician of the opposition killed by the Fascists in 1937]. I had them hanging behind the shutters of a window, so that when the shutters were open, the photos faced the wall and nobody could see them.

The book explores the experiences of farmers in the poorest rural valleys of northern Italy, valleys that stayed poor even after the economic boom of the sixties. Mascarello recounts the way the Fascist carabinieri broke into his house and turned it upside down looking for "subversive volumes." He then gives a description of the inhabitants of Barolo, a hill town in his native Langhe region that is laid out around a nineteenth-century castle: "They talk exclusively about things related to the countryside, about prices, about the red spider [a disease that attacks grapevines]; otherwise they play *tressette* [a card game]."

With its warm cellars and inviting restaurants, the area around Alba in Piedmont is now a popular destination for gastronomic tourism. But at the end of the seventies, it wasn't much different from the place described by Rino Mascarello. His son Bartolo, born in 1926, followed his father's path and took up winemaking. By the seventies, Bartolo Mascarello was already one of the very few Italian wine producers with an international reputation. Among his friends was Revelli, who regularly spent the summer months in the Langhe region at the castle of Verduno, and many journalists of *Il Manifesto*, a newspaper founded by radical leftist intellectuals who had quit the Communist Party in 1970. Bartolo Mascarello's wine cellar was visited by various "historical" leaders of the Italian Left, including the Socialists Pietro Nenni and Antonio Giolitti, the Communist Giancarlo Pajetta, and Lucio Magri and Luciana Castellina. Other notable guests were the publisher Giulio Einaudi, the writer Carlo Emilio Gadda, and the journalist Giorgio Bocca, who, in order to define the sensorial component of Bartolo's wine, invented the expression "barolesque aroma." For years, Mascarello's company headquarters was a cultural meeting place where wine lovers, intellectuals, journalists, and politicians would drop by, attracted in part by the extraordinary and rare wines, but mainly by the personality and the warmth of the host.

Bartolo Mascarello was viewed as among the last of a dying breed, a hyper-traditionalist who adhered to the Barolo tradition of fermenting grapes in large chestnut-wood casks, called *botti*. He shunned the technique—imported from France—of using small oak barrels, known as *barriques*, with a capacity of only 225 liters. Bartolo's opposition to the big industrial warehouses that have disfigured the landscape of the hills around Alba is famous. In his final years, confined to his home by illness, he started to paint, with some artistry, the labels for his wine.

Bartolo died quietly on a sunny morning in early March, 2005. In his touching obituary for the prestigious Italian newspaper *La Repubblica*, Giorgio Bocca wrote:

> What makes Mascarello's Barolo so special? Nothing much, except perfection. And what made Bartolo special? Nothing much, except integrity and wisdom, and such a fullness of life that you couldn't help walking faster when you were about to ring his doorbell, enter his office, and find him sitting at his desk invariably with the *bonet* [a beret with a peak] on his head, and with his narrow face, his light-colored eyes, and in his hand the most recent wine label inscribed with the slogan: "No *barriques*, no Berlusconi." That was his way of saying no to any French paraphernalia for making wine with wood flavor additives, and no to ruthlessness in politics. And to think that there was somebody who dared to report him to the carabinieri."

Some time before his death, Petrini visited Bartolo Mascarello in his house in the village of Barolo. He gave a warm welcome and then, with the wit characteristic of an intellectual fond of his origins, he recounted the story of his first meetings with Petrini, his blue eyes sparkling with irony just at the thought of it. The story begins with a visit he received from Petrini in the seventies. Petrini was with his friends, former union workers or leftist militants active at the PCI. They all wanted to learn the secrets of the cellar, sample some wines, and talk about politics and the workers. As Bartolo told it:

> And they were reenacting the old ritual called "Singing for eggs" [in Piedmontese dialect, *Canté i'euv*], a secular pilgrimage similar to Christmas caroling that is traditionally performed on farmyards before Easter. The farmer is serenaded and then repays the singers with bread, salami, and Nebbiolo wine. Petrini and his friends decided to come to

see me in between songs. I had become a *refugium peccatorum*—a refuge for sinners. It was through me that they could get acquainted with the quite uptight world of the Langhe wine producers. They had even brought along Chris Hamblin, a Scottish cellist from the Shetland Islands, whom I was very happy to take in my house through the days of the show.

The arrival of such loud and disheveled "hippies" with their guitars was more than the conventional people of the Langhe could bear. "I had welcomed these young men, and I liked Carlo Petrini's provocative wit and his ability to excite young people. He had come to visit me in Barolo for the sheer fun of it, but in a short time he managed to turn a country fair into an international event. I have to admit that we wine producers were then miles away from thinking what wealth could come out of a good campaign for the image of our territory."

At the time, the wine producers of Barolo were embittered by the difficulties of exporting their wine. Riding the energy that Petrini had brought to the Canté i'euv, they gathered in Bartolo's living room and came up with the idea of founding a club—something like the then-trendy gastronomical academies, but with the specific goal of spreading the culture of good food even among ordinary people, and in particular among the kind of young men and women who attended popular music concerts.

And so the forerunner of all the Slow Food associations was born: the Libera e benemerita associazione degli amici del Barolo. All the participants in those legendary drinking and singing sprees immediately joined, and between their Dolcetto wine tastings and the rallies against the atomic bomb, the gang from Bra soon attracted hundreds of members. The first official meeting took place in November 1981, in the Barolo castle. The association's slogan was: "Barolo wine is democratic, or at least it can become so." As the slogan attests, the participants balanced the irony of their tone with a genuine desire to enhance the reputation of their native region.

Giovanni Battista Rinaldi, mayor of the town of Barolo, president of the *enoteca comunale* (the town's own stock of vintage wines), and a wine producer himself, offered his castle for the event. Rinaldi, who passed away in 1992, was an old-fashioned gentleman, a refined oenologist, and a gourmet; in a town that was detached from the outside world and run by Christian Democrats, he was an open-minded man of principles. In 1970, while mayor of Barolo, he organized a fund-raising drive for the city to buy the castle of the Falletti family before a liquor factory could get it. For the workers who maintained the vineyards, that castle represented a strong link to their past.

Of course, things were not always rosy between the club members and the Langhe wine producers. Bartolo Mascarello, for instance, began receiving strange phone calls: "Stop helping Petrini and his friends: don't you know they are all communists?" To which Bartolo replied, somewhat amused: "Really? Petrini is not a bad guy; he won't bite."

Both Mascarello and Rinaldi played a major role in Petrini's oeno-gastronomic education, but he learned a lot from another aficionado of Barolo wines as well, the oenologist and wine enthusiast Roberto Ratti. Ratti owned a vineyard at La Morra (a hamlet in the Langhe not too far from Barolo) and was very active in promoting wine culture, publishing books on wine, and organizing wine-tasting courses. After his untimely death in 1988, Ratti's son Pietro along with his nephew Massimo Martinelli inherited both his cellar and his savoir-faire. Petrini recalls Mascarello and the others in this way:

> In recent years, Italian oeno-gastronomy has come into the spotlight. Barolo and Brunello have become famous. We have done a great job, and yet we cannot get all the credit for it. We also have to credit all those who worked toward our goal in a time when a national oeno-gastronomy was still beyond the horizon. Among these people I count Bartolo Mascarello, with whom I often had friendly disagreements. I told him many times that so long as his wine labels declared "No *barriques*, no Berlusconi," I could agree only with the second part of the sentence. But this does not take anything away from my personal affection for him, nor from his formative influence on me. Bartolo was one of the great figures of Italian culture and ethic civility. Although younger than most of them, he belongs to the same straight-backed, eminently ethical generation of Piedmontese characters like Norberto Bobbio, Alessandro Galante Garrone, Primo Levi, and Nuto Revelli.

FROM RADICAL POLITICS TO WINE BARS

The founders of the Slow Food movement didn't emerge just in Piedmont and Tuscany. The town of Mira, near Venice, was also the scene of an important moment in the movement's growth. A few months before the outing to Montalcino, the members of the Barolo group organized an oeno-gastronomic week at the Palazzo dei Leoni in Mira, on the Brenta River, from May 25 to May 27, 1982. Wine and songs, politics and food, commitment and pleasure. Among the participants in these seminars were professors like Giovanni Battista Rinaldi, young restaurateurs like Marco Brezza from Barolo, and Massimo Martinelli, Roberto Ratti's nephew, himself an oenologist and wine producer from La Morra. For the Bra group, this was their first attempt to promote wines of the Langhe region away from home.

In Mira, the group met two young activists named Galdino Zara and Roberto Checchetto. The two had been factory workers and union organizers at the Mira Lanza chemical industry until 1980, when they quit and opened a wine bar in Mirano, Il Tastevin. In 1984, the pair went on to open a cooperative restaurant: La Ragnatela in Scaltenigo di Mirano. Zara is now a governor of Slow Food, and Checchetto is one of the original authors of the guidebook *Vini d'Italia*.

Their stories were quite similar to those of the Bra group: both were thirty-something, tired of politics, disillusioned by the defeats of the unions, and beaten down by the conservative backlash that followed 1968. Today Zara and Checchetto, with five other partners, still manage that same tavern just a few kilometers outside of Venice. The Ragnatela, in particular, offers excellent fish; the kitchen is decorated, somewhat ironically, with portraits of Lenin and Che Guevara. Here is the journalist Petrini reviewing the "Magnificent Seven" of the Ragnatela on May 7, 1987, in *L'Unità*:

> How many comrades, after having been involved in factories' and unions' politics, have decided in recent years to embrace the fascinating, socializing world of restaurants and have opened taverns and inns? Undoubtedly, a great number. Some of them have quit afterwards, so many are the difficulties connected with this profession. But others have stuck with it and have created a network of places where good food can be enjoyed without the air of pomposity typical of certain high-class

restaurants. And so we have traveled to the banks of the Brenta River, where the use of the local dialect is mandatory, . . . to dine at a lovely little restaurant that offers great food at a modest price. The credit for this little gem goes to the co-op that runs it, seven magnificent characters who belong to the above-mentioned category of people.

In Rome in the late seventies, another group of former radicals opened one of the first Italian "wine bars" (it used the English name, as opposed to the more familiar *enoteca*). Close to the Colosseum in the Umbertino neighborhood, it was called Cavour 313 (from the street name and number). The band from Bra, in Rome for a convention of the Arci, found a safe harbor there. Gigi Piumatti, who today is the editor of the *Vini d'Italia* guidebook, remembers that it was around the tables at Cavour 313 that Petrini's plans took off. From cultural operator, he became a communicator. The publishing firm of Gambero Rosso Editore was born here, parented by a group of leftist intellectuals, journalists, and wine enthusiasts. Cavour 313 offered wine courses and wine tastings for their guests, their education beginning right at the table. In Rome at that time, a wine list with thirty-five Piedmontese wines was something extraordinary. Nor were there many specialized publications about wine in Italy: the primary reference book was the massive *Catalogo Bolaffi* by Luigi Veronelli (also known as the "Wines' Peerage"), which provides a summary profile for each wine it lists. Andrea Gabbrielli, who at the time was the editor of the gastronomic monthly *Gambero Rosso,* and who later became the editor in chief of *Vini d'Italia* and is now active in the Slow Food Condotta of Rome, has vivid memories of the endless, wine-inspired tirades among the guests:

> Unlike Veronelli, who was an anarchist and a philosopher of individualism, Carlin had a knack for organization. He inspired a genuine interest in food culture, which he refused to see as an exclusive privilege of the intellectual right or the bourgeois gourmets. We were young and leftist and wanted to learn some basic concepts in order to explain them in an accessible way that could be easily understood by people in their twenties. Our important insight, which is still valid today, is that young people go to the Salone del Gusto or to Vinitaly because of their interest in the environment but also because of their passion for good-quality food.

At about this time, Petrini met Veronelli himself. Veronelli was Italy's most famous journalist specializing in wine. Born in Milan in 1926, he was an anarchic oenologist and theorist of peasantry. By the time he died in Bergamo in 2004, he had become something of Italy's answer to Robert Parker. Veronelli nurtured the cultural growth of Petrini and his associates and anticipated the Slow Food philosophy that favored quality products associated with disappearing communities. One of his first books, *Alla ricerca dei cibi perduti* (Remembrance of foods past), was edited by his friend Giangiacomo Feltrinelli and published in 1966. It was reissued by Derive/Approdi in 2004. In it, Veronelli makes this comment about Piedmont: "In the fall, there is no place I love more than the Langhe. I love to walk through the countryside there, which is half cultivated and half wild; I love to inhale its aromas, full of herbs and must. I also love, glutton that I am, being harassed by that powerful, intoxicating smell of truffles."

Petrini has explained his relationship with Veronelli and how it deepened through the years:

Veronelli is undoubtedly the precursor of all modern Italian gastronomy. In his first fifty years of activity, he accomplished a great deal. His innovative gift for communicating about food could be compared with Giovanni Arpino's or Gianni Brera's about sport. He acknowledged the peasant world in the same way the Terra Madre assembly recently did. Veronelli personified the figure of the modern gourmet as we know it. Through his wine stories [and] his trips, . . . he has been an inspiration for an entire generation. The dates of his publications confirm it: *Il Gastronomo* magazine came out in 1956; *Vini d'Italia* in 1959; his *Guide all'Italia piacevole* [Guides to a pleasurable Italy], a nine-volume work, was published in the sixties. Having read his articles for years I can state that, after the battles about olive oil, his decision to join forces with the youth of the social center for the Fiera dei Particolari and for the project "Terra e Libertà-Critical Wine" was something extraordinary. I was stupefied somebody seventy-seven years old could find the strength to adopt such stances. He collected these essays in his last book *Le parole della terra* [Words of the soil]. Veronelli knew I agreed with him in fighting against raising prices and the requests of the DOCs, the local guarantees of origin, even if I was puzzled about giving localities jurisdiction over food. As I stated during the assembly of the Terra Madre, I think that each food community should codify the rules related to its own products.

LA GOLA: FOOD FINDS ITS VOICE

The first issue of *La Gola*, a "monthly magazine about food and material life techniques" (by its own definition), came out in Milan in October 1982. Until 1988, when its publication ceased, *La Gola* was the only periodical in Europe completely devoted to food culture and designed for cultivated readers; the articles were contributed by writers, poets, and artists. The editorial board could not have been more heterogeneous. Gianni Sassi (who passed away in 1993) was the editor in chief; in the seventies, he had been the editor of *Alfabeta*, a literary periodical to which Umberto Eco contributed. Sassi was also a graphic designer, painter, publisher, and record producer. As an artist, he was associated with the Fluxus group that was linked to John Cage, and he was a music lover.

In the first issue of this elegant large-format publication (the layout was designed by Sassi), the articles were scholarly but off-beat: "La cena di Brummel" (Brummel's dinner), written by Giuseppe Scaraffia; "Il cibo di Omero" (What Homer ate), edited by the scholar of Greek Jean-Pierre Vernant; three pages were dedicated to gastronomy itself, including an article on black cabbage by Porta, and various portraits of restaurateurs. Significantly, the very first issue included this statement from Luigi Veronelli: "In the act of feeding, the biological being and the social one are strictly connected," because every one of us is "omnivorous: fed by meat, vegetables, and imagination."

In *La Gola*, there was a smart mix of snobbish and eccentric topics — recipes, the history of cooking, anthropology, and the science of communication, discussions of the excellence of certain products and of diets, articles on "supermarket obesity," and detailed reports on different regions. Among those who contributed articles were the food scientist Marco Riva, the food historian Massimo Montanari, and the writer Folco Portinari. The 156 issues of *La Gola* amounted to a virtual encyclopedia of gastronomic science, and there is no doubt that they were a source of inspiration for the "slow" philosophy.

Carlo Petrini was closely tied to *La Gola* from the very beginning: he went to Milan to gather inspiration from the editors, and in exchange he offered ideas for essays, topics, and discussions. His name appears in the magazine's masthead as one of the contributors in the issue of April 1983, when Arci Gola was first taking shape. Indeed, the association's name arose out of the meeting of Sassi and Petrini. At its beginnings, the Arcigolosi group wanted to create a market for goods of indisputable quality. In an article in that 1983 issue, Petrini explains: "Arci Gola will bring together organizations and companies scattered all over the nation that will share some cultural premises and be committed to a coordinated and concrete promotional campaign on a local and national level. We are talking about wine shops and restaurants, public organizations, and groups like the Libera e benemerita associazione degli amici del Barolo of Bra [in the Cuneo province]. The latter, for example, seeks out DOC wines and products of excellent quality made by producers of its region, in order to sell them at fair prices."

Alberto Capatti, who was a member of the original group of *La Gola* magazine and today is the dean of the University of Gastronomic Sciences founded in Italy by Slow Food, explains:

In the early eighties, industrialized food processing, small production, and gastronomy were not in conflict. *La Gola* was all for making these three elements converge. At that time, the food-processing industry was not considered an adversary, as it became later. Neither was there a conflict with small producers of high-quality goods, winemakers for instance, or with the intellectuals. We wanted to get along, and in Milan at that time we believed we could create an innovative and effective nexus linking design, fashion, and food. My relationship with Petrini also started for political reasons, I believe. The first thing he said to me, I remember, struck me as a rather odd idea: he wanted to create a kind of universal cellar where the wine producers had to deposit their wine so that it could become collective memory. At the magazine there were many discussions, but no sense of partnership; the spirit of cooperation was instead deeply embedded in Carlin.

THE BURGUNDY PYRAMID

One cannot come away from the so-called "Trois Glorieuses" in Beaune, the capital of France's most famous wine region, Burgundy, without understanding the significance of *terroir* in determining the success of a great wine. *Terroir* is that magic combination of soil, climate, and light that can make the wine from one particular vineyard outstanding. Over the course of three days, the city of Beaune comes to life in three Pantagruelian banquets while the hospices, the old local wine institutions, put their products up for auction. The event has been taking place continuously since 1860 and is held in November in conjunction with the Wine Fair.

Following their formative trips to Tuscany, Rome, and Milan, Carlo Petrini and his group decided to move closer to the homeland of every gourmet: France, and in particular Burgundy, the gastronomic center of the country. In Petrini's words:

We realized that those great French bottles, the dream of any wine enthusiast—names like Romanée-Conti, Montrachet, and Gevrey-Chambertin—contained something that went beyond the vast rural tradition of the Langhe, even taking into account the mythologizing of recent literature. Those famous labels combined entrepreneurial talent, a thousand-year-old history, and a good communication strategy. Most of all, the French had a special skill in selling the overall image of their wine-producing regions, which involved the landscape, hospitality, cuisine, wine, and the team spirit of the *vignerons*, which was so different from the individualism of the Tuscans and Piedmontese. The vineyards of Burgundy are among the most ancient in France: some now-famous wine-producing regions were laid out by medieval religious orders like the Benedictines in Cluny and in Cîteux. Later on, with the creation of the Clos de Vougeot, the best Burgundy wines became established. Centuries went by, and those properties were parceled out: today any winemaker can classify his or her bottles according to a ranking system that recognizes four qualities of soil: regional and sub-regional denominations, communal denominations, *premiers crus,* and *grands crus.* This explains why often on French wine labels the place of origin is not given. It's enough to say Romanée-Conti, and it's clear what that means. It's a kind of hierarchy that has established itself vintage after vintage through decades: it gives shape to a kind of pyramid, the Burgundy pyramid that benefits everyone, the ones at the base and the ones at the top.

Between 1981 and 1986, Petrini and his associates had been anchoring their education in wine. They began with the courses of Massimo Martinelli at La Morra, which were offered at the town wine cellar, and from there they started to organize their movement.

Martinelli, born in 1943, is a healthy man in his sixties (thanks, he says, to Barolo). An oenologist and wine producer, he lives in La Morra, one of the best villages for Nebbiolo-based wine in the Barolo region. He recollects that in the eighties, local chefs organized theme nights at the town wine cellar:

> At that time, there was no real oenological culture in Italy. It was taken for granted that in Piedmont we had good wine, but this was basically implied, a reality which went without saying. My uncle, Renato Ratti, invited an Alsatian guy named Jean Siegrist, a professor of wine tasting at Beaune, to the Istituto enologico di Alba. That course inspired me: I was interested in what he had to say about different aromas and the ways to identify them. Then I started putting together different aromas in my own lab, following the example of Pinot Gallizio, the pharmacist-painter who taught herbal medicine at the Alba institute. That's where I learned to make infusions and to extract perfumes from herbs, fruits, and flowers.

At the wine-tasting seminar in Mira, Martinelli had presented the aromas that constituted basic knowledge for the wine expert: tobacco, butter, honey, eucalyptus, seaweed, pepper, anise, coffee, rose, and peach. He presented even the smell of cork, the worst flaw a bottle can have, which he had obtained by making an infusion of flawed corks.

One day, Martinelli read in a French wine magazine that the Beaune Professional Committee offered (then as now) weekly courses in wine appreciation. He made some telephone calls and quickly organized the trip. He and the others knew that the only way to improve their oenological competence would be to attend the course at the Ecole des vins de Bourgogne, which was established in Beaune in 1974 to train laymen and experts in the sensorial analysis of wine.

In January 1986, a group of five left Piedmont headed for Burgundy: Carlo Petrini; his "lieutenant" Gigi Piumatti; the oenologist Renzo Tablino; Piero Sardo, the intellectual from Bra who offered the group some theoretical foundation; and Martinelli himself. At the school in Beaune, the Arcigolosi had their first encounter with the very strict rules of professional wine tasting: they had something between twelve and twenty labels to evaluate, and the goal was to be able to distinguish the different wines and accurately assess their flavor components and profile. And yet, a knowledge of sensorial analysis and in-depth wine-tasting techniques, as important as they are, was only one aspect of the overall education that Petrini and his colleagues were seeking.

While in France they immersed themselves in classes on theory, dinner parties, visits to local restaurants and wine cellars, and of course, wine tastings. One day, during an afternoon outing in Côte d'Or, home to Burgundy's most famous vineyards, Petrini asked, "Isn't the famous Romanée-Conti from around here? Why don't we go there?" Martinelli replied, "Look, I know that cellar, let's try it." No sooner said than done: the five of them showed up, unannounced, at the best-known domaine in France declaring, "We are some curious Italians, can we please pay you a visit?" The proprietor offered an icy welcome: "That's impossible, you need to reserve months in advance." The group insisted, "Could you please do us a favor? We have to leave in five days." The Frenchman turned the pages of his register and offered them an appointment on Friday at seven-thirty in the morning. The Italians responded to the challenge. The night before they looked through their Michelin guide and dined in one of the most "starred" restaurants in the area, the Lameloise in Chagny-en-Bourgogne, run by the chef-patron Jacques Lameloise. The group enjoyed a hearty supper and showed up the following morning at the Domaine Romanée-Conti. "It was the earliest wine tasting of my entire life," remembers Martinelli. "When we tell this story no one believes us. But our French, Dutch, and German classmates in Beaune had to acknowledge: *les Italiens* got there first, we beat them all. We had a chance to talk to major and minor winegrowers, and we learned about the profound differences between France and Italy at that time: French wine producers had an esprit de corps, they knew that the land is a common property."

The team of friends returned to Piedmont intent on applying their newly acquired knowledge. They began planning wine-tasting courses and arranged meetings with wine producers in order to share what they learned in France. They organized a weeklong meeting in the Langhe in 1987, open to all the Arci members of Italy. The meeting turned out to be a rehearsal for the big conventions that would take place in the nineties in Piedmont, Tuscany, and Friuli-Venezia Giulia. Meetings like this initially generated some skepticism among local winegrowers, but then, because of growing interest in Burgundy's model of success, they became a template for many cultural events.

Montalcino, Barolo, Rome, Milan, and Beaune: these were the stages in the complex, mainly oenological, itinerary that led to the formal establishment of Arci Gola in the summer of 1986. Prior to that point, the leftist intelligentsia considered these initial, tentative steps as typical of nothing more than a "fraternity of *buontemponi* (fun-loving men)," according to the definition given by Petrini himself. However, that "fraternity" was bound to go a long way, even at the cost of cutting off some of the roots that had been growing in the previous twenty years.

chapter 2

THE ROOTS: 1949–1982

VIA MENDICITÀ ISTRUITA

Carlo Petrini was born on June 22, 1949, to Maria Garombo, a nursery school teacher, and Giuseppe Petrini, a craftsman. He came into the world in Bra, a city known for its cheese, and he was delivered by a midwife named Maria Gola. The word *gola* in Italian has several meanings. One of them is "throat"; at the same time, the word has long been a synonym for epicure or gourmet, and it is suggestive of a passion for food and gastronomy. For a man who was going to become the most famous eco-gastronomist of Italy, it's tempting to see this as a case of predestination.

Petrini was born in the middle of the Cold War, at a time when Italy was emerging from the virtual famine that followed World War II. Theaters were showing *Riso amaro* (*Bitter Rice*), a neo-realist film by Giuseppe de Santis that denounced the harsh working conditions of the women laborers of the Po Valley rice fields. The shot showing Silvana Mangano's beautiful legs immersed in the rice fields became an icon of the times. Following the period of the monarchy and the papacy of Pius XII, the first governments of the Italian Republic were being formed.

At that time in Bra, the smell of tannin coming from the leather factories prevailed over the aroma of cheese. Bra, the city's namesake cheese, isn't actually produced in Bra. Rather, it comes from the hills around Cuneo, a few miles from the Alps and the French border; Bra, however, is where the cheese is seasoned and traditionally sold by the local retailers. Following the war, Bra was both a commercial center and a working-class town, full of labor cooperatives in the tradition of nineteenth-century associations like the Society of Mutual Aid. A typically Italian phenomenon, this institution was created to enable the poorest members of society to organize and secure help for themselves. It was one of the first examples of welfare, launched by the local crafts-people themselves: cobblers, market vendors, and tanners.

Petrini received a Catholic upbringing. He studied at a boarding school run by Salesian friars, went through the student protests and upheavals of 1968, and was influenced by secular French culture. Catholicism, peasant culture absorbed with a dash of Marxism (not so much that of Marx himself, as a Marxism interpreted by the French historian Fernand Braudel and the English philosopher Bertrand Russell), and the quickness and vitality typical of those who begin working at a young age: these are some of the distinctive traits of the founder of Slow Food. Petrini has never abandoned his roots:

To be born in Bra and never to forget it: it has marked my life. Our international headquarters are still in Via Mendicità Istruita, a small street that goes uphill and leads you to a square with the statue of Giorgio Cottolengo, the saint who was born in Bra in 1786 and who founded the Turinese shelter for the homeless and derelict. When I travel around the world, I have often been asked: "Why *Mendicità Istruita?*" It is not easy to explain our address. In the eighteenth century, the Accademia degli Innominati was here. The name of the street comes from the educational institution founded to house destitute young women, and, as the words indicate, to educate them: the Ritiro della mendicità istruita. In Italian, it means educating a person who lives off charity. I am fond of the name; it's evocative, and we never wanted to move, even though in twenty years the main office has become too small: rather, we opened more offices in town. At the end of the nineteenth century, the capital of wine in Piedmont was Bra, not Alba. In Alba there were only the Calissano and the Pio Cesare wineries. Here there were at least ten of them. Bra was actually where Barolo was produced. It was a man from Bra who defeated the oidium, the fungus that attacks vine leaves. In fact, Bra has always been an excellent spot from which to observe the value of the oenological and gastronomical patrimony of the neighboring region of the Langhe.

I have a strong sense of the region, which I have never really left, despite all my travels. My family was a quiet one and belonged to the town's typical bourgeoisie, with Socialist and Communist roots on my father's side, and Catholic ones on my mother's, who came from generations of greengrocers. I have a sister, Chiara, born when I was eight, with whom I am very close: she has always stood by me, even in the most difficult times. My father was a car electrician; at one point he started putting together car horns, with the idea that I had to help him and learn a profession. After my elementary school years, my parents sent me to study with the Salesian friars and from there to the technical school in Vallauri in Fossano, a town some 20 kilometers from Bra.

My grandfather Carlo was relatively well known in town. A Socialist railway man, he was a member of the city council during the first leftist administration of the Red Biennial 1920–22 [a period of workers' strikes partly inspired by the Bolshevik revolution in Russia]. At the Livorno convention of the Italian Socialist Party, when the Communist wing collided with the Social Democratic reformers, he chose the Communist Party.

I got my high school diploma in the fateful year of 1968, although it had no particular significance to me. The protest wave hit Italian higher education only in 1969. In any case, the student movement gained strength mostly in the high schools. A bit of a disappointment to my parents, my best grades in school were in the humanities. I went to the exam for my diploma with three failing grades: engineering, technology, and technical design. I somehow managed to pass the exam in two disciplines, but the teachers decided I had to be examined again in September in engineering. When I showed up to take the exam for the second time, the teacher asked me some easy questions. At the end, the president of the committee asked me: "Would you promise that you'll never become an engineer?" I nodded vigorously, and they gave me the diploma.

In September I registered at the University of Trento, in the department of sociology, as a working student. My first job was as a salesman of food products, which lasted for several years, until I devoted myself entirely to the associations we had founded and to their economic aspects.

The University of Trento in the years of the student protests witnessed occupations, rousing assemblies, and collectives. All the leaders of the student protest movement attended the university, and some of them actively participated in the violent "years of lead." However, Petrini did not spend much time at the sociology department: he went to Trento mainly to take exams. He had a job selling candy in the province of Cuneo in eastern Piedmont and otherwise kept busy with his involvement in various social service agencies. Petrini has vivid memories of those years:

> My social and political upbringing did not take place at the University's sociology department, but rather in a Catholic organization of which I had become the president in 1966, at the age of seventeen. This was the Conferenza di carità under the auspices of the Società di San Vincenzo De Paoli, which was established in the middle of the nineteenth century. The most important branch of the Society in Piedmont was located in Bra, which had 130 members, and I became its president, the youngest in Italy.

FROM CATHOLIC TO COMMUNIST

People who have known Carlo Petrini since his youth say that he was already a leader then, ready to embark on any kind of risky adventure, provided it furthered the causes he cared about. One such venture was to raise money for charitable purposes by selling knickknacks collected from people's basements: this was a small-scale revolution at a time when the traditional form of charity consisted in offering food stamps to the poor.

With the money from their bric-a-brac sales (20 million lire, equal to about $175,000 today), the group opened a school for illiterate adults. Petrini had read about Henri Groués, a French Catholic priest known as l'Abbé Pierre, founder of the Emmaüs organization. Emmaüs is devoted to helping the poor and homeless, as well as refugees; over the years it has grown into a large movement with branches across France. Abbé Pierre had also organized the first community service camps for youth, and Petrini wanted to try that type of fund-raising in Bra.

As usual Petrini had by his side Azio Citi, a former classmate from his elementary school days. "Carlin believed in human values, but I would not define him as Catholic; rather, he had ideas and succeeded in getting people involved in a project. He was always cheerful and smiling. In our branch of the San Vincenzo De Paoli, there were not only observant Catholics but also laypersons like me who had decided to join in order to feel useful. Giovanni Ravinale was also a member, and he accompanied us on our cultural and political travels. From time to time, one of us would dress up as Santa Claus and go and play around in an orchestra. Strangely enough, Carlo was always the conductor."

Nevertheless, it was impossible to be young at that time without joining some political group. In the United States, peace marches against the war in Vietnam were attracting hundred of thousands of young people, and in Italy, divorce was legalized. Dario Fo was transforming Italian theater with irreverent comedies that criticized the police and the Christian Democrat regime. These were the "hot" years, characterized by terrorist attacks and tension between the Right and the Left. Although already active through their Catholic association, it was natural for Petrini and his friends to respond to these events by creating a cultural club in 1971 called the Circolo Leonardo Cocito, named after a hero of the local resistance against Nazi Fascism.

On April 28, 1971, the radical leftist review *Il Manifesto* became a newspaper, and the idea of organizing a political power to the left of the Communist Party gained momentum. At the beginning, *Il Manifesto* had only four pages with no photographs and no advertising and was sold for 50 lire (something like 40 cents today), rather than the 90 lire charged by other newspapers. In the publishing world, it was an unexpected coup, and the paper has remained popular even today among young people, intellectuals, and union members. Attracted by the ideas nurturing the columns of *Il Manifesto*, the young members of the Società di San Vincenzo decided it was time for a change. They gathered at their Circolo Cocito, but there was little consensus among them as to the future of the group. One of them had even joined a political organization with Maoist overtones. Finally, they decided to join *Il Manifesto*, which had also become a small political party that debuted at the elections of 1972. The results of the vote were a disappointment (*Il Manifesto* gathered only 0.6 percent nationally, with 156 votes in Bra), and the members of the Circolo Cocito immediately ditched the newly born political force. (Two years later *Il Manifesto* merged with another independent leftist party called Partito democratico di unità proletaria, or PDUP. Unconnected to the PCI, the PDUP was relatively popular during the period of youth protests, but has since faded from existence.)

SLOW COMMUNICATION:
A JOURNAL, A RADIO STATION, AND A CO-OP

In those years the radical Left kept splitting into different movements, groups, and parties, which, without the support of the PCI, usually survived just one round of voting. In 1973, the state coup in Chile brought to a bloody end the government of the Socialist Salvador Allende. In Italy, Enrico Berlinguer, then the leader of the biggest European Communist Party west of the Berlin Wall, began to develop his theory of the "historic compromise" with the Christian Democrats. This involved forming a special relationship between the most important opposition party, the Communists, and the Christian Democratic party, which had been in power since the end of World War II. (A similar "great coalition" came into power in Germany in 2005 under the lead of Chancellor Angela Merkel.) It was a choice the radical Left disliked.

Back in Bra after his mandatory military service, Petrini tried to emerge from his isolation. Over a period of several months, he undertook two initiatives with the Circolo Cocito: a political journal and then an independent radio station. In September 1974, the first issue of the monthly *In Campo Rosso* (In Red Domain) appeared. The editor in chief was Grazia Novellini. As the only professional journalist on the staff, Novellini (today one of the pillars of Slow Food Editore, the organization's publishing arm) was, according to Italian law, the only one in the group who could assume responsibility for the publication. Novellini recounts: "As always, it was Carlin who came out with the idea of founding a magazine. Apart from one's natural inclination to want to pick out a nice place to eat now and then, very little attention was being paid to food at that point. Our goal was to become more visible in Bra and to create a counter-power in the radical Left. We felt we were the only ones in the opposition." That year, Jean-Paul Sartre published *On a raison de se révolter*, Leonardo Sciascia published *Todo Modo*, and Michelangelo Antonioni brought his film *Professione: Reporter* to screens all over the world.

Rereading the early issues of *In Campo Rosso* (a name which leaves little doubt as to the journal's political credo), one is struck by how typical the language is of its time: an uncompromising and tough language that stakes out its opposition to businessmen, bureaucrats, and the local Church in a single *J'accuse*. The tone is witty, satirical, and ironic.

Dominated by conformism, Bra perceived very little of the turmoil in the world, and the members of the Circolo Cocito tried desperately to find a way out—anything in order to engage in a discussion and to provoke the reader.

On June 17, 1975, at ten in the morning, history was made when the city resounded with the refrain of a well-known song by the Italian songwriter Francesco de Gregori, who is still very popular today among liberal and progressive youth: "*Hanno pagato Pablo, Pablo è vivo.... Hanno ammazzato Pablo, Pablo è vivo*" ("They have paid Pablo, Pablo is alive.... They have killed Pablo, Pablo is alive"). The voice of de Gregori was being broadcast by an independent, noncommercial radio station, the first one in Italy.

In July 1974, the Italian constitutional court had declared RAI (the state-owned broadcasting network) an illegal monopoly. Up until then, RAI had been Italy's sole broadcaster of television and radio programs. After the historic ruling, the Italian parliament took measures and, in April 1975, approved a law that opened the doors to the creation of independent broadcasting companies. (Ironically, the new law ultimately made the fortune of Silvio Berlusconi, who built an empire in telecommunications and went on to become a major conservative force in Italian politics, most recently serving as prime minister from 2001 to 2006.)

It was against this judicial background that Radio Bra Onde Rosse, or Radio Bra Red Waves, aired its first programs. The station was located in a little attic overlooking the roofs of the city. An extension of the Circolo Cocito, it had no permit and aired programs that challenged the local establishment.

Petrini's friend Azio Citi was a leading figure in these first transmissions and recalls:

> In the little local markets close to the harbor of Livorno, on the Tuscan coast, where there are some American military bases, you could find a lot of Army surplus. We went there and bought the radio of an American tank used in the Korean war. It was not a very powerful transmitter, to be sure, and we could not broadcast beyond the nearby hills. But our signal was received all over Bra and in many places in the Langhe territory. Our radio had no transistors, only fuses, which needed to heat up. So if you wanted to start a program at, say, eight, you

had to get to the office, at the very top of a building in the historical center, at least one hour in advance to set everything going. After that we had to check the wave emissions with an SWR-meter. We got all our information from the newspapers of the militant Left. We had neither the journalists nor the money to buy a telex with the press agencies, yet our sources for the local news were excellent. At the beginning, there was a lot of heated discussion about taking advertisers, and finally we decided not to do it. When Carlin was elected in the city council, we began broadcasting recordings of the council sessions forty-five minutes after they had taken place: that was the time necessary to take the recorded cassettes, by foot, from the city hall to our office. They confiscated our equipment twice, but we weren't intimidated and held our ground.

The pirate radio experience was short-lived. On July 14, 1975, the station's equipment was confiscated by the police for the first time. Across the country, there was a great deal of support for the station, and a month later Radio Bra Red Waves was back on the air. The Italian intelligentsia of the Left vigorously positioned itself against the confis-cations of radio equipment and the criminal charges brought against the station. As Petrini describes it:

> The only way we could make the station work was with the help of vol-unteers who were willing to collaborate with us. I remember that the writer Dario Fo was an enthusiast. He came to Bra and stayed a month. Together we watched over the equipment that had been confiscated by the magistrates, always ready to put it back in service, and telling the policemen that the fuses could not possibly go cold. Dario told me: "Be brave Carlin, go on, this is going to be the free press of the next century."

But on October 9, the judiciary again ordered the station to be shut down. Proceedings were initiated against it, then suspended, and finally the case was remanded to the constitutional court.

Ultimately, it was the court ruling in the case of Radio Bra Red Waves that resulted in the liberalization of independent broadcasting in Italy. Following the decree of July 28, 1976, the station was left alone for a few months. However, once the novelty had worn off and national interest in the case waned, these militants of independent radio could hardly cope with the daily routine: broadcasting had become increasingly demanding. Petrini and his associates continued transmissions until 1978 and then closed. The kidnapping of the Christian Democrat representative Aldo Moro by the Red Brigades, radical leftist terrorists who were then steeping the country in blood, was the last piece of news the radio aired. The kidnapping came to a tragic end with Moro's murder. The periodical *In Campo Rosso*, at that point a bi-weekly, continued until 1985, and a less politicized weekly paper rose from its ashes.

The next two ventures launched by Petrini and his associates sought to provide a financial foundation for some of their other activities, while also establishing a gathering place that might attract a wider public. In that same fateful year of 1975, the group opened a cooperative grocery store in Bra and a political bookstore in the nearby town of Alba. As Petrini recalls:

> In 1975, we opened a grocery store with the idea of selling products from small local producers at reasonable prices; that way we could do a bit of self-financing. It was called Spaccio di unità popolare [Store of popular unity]: from that moment on we decided to join the official partnership of the Left, that is to say the Arci. That way we were not confined to offering certain services only to our members. We were selling everything, from groceries to detergents: our goal was mainly to play our part in keeping prices down. The local retailers did not like us at all, but we became very popular with consumers.
>
> The 1975 elections were a success: I became a member of the city council, for the PDUP, and I was alone in opposing the "historical compromise." Until that moment I had kept working as a salesman to support myself, but with the store established I decided to give up job security for the sake of the new enterprise. My salary was 300,000 Italian lire a month [at the time, less than $200]. In the same year, we embarked on a new adventure in Alba, opening a bookstore that aimed at being a cultural club as well. We called it the Cooperativa Libraria La Torre [Tower book co-op]. I was able to raise money to start it by organizing some concerts, and then I began wandering around publishing houses to get remainders. Our bookshelves were full of political essays, but we sold nothing.

Almost overnight, the bookshop, housed on the first floor of a medieval tower in the center of Alba, became a center for cultural events and meetings, similar to the Circolo Cocito in Bra. In these two sleepy provincial towns, Petrini continued to fulminate, carried along by the wave of political victories for the Left then sweeping across Italy. From Rome to Turin, there were now several "red" municipal administrations. The bookshop and the store represented other ways to be in politics. Checca Barberis, who remains a member of the co-op that manages the bookshop, recalls:

> Carlin was the driving force, organizing debates with eminent writers and bringing in artists who later became famous. Furthermore, Carlo read, or rather, he devoured books. A text by Fernand Braudel especially intrigued him. Braudel was the French historian who, thanks to the *Annales* and his *Maison des Sciences de l'Homme*, had first emphasized the social and anthropological aspects of history. Carlin particularly enjoyed reading one essay published by Einaudi: *Civiltà materiale, economia e capitalismo* (Consumer civilization, economics, and capitalism). After reading that study, he started to look at the peasants of the Langhe district from a different perspective.

SLOW MUSIC: THE CANTÉ I'EUV AND TENCO

The traditional chant of the old Piedmontese festival known as Canté i'euv goes something like this: *"Dateci, o dateci le uova / delle vostre galline / i vostri vicini ci hanno detto / che avete le ceste piene"* (Give us, o give us the eggs / of your hens / your neighbors have told us / your baskets are full). It was typically performed by a group of men, including one dressed as a friar, accompanied by a little band with a violin, a trombone, and an accordion. Cloaked in the traditional black capes of the Langhe, the group would wander from farmhouse to farmhouse singing the ancient propitiatory ritual. The farmer, having been woken up in the dead of night, would dip into his reserves of eggs, cheese, salame, and good vintage wine, and head down to the courtyard. Originally, this ritual called for unannounced visits to the courtyards of farmhouses up in the hills, and it often inspired picturesque verses mocking the proprietor's cheapness. In more recent years, the itinerary of the beggars has usually been announced, and in the nights preceding Easter, food and drink were consumed on the spot, the songs dragging on until dawn.

Petrini has never skipped this ritual of spring in Piedmont, known as the festival of "singing for eggs" (the name *Canté i'euv* comes from the local dialect). There are a few favorite activities he would not give up for anything in the world, and his devotion to them has only strengthened over the years. In the summer, there is the feast of San Firmin in Pamplona, with its famous bull-running race; in the fall, he spends a week in Sanremo, on the Riviera, for the Tenco Festival (a three-day gathering of Italian and international singer-songwriters); in December, he attends the great feast of *Bue Grasso* (Fat Ox) in Carrù, in southern Piedmont; and in the spring, he never misses the nights of egg collecting in the Langhe. A fan of popular music, Petrini has dragged along all his singer, actor, writer, and politician friends since the seventies to "sing for eggs" with him on the hillsides above Bra:

> When I travel around the world and bump into someone who looks familiar, I find out very often that our acquaintance dates back to a Canté i'euv some twenty or thirty years before. I still love to do it: closing up shop to go to the farmhouses. People may be sleeping, yet at a certain point a light goes on, they give us something to eat, and we all dance and have fun. I always tell my Slow Food friends: if you are no longer capable of having fun, you'd better give up. Canté i'euv was almost disappearing as a tradition: we rediscovered it and gave it new strength. Really, that contact with the simple food of the farmhouses turned out to be an important moment in my experience. I have to admit that, more recently, good wine has become the main destination of our nighttime wandering. That's because we have never believed the fantasy according to which "peasant's wine" is excellent. Through the years, we have become more demanding.

In 1975, songs like *"Hacia la libertad"* by the Chilean group Inti-Illimani were the soundtrack of the Left, while Pink Floyd was in full swing with its immortal "Wish You Were Here." In Italy, poet and songwriter Francesco Guccini, a.k.a. *maestrone*, had leapt to popularity, particularly among the youth of the time. Guccini was from Modena, in the heart of Emilia-Romagna in central Italy, and had grown up in Pavana, in the Appenine hills above Pistoia. He sang of daily life among the poor and downtrodden, with lyrics that were often bitter. Here is a verse from his "Canzon delle osterie di fuori porta" (Song of the taverns on the outskirts of the city): *"Sono ancora aperte come un tempo le osterie di fuori porta / ma la gente che ci andava a bere fuori o dentro è tutta morta. / Qualcuno è andato per età, qualcuno perché già dottore / e insegue una maturità: si è sposato, fa carriera ed è una morte un po' peggiore."* (The taverns on the outskirts of the city are still open the way they used to be / but the people who went there to drink are all dead. / Some are gone because of age, and some, with diploma in hand / have sold out: married, had a career, and died a bit worse off.)

Guccini had been one of the first performers at the festival launched by Sanremo's Club Tenco, dedicated to the arts of the singer-songwriter. The club, named after the Italian singer-songwriter Luigi Tenco, was founded in 1972 by Amilcare Rambaldi. In 1974, Rambaldi organized the first festival, inviting Italian and international singers for three days of performances at the Teatro Ariston of Sanremo. Rambaldi had a flare for spotting talent, and he had invited Guccini and Roberto Vecchioni—both of whom are now major names in Italian music—to the festival at a time when they were still totally unknown.

Guccini helped open the doors of the Tenco festival to Petrini and the others. He describes this time in the book *Carlin e gli amici del Club Tenco* (Carlin and the Club Tenco friends, 2004):

> If I remember correctly, I met Carlo Petrini (to me he has always been Carlin from Bra) in 1976. He came to my house—I can't recall if he called me first (still, now that I know him, I am almost positive he didn't)—with two other men from the Langhe, Azio [Citi] and the late Giovanni [Ravinale]. He claimed that they had founded a "free radio station," the first in Italy (there are at least six hundred other radio stations which claim to have been the first free radio in Italy). He said that Dario Fo had already been to see them, and he wanted to know whether I could participate in a concert in Bra. And for free, needless to say. I was at the time (and still am) deeply fascinated by the Langhe, by the Piedmont writers Cesare Pavese and Beppe Fenoglio, by the *trifola d'Alba* [white truffle] and the *bagna cauda*, by the fall with its first fogs and the reddened rows of Nebbiolo, by the legendary names Barolo and

Grinzane Cavour, by Piedmont with its jagged, shiny mountain tops, and all the literature about it . . . so I accepted.

Two years later Guccini returned to the province of Cuneo to play for prisoners at a local jail. After the concert, Guccini and the Bra trio all ended up in a *piola*, a typical Piedmontese inn. The Emilian songwriter continues:

The *piola* turned out to be noteworthy: I ate well and drank better. Not only that, I also discovered the incredible talent of the three men. As soon as we finished eating, cheered up by a few glasses of alcohol, they took control of the situation and blew the audience away with some excellent cabaret pieces. We were chatting away and ended up talking about popular traditions. They mentioned the practice of the "Cantare le uova," and I replied that similarly, in Pavana, we had the "Maggio," and invited them to come to see it. Obviously, I went "singing for eggs" with them, and, with Carlin in the lead as always, we also organized a "Pavanese" expedition to the Langhe. Then there was the "twinning" of the three cities—Dolceacqua [a small town above the Ligurian coast, close to the French border], Bra, and Pavana. Step by step, our friendship was getting deeper. . . . Soon enough, Carlin and his friends showed up at Club Tenco, where they threw everybody into hysterics every year.

Petrini remembers those years with some longing:

The *maestrone* took us to the Tenco festival in 1978. We were reluctant to perform during the show; instead we held court backstage in the so-called "infirmary," where the singers were provided with medicinal glasses of wine. Only twice, in 1990 and in the year that followed, they persuaded us to go on stage. In Sanremo we were known as the "Trio from Bra," the Tall, the Short, and the Fat. The roles were established and never changed: I was the "good host" and took care of the direction; Azio was the true artist of the group, while Giovanni poured in his irony, with the quick wit he had inherited from his father. Those were memorable years. From then on, Sanremo became a fixed date for us, and our fellowship was to be severed only by Giovanni's passing.

One of the most poignant moments of that adventure, which lasted more than twenty years, was when we brought the singing duo of the Nete Twins to the 1980 Tenco festival. The twins were two ladies in their late sixties we had met on May 1 of that year at a patron-saint feast in the hamlet of San Giuseppe Monforte, a small village in the Langhe. They mainly did songs from the twenties and thirties. One, Anna (she preferred Neta, the Piedmontese abbreviation of Annetta) Costamagna, passed away in 2002; the other, Domenica, known as China, died in 1987. They were self-taught and played the guitar and the mandolin; they had never performed anywhere other than Trinità, their home town, in the province of Cuneo. We took them to Pavana, in Tuscany, for the traditional summer reunion with Guccini, where we usually went to eat mushrooms and sing. When we got to Savona, on the Ligurian Riviera, the twins candidly admitted they had never seen the sea before.

They fascinated us with the way they could make themselves match like two peas in a pod, as well as with their songs, played in the style of the days before radio — a repertoire that was, nevertheless, fundamental for the festivities. For those of us fortunate enough to have enjoyed the art of the twins in those seven years before China, the mandolin virtuoso, passed away, they were unforgettable. We brought them everywhere, to Paris, to the beach on vacation. But once, when they saw the fare of the Hotel Royal in Sanremo, where Club Tenco had invited us, they asked me: "Carlin, why don't we go back home, and tell them to just give the money to us?" After her sister Domenica died, Anna refused to sing ever again.

Piero Dadone, a journalist from Cuneo, described the Nete twins in his book *Non ti fidar di un bacio a mezzanotte* (Do not trust a midnight kiss). The book, which is dedicated to Anna, features a CD of songs by the Nete twins, together with the complete lyrics of their repertoire. Dadone says: "The Nete sisters, now deceased, lived through the war in Libya, the First World War, Fascism, the Resistance, World War II and the economic boom that followed, and the turmoil of '68; they prided themselves on their fearlessness. And it was at that time that Petrini and his pals from Bra became the sisters' promoters."

SINGING FOR EGGS: MUSIC AND POLITICS

The founder of Slow Food is well known to have great organizational skills. After his first visits to Sanremo, he seriously considered becoming a cultural impresario. His cultural activities were, however, always attached to the land and its traditions. They were never an end in themselves, but rather a way to reconnect people to food, tradition, and culture in the largest sense of the word. He says:

> In the mid-seventies, I started seeing the Piedmontese writer Nuto Revelli regularly. He was the author of *Il mondo dei vinti*, a book in which he had collected stories about the poor peasants of the Langhe. He inspired us to immerse ourselves in the world of the country people, although his own approach was rather different from our own. It wasn't gastronomical. He was interested in exploring a dying peasant world as something to be carefully studied and described. We, on the other hand, wanted to interact with that world. Nuto and I always liked each other, to our last meetings just before his death in 2004. All the while, I nurtured another passion of mine: popular songs of the Langhe that we learned at the taverns we went to. I went about this systematically, and between 1971 and 1977, I recorded several cassettes thinking that I might establish a center where I could preserve and promote oral culture.

Tavern sing-alongs and large public gatherings are not, in the end, all that different. This explains how the Langhe Arci, with the help of the Circolo Cocito, presented an international popular music festival in a series of towns in the Piedmont region from April 4 to 8, 1979—a kind of modern-day Canté i'euv, the festival was modeled after the old Langhe tradition. Groups came from France (Lyonesse, Grelot Bayou), the U.K. (Chris Hamblin, Magic Lantern), Ireland (Na Fili), and from all over Italy (Canto Vivo, Prinsi Raimund, Astrolabio, Viulan, and many others) to participate in it. The streets were filled with the sound of the Irish musicians and the pipes of Alain Cadeillan and the Perlinpinpin Folc (a group that collects and performs the music of Gascony). People danced to Occitane and Briton songs, and the Tuscan *Cantar Maggio* (May song) mingled with songs of the Canté i'euv of the Langhe. The festival lasted four days and four nights, with 67 performances by 117 musicians, and thousands of people filling the theaters and squares. In Diano d'Alba, a small town a few kilometers from the capital of the Langhe, there was a traffic jam of epic proportions. Young people carrying tents and calling in loud voices stunned the straightlaced local population and caused some problems for the organizers, who were unprepared to manage such an overwhelming crowd of visitors.

The following year, the festival was held in March on an even larger scale, with 150 events and a greater emphasis on international participation, with groups from India and all over Europe. The violin was accompanied by the *ghironda* (barrel organ), the tuba played alongside the cello (the latter was also the graphic logo of the event). Contributions promised by the local authorities were late in arriving, but the group from Bra did not lose heart: they steeled themselves and borrowed whatever money they needed to avoid falling short of expectations.

Throughout their cultural activities, Petrini and his leftist friends never lost sight of their longstanding goal of effecting political change. After the successes of the festival and the co-op store, their leftist political group gathered 8.6 percent of the votes and became the fourth most popular political force in Bra. In the election of June 8, 1980, they won twice as many votes as they had five years earlier. From April 8 to 12, 1981, shortly after yet another devaluation of the Italian lira (6 percent this time), the Canté i'euv was held for the third time. This time, Hungarian and Moroccan musicians joined the Italian popular music groups. There were more people, more expenses—and more disagreements as well, about damaged schools, ruined flower boxes, and dubious tax irregularities.

Petrini was about to go through a "black year" that kept him out of politics. On November 23, 1980, an earthquake devastated Campania and Basilicata, causing three thousand deaths and leaving three hundred thousand homeless. The whole country mobilized to help the stricken areas; Piedmont sent trailers, food supplies, tents, camp beds, and other basic necessities. Petrini found himself heading and organizing the local relief operations. People close to him knew that he was not particularly interested in accounting and tended to maintain a detached attitude toward money. Yet when he was late with a payment for a batch of mattresses he had bought on behalf of the city of Bra, he was placed under investigation by the local judiciary. Meanwhile, the funds promised by the Piedmont region to finance the singing festival had not materialized.

As a consequence, the Arci Langhe accumulated a deficit of 1 hundred million Italian lire (comparable today to $240,000)—at the time, a relatively conspicuous amount.

As is often the case, necessity was the mother of invention, and Petrini started focusing on food and wine, setting aside songs and politics. He resigned from his seat at the city council (on account of insufficient evidence, the charges of the misuse of public funds were dropped) and began getting involved in catering and social tourism. He recalls that terrible year:

> I had just returned to the city council and found myself at the center of a double frontal attack. On the one hand, because of the Irpinia funds for the earthquake relief; on the other, there were some anonymous letters accusing me of allocating public funds to the Canté i'euv. It looked as though everything was becoming a bitter political fight, and it's probably true that we had pushed the establishment too far, too. In the meantime, while I waited for Piedmont to make its promised contribution to the festival, suddenly the provincial government backed out and blocked the payment. It was a tough year, 1980. *Primum vivere* [live first]: at that point my goal was not to be overwhelmed. I had to rethink everything I was doing. Today nobody ever resigns under any circumstance, but I wanted do the right thing and so I left the city council: I wanted to devote myself entirely to getting the funds back and defending myself. Still, the money was not coming in, inflation was galloping at a rate of 15 percent, and the banks were strangling me. I had to become an entrepreneur and exploit my contacts with wine producers and tavern owners, as well as my experience and knowledge of the territory. From the beginning, however, I tried to balance considerations of economics and quality, and it wasn't long before we created restaurants, a co-op, and tourist activities for young people who lived in the city.

PINA AND MARIA, THE FIRST "SLOW" COOKS

Maria, born in 1921 and raised in Roreto di Cherasco (a small town in the plain between Alba and Bra in southern Piedmont), adds forty egg yolks for each kilogram of flour. Pina, who is twenty years younger and from Treiso (a small village in the hills of the Langhe), uses half that many:

eighteen eggs yolks for each kilo of flour. So here are two different recipes for *tajarin*, the traditional fresh pasta made of dough rolled out incredibly thin and then hand-cut with a knife. If the Nete twins were the soundtrack of the beginnings of Slow Food, Maria Proglio, née Pagliasso, the beloved "mamma," and Pina Marcarino, née Bongiovanni, a fiery stove warrior, were Slow Food's first cooks. To be sure, Pina and Maria may have their differences when it comes to the number of eggs needed for *tajarin*; nevertheless, they were closely united in their professional and human adventure.

Pina and Maria are the real soul of two of the four historic restaurants that were founded by Petrini and his associates. The first two were the Osteria dell'Unione, which was opened as an Arci club on May 1, 1982, by Pina Bongiovanni and her husband, Beppe Marcarino; and the Boccondivino, which was located in the courtyard of Via Mendicità Istruita and opened on December 1, 1984, with Maria Pagliasso at the stove and Carlo Petrini, Silvio Barbero, and Gigi Piumatti serving at the tables. The Osteria dell'Arco opened on April 1, 1986, in an alleyway in the historic center of Alba, with the cook Beppe Barbero (a disciple of Maria) in the kitchen and Firmino Buttignol in the dining room. And finally, the Arcangelo di Bra operated out of an elegant villa on the hill from March 1987 to June 1994, with Carlo Arpino, brother of the writer Giovanni Arpino, as the cook and pastry chef.

Pina Bongiovanni belonged to a family of innkeepers: in the thirties, her father Cesare bought a little inn in Treiso that had a lovely *topia* (a vine-covered pergola), under which old folks had the habit of drinking a glass of Barbaresco wine while playing cards. Pina was a kid then: she was only four when World War II ended. After all the fighting between Fascists and Partisans during the *Liberazione* period, her father decided to retire, so the Osteria dell'Unione stayed shut and abandoned for thirty years. Then in the seventies, Pina and Beppe met Petrini at the Cooperativa Libraria La Torre of Alba, and he persuaded them to reopen the family inn. Pina recalls:

> The license to keep the inn open had expired, and at the city hall of Treiso they did not want to issue one to us. It was Carlin who said: "Let's create a 'private' club under the auspices of the Arci, a place to take members of the club to eat." And that was that. When in 2005, Romano Prodi

renamed the coalition of the Left the "Unione," I said to Beppe: "See, we are still fashionable!" In the early years, you needed to have a membership card to eat here. I served only bread and salami, then came *tajarin*, *agnolotti del plin* [very tiny stuffed pasta pieces, made with a particular pinch to hold the filling], rabbit stew, and poached veal in tuna sauce.

Today you can have the same plates made to order by her daughter Patrizia. Arci Gola and the manifesto of Slow Food were born on those tables.

Maria Pagliasso, on the other hand, grew up in the Maiulin inn, a rest stop for cart horses in Roreto di Cherasco. Her father worked as a stableman, and she stayed in the kitchen to feed the hungry drivers: fish from the Tanaro River, *bollito* (boiled meat), and eels. Once the old family inn shut down, Maria went to work as a cook in many other places, including a clinic and some elegant restaurants.

One day her daughter Lucetta, who hung around with Petrini's group, described the difficulties of her mother's situation: "My mother was about to fall into a depression after Dad's death. She was at home, she was retired, and after a life of work, she couldn't remain idle." Petrini came up with an idea: why not re-open that vegetarian cuisine restaurant that had just closed in Via Mendicità? Carlo wanted Lucetta's mother to invite him over for lunch. Maria recalls: "I put together a great menu, I knew he loved to eat well. There was *finanziera* [a Piedmontese dish with meat, chicken livers, and vegetables cooked with vinegar], risotto, *bonet* [a cocoa pudding with amaretti cookies]. At the end of the meal, he says: 'My dear Maria, I came here to tell you that starting December 1, we shall open a restaurant in Via Mendicità, we'll serve at the tables, you will be in the kitchen. Do you accept?' At first I said no, but with him it was impossible . . . and I now have been in that kitchen for twenty years, teaching many cooks. I have gotten real gratification from that work, like that time when the Ceretto brothers, Bruno and Marcello, the producers of Barolo, took me to America to cook. I loved it so much."

Today, the menu of the Boccondivino, the restaurant on the first floor of the courtyard in Via Mendicità Istruita, a few meters from the office of the international president of Slow Food, offers the same dishes, made with products coming from the Presidia of the "little snail" movement: poached veal in tuna sauce, tongue with pickled vegetables, risotto with leeks, and Saras del Fen (ricotta cheese wrapped in hay), chickpea soup, meat braised in Barolo. (More is to come on the protected foods of the Presidia in Chapter 5.)

THE COOPERATIVE OF THE TAROTS

In April 1982, the Cooperativa I Tarocchi (Cooperative of the tarots) was established to provide better management for a series of new economic enterprises, centered now on wine and restaurants. Giovanni Cravero, Carlo Petrini, Silvio Barbero, Firmino Buttignol, Anna Ferrero, Gigi Piumatti, and Marcello Marengo were among its founders. The most effective from the very start was Buttignol. A factory worker from Friuli in his thirties, he had been a welder and a union representative with Barbero and was now on unemployment with two small children. After having joined the Free and meritorious association of the friends of Barolo, he had started working with them: he tasted, bought, and resold wine, and then threw himself into the adventure of running the cooperative. In Italy, there is a popular card game played with the distinctive cards of the tarot deck. Instantly recognizable as a name, tarots were a good choice to symbolize the chain of restaurants and wine bars the Bra group wanted to open all over Italy. The Osteria dell'Unione, which was only an affiliate since it belonged to Pina and Beppe, and the Boccondivino were supposed to be the "first cards of the deck."

Today Buttignol is the president of the I Tarocchi co-op, which has sixteen employees and sales of $1.2 million per year. He remembers the co-op's beginnings:

> At that point, Silvio and I were both union members. We got involved in the cooperative in stages: I started working for it first, then he joined. Carlin convinced us that an ambitious project was about to take off, the first goal was hence to raise funds. I therefore began organizing camps for young middle school students from Rome. We hosted them in some farms in the Langhe or in small hotels, and took them through a socio-historical itinerary, explaining the local economy as well. We played a French game to teach them to recognize different aromas; it was called *le nez du vin*, the nose of wine. We found out that these young people could not recognize basic smells. If they smelled the essence of

an apple, they would say: "It smells like shampoo." They would identify clove as the toothpaste from the dentist. We were stunned, and we realized that those kids lacked any contact with the reality of the soil; many of them had never even seen a cow before. We told them about vineyards, castles, and local traditions: students and teachers were both passionate. We also started some summer camps, and took them canoeing, horseback riding, and biking. The nature we introduced them to was a far cry from that of the boy scouts; rather, it was related to peasants and to the products of the soil. It was tiring but exciting, too: it was oeno-gastronomy applied *in loco*. All these activities went on for at least six summers. Then Boccondivino got started: we took turns, and everybody, Carlin included, served at the tables. Just like today, the restaurant was closed on Sundays. There was only one reason for that: nobody wanted to do the weekend. In the kitchen, Maria Pagliasso was a master sergeant—she would get mad at Carlo if he got caught up in conversation with clients he knew and was late taking the ready dishes to the tables. The passion for wine and gastronomy caught everyone. Thanks to Maria, who also prepared food in the summer for the students at the farmhouse, we learned about the authentic cuisine of the Langhe. In 1986, after the experience of the Boccondivino, I opened a new restaurant in Alba, which was an offshoot of the I Tarocchi co-op. It was in Vicolo dell'Arco, a couple of steps from the central Piazza Duomo. In 1994, it moved to a courtyard in Piazza Savona, where it still is.

The Arci Langhe was also at the origin of an innovative project having to do with wine. From 1980 on, its members published a yearly catalogue of local wine producers, which offered labels that are famous now but were still unknown at that time. Ever industrious, the Arci Langhe also joined forces with the environmental organization Legambiente to publish a small book titled *Trekking: Andar per Langa* (Trekking: a walking guide to the Langhe). Appearing in June 1982, the book spoke tellingly of the group's approach to the land, stating in its introduction that "The secret of walking through the Langhe lies in its rhythm: quiet, sweet, in a word, human."

However, despite the many activities, Petrini was beginning to get restless. With the worst period behind him, he was ready for a new adventure. Here's how he sums it up:

The Cooperativa I Tarocchi started with multiple goals, but soon found itself at an impasse, whether to continue focusing on oeno-gastronomical issues or to carry on organizing social tours and offering camps for children. To tell the truth, the support we were getting from local organizations was beginning to fade. We waited forever for funding, and with skyrocketing inflation, the money we did get was always worth 15 percent less than the amount we'd asked for. Having to acquire wine from small producers for our restaurants, we began to resell it to other Italian restaurateurs. The members of the group did not always agree on how to proceed: some, maybe the ones who had been union members or leaders in the student struggles, could not understand why they had to be at the stove or serve at tables and wanted to keep organizing tours. And yet, it never occurred to me then that we were going through a kind of political "splitting": creating associations has always been a way of doing politics. Backlash? Far from it. The truth is that, thanks to French gastronomical culture, to *Gola*, and to my contacts with the Arci of Rome, I was ready for a change before the co-op was. It was nevertheless clear that there was a new market to discover and that the market in question was developing quite fast. We sold the first *novello* wine [a wine that is harvested and sold almost immediately, like the French Beaujolais Nouveau], the Santa Costanza di Banfi, and, at the same time, we started disseminating a national oenological culture through our restaurants. The Boccondivino was the first local restaurant to introduce a wine menu with non-Piedmontese labels. From time to time, we received a case of Romanée-Conti and looked at it, enraptured. Those were tumultuous years: we were all learning a new profession. Fortunately, a lot of people were very generously offering courses and guiding wine tastings and symposia.

The time had come for the birth, on November 26, 1983, of the Arci's oeno-gastronomical league, the Arci Gola. At the beginning, it had no formal membership, but it quickly grew in autonomy until it was ready for its official establishment in 1986.

chapter 3

THE IDEA: 1986–1989

ARCI GOLA: AN IDEA WHOSE TIME HAD COME

The writer G. K. Chesterton, who created the character of Father Brown and was himself a Catholic thinker of engrossing optimism, once wrote: "An idea, if it doesn't try to become word, is a bad idea." And went on: "The word which doesn't try to become action, is a bad word." The idea came in 1986, and the words were "Arci Gola," which later became "Slow Food." The movement gained momentum by means of articles, books, and seminars. Slowness, a style of life whose slow, human rhythm was juxtaposed with the "fast life," was the fundamental concept that the group proposed for *Homo sapiens* and *edens,* a human being in the pursuit of intellectual and material pleasure.

The four years during which this idea matured and then spread across Italy and into the world were years of profound changes in Italy, as the nightmare of terrorism, which had lasted from the late seventies into the early eighties, brought an end to the Italian Left. Petrini and his associates, nurtured by a vision of life that was at once ethical and hedonistic, had somehow managed to escape the years of bloodshed and ideological conflicts unharmed.

It was thanks to the nationwide network of the Arci—the Italian recreational and cultural association established in 1957 by the PCI—that Petrini's national association, Arci Gola, could take off. Enrico Menduni was president of the Arci organization, which had 1.2 million members, from 1978 to 1983. He was a controversial intellectual with ties to the PCI. He would later leave a promising political career to become, first, a member of the board of RAI, the national public television network, and then a professor of communication sciences at the universities of Siena and Rome.

Menduni understood the difficulty a Communist organization would have in attempting to advocate for the environment and for civil rights. He explains:

As an organization, Arci was sclerotic. I decided to work to update it by encouraging the birth of groups interested in such topical issues as women's rights, youth, freedom of information, gay and lesbian rights, and the environment. In those years, the movements that in some way anticipated and led the changes in Italian society were born. Carlin Petrini and his associates from Bra were among these groups. They wanted to found a national oeno-gastronomical league proceeding from their local experience. I persuaded them to call it "Arci Gola." I asked Gianni Sassi for permission to use the name. Gianni had created the monthly *La Gola* in Milan, and had designed for Arci a beautiful poster with a naked man, all painted white, who was sitting with his legs crossed, and the inscription: "You can't do it alone." Thinking back to those years, the group from Bra seems like something out of a song by Paolo Conte, somewhere in between jazz and ribaldry. A strong individualism animated Petrini and his associates, and, although part of a movement of the Left, they nevertheless represented something peculiar: the pleasure they took in hanging out at a *caffè*, eating and drinking, was expressed with a certain refinement, a sophistication quite distinct from the workers' movement. Not by coincidence their roots were between Liguria, Piedmont, and Lombardy, in the north of Italy: we perceived them as almost "French."

Today, judging by the itinerary of Carlo Petrini, it seems to me that he has avoided the pitfall of becoming a theorist of late-bourgeois pleasure, and he hasn't sold out. He has managed to get involved in exotic things like chili pepper chocolates while staying faithful to his origins, and when it seemed that he only wanted to promote a sort of mass hedonism, he made it clear that he had not forsaken his ideals.

Arci at that time served as an umbrella organization for a series of quite different associations. Some of them supported hunters' interests, a very popular sport in some Italian regions; others were devoted to kids' soccer; still others fought for environmental causes. Each of these associations, however, had a membership fee, which meant that money was always flowing into the center; that way, the national presidency of Arci was capable of financing the activities of the smallest groups. The largest contributors to the national budget were the sports and hunting societies. That financing system did not please everybody, especially the hard-core Communists, who could not put up with the eccentricities of the environmentalists and the neo-gastronomists. When, in 1983, Menduni was forced to resign on account of an illness that kept him out of public life for two years, Arci's chairmanship was assigned to an executive who transformed it into an organization whose constituent associations were more independent of one another. The first to break away were the environmentalists, who founded their own "environmental league," Legambiente, which now has initiatives in marine and coastal monitoring and sponsors voluntary work to defend nature and reduce pollution.

The decision made by the environmentalists turned out to be contagious. Petrini and his associates understood that the time had come to take the big leap towards autonomy and "*battere moneta*" ("beat the bushes"), in Barbero's words, by assessing their own membership fees.

An Arci gastronomical league promoted by the association of the friends of Barolo already existed, but its main function was to increase the value of the local cuisine and produce. However, the group could not organize its own business, since it had not yet been formalized. The league replaced its old logo, an image of eggs crowned by the Langhe hills, with a new one, created by Sassi—an image of a big pot with a man in Renaissance clothes standing next to it, taken from an old engraving. An assembly was convened, which took place on July 26 to 27, 1986, at two highly evocative sites: the Fontanafredda estate in Serralunga d'Alba (royal vineyard and former residence of the mistress of King Victor Emmanuel II of Savoy) and the library of Silvio Pellico, an Italian intellectual of the Risorgimento.

The goal of the conference was to promulgate a new philosophy of taste, in which pleasure and knowledge had equal importance. Petrini was unanimously elected president. As usual, praise of conviviality and an insistence on the right to enjoy oneself were the dominant themes, but a new approach was also beginning to take shape: cultivating an awareness of food culture as the first step in the effort to conserve distinctive local food products. The environmental protection of oeno-gastronomical culture and of places of pleasure such as cafés, pastry shops, taverns, workshops, old mills, bakeries, and wine cellars was another topic of interest.

Obviously, the conference offered plenty of occasions for conviviality. At the inn and restaurant called Real Castello di Verduno, which is run by the Burlotto sisters—Liliana and Lisetta in the kitchen and Gabriella in the dining room—the delegates were offered beef tongue in green sauce, the peasant *minestra del battere il grano* (a broth with chicken livers and herbs), *giura* with cream of zucchini, and to conclude, *bonet*, a pudding with chocolate and amaretti. One particularly noteworthy specialty of the house is braised beef, called *giura*. In the local dialect this is the name given to cows at the end of their career, when they are headed to slaughter. A humble dish of the Langhe lowlands, *giura* is cooked very slowly and was traditionally put on the stove before the farmers went out to work in the fields. At the Osteria dell'Arco in Alba, other guests savored the risotto with Barolo, while at the Boccondivino in Bra they had Maria Pagliasso's famous chicken with vinegar butter. Finally, Ristorante Brezza in Barolo served up *plin,* tiny ravioli in roasted meat sauce, herbed rabbit, and Barolo zabaglione.

THE TRAGEDY OF METHANOL-TAINTED WINE

When Arci Gola was first established the name was composed of two separate words. Later on, the two words were fused—Arcigola—making a pun on the prefix "arch-" to suggest a kind of "arch-*gola*," or "arch-gourmet." However, this "new" name coincided with a bad moment in the oenological history of the Langhe. March 1986 was marked by the scandal of methanol-tainted wine, which caused nineteen deaths across northern Italy. That event is to be considered a kind of divide in the history of Italian viticulture. Because it was such a traumatic event, the scandal made it clear that Italian winemakers had to make quality their highest priority.

It was not easy, at first, to grasp the significance of this crisis. Initially, it did not attract a lot of attention. A doctor in a Milan hospital had made a connection among the suspicious deaths of three Milanese, who had died between March 2 and March 13 after having experienced a terrible stomachache, vomiting, and headache. He suspected that "perhaps these people drank some poisoned wine." It turned out to be true, and on

March 29 the news hit the front pages: "Wine and methanol: a massacre." The ambrosia of Bacchus had never before been connected with a common poison. The newspapers started referring to a "killer-wine." The number of victims jumped to ten, and it was said that they had all died while drinking a sort of Barbera (at least that was the inscription on the magnum bottle), produced by a company in Incisa Scapaccino (between Asti and Alessandria). The stock of bottles was produced by some "narzolini," retailers from Narzole. Narzole is a little center in Cuneo province where brokers used to buy and sell loose wine at low prices (the town has no grape production of its own). To get a higher alcoholic content, one retailer had spiked the grapes with a high percentage of methyl alcohol. At the time, there were no controls on the sale and use of methyl alcohol, yet just 5 milliliters of it could cause eye damage, while 150 could be lethal.

Days passed before the police were able to piece together the whole complex process and understand that the adulterated stock of magnum bottles had been sold in supermarkets for 1,800 Italian lire (a little less than the current $2) and had been produced using raw material sold to the Incisa-based company by Giovanni and Daniele Ciravegna, a father and son from Narzole. For oenology, the consequences of this transaction were devastating, to say nothing of the tragedy that hit so many families. The newspaper *La Repubblica* wrote on April 12, 1986: "The bells toll on the vines of La Schiava, of Soave, of Ribolla, and of Lambrusco. All over Trentino, Veneto, Friuli, and Emilia, a dreary toll is heard. Those methyl victims dragged down orders for wine, closed the doors to the export of wine, and cut by half domestic wine consumption."

As if that were not enough, that summer the aqueducts of the Po Valley were polluted by *atrazina*, a herbicide. From Bergamo to Ferrara, from Mantua to Casale Monferrato, health authorities ordered every household to turn the faucets off. The cause? The indiscriminate use of pesticides in agriculture: toxic runoff from the fields had gotten into the aquifers and polluted the water supply.

And there was more to come: that dreadful spring ended with the disaster of Chernobyl, the Russian nuclear plant where there was a meltdown of the core, releasing a radioactive cloud all over Europe. The consumption of leafy greens plummeted; there were doubts about the quality of milk, of meat, and of the mushrooms coming from Eastern Europe.

The relationship between humans, the environment, and food was changing. The following years brought more tragedies: mad cow disease, chickens poisoned with dioxin, hormone-laced meat. Food counterfeiting led to talk of *cibo impazzito* (food gone crazy), according to the definition of journalist Jean-Claude Jaillette in his book, *Les dossiers noirs de la malbouffe* (The dark files of bad food), which denounced the inefficient European controls on food safety. Drawing on his extensive research, Jaillette wrote that "the food industry is afflicted with an arrogant desire to impose its products ever more widely, regardless of cultural differences, on people all over the world," and it has forgotten that "there can be no beneficial and long-lasting progress if one does not take into consideration the experience that peasants have acquired through the years and their universally acknowledged culture."

Arci Gola was still in its infancy, but the ideas embraced by the group were beginning to gain wider attention. In Italy and elsewhere, people started talking about the relationship between food and the community; questions were raised over such issues as chemically altered products, excessive use of electricity, and the sacrifice of quality for the sake of easy money.

On June 5, 1986, yet another blight struck. This time, the damage was not man-made, but a hazard of nature: hail. Twenty minutes of fury from the sky were enough to strip the vineyards of the Barolo DOCG of their grapes, damaging 50 to 70 percent of the harvest in the Langhe. In the Langhe, where feasts and singing accompany every grape harvest, wine is considered a gift, despite its cost in labor and sweat. And the fuller the casks, the better. Until the early eighties, the wine from Nebbiolo grapes—the basis of Barolo—was still often sold in bulk at the winegrowers' cooperatives. Sometimes retailers paid more for Dolcetto grapes than for Nebbiolo, because nobody in Italy wanted Barolo anymore. At the same time, younger winemakers were breaking from tradition, trying innovative methods for making wine from the difficult Nebbiolo grape. They sought to emphasize quality over quantity—and the paltry harvest of 1986 presented them with a particular challenge. As ever, Petrini and his associates from Bra shared the pains of the Piedmontese winegrowers and looked for ways to help them regain their footing after the many setbacks, both environmental and natural, that the year had brought.

ELIO ALTARE, THE REBEL OF BAROLO

The winegrower Elio Altare was born in 1950 and grew up in the village of La Morra, one of the most famous subsections of the Barolo DOCG. An intelligent and curious boy from a winemaking family, Altare was eager to carry on the family business. He spent several years studying agriculture and came home full of ideas for new ways of doing things. To his father's dismay, Altare wanted to radically prune the vines so that they would produce far fewer grapes — the remaining grapes would, he said, be sweeter and filled with the taste of the soil. In addition, he wanted to ferment the wine in small casks, or *barriques*, like the ones he had seen on his trips to Burgundy, and throw away the old ones, which were big and difficult to keep clean. He felt certain that the smaller casks would help extract the wine's aromas, which tended to be hidden by the grapes' tannins and sodium tartrates. His goal was to produce a more elegant Barolo than that of his grandparents, because, as he said to his disapproving father, "wine is pleasure."

Altare was convinced that much of the wine of Barolo was performing at less than its potential. As he put it, "If Barolo is not selling, it's because it is not being made correctly." In the early eighties, he began to experiment with a variety of new approaches. He chose to briefly macerate the grapes at a controlled temperature using techniques that involved modern systems of fermentation. In 1985, Altare's father died and he began to more vigorously pursue his innovations. He recalls the challenges he faced, both as a modernizer and in the aftermath of the hailstorm of 1986, which destroyed 50 to 70 percent of the harvest in the Langhe:

> I wrote it all down in the little journal I keep: during the grape harvest of 1986, I convinced my harvesters to inspect the bunches one by one and clean out every ruined grape before pressing them. It took them four days, and they looked at me if I was out of my mind. Everyone opposed me on this. Fortunately, it turned out to be an exceptional year for wine, like the previous one. The first people to realize this were Carlo Petrini, whom I had met when he picked my Dolcetto for the dinners at the convention when Arci Gola was established; and an American journalist, Robert Parker, who, in the magazine *The Wine Advocate* listed my Barolo Vigna Arborina 1985 among the best Italian wines he had tasted. They called me an innovator because I used the

barriques instead of the old casks. It's true, I took a chainsaw to them. All over the world, 225-liter casks were being used to refine wine. With Carlo, we understood each other at first glance. He is a person who inspires confidence, and he wanted to help us younger people find a new way. He was willing to take risks if he believed in you.

A group of young winegrowers including Luciano Sandrone, Gianni and Roberto Voerzio, and Giorgio Rivetti began some "casual" wine tastings with Altare, comparing, for example, the French Pinot Noirs and their lightness with the ancient tannicity of Barolo. These modernizing young winegrowers found they had much in common. Alongside their concern for the techniques used in their winemaking, they shared an equal concern for the soil of their vineyards. Altare recalled the artificial fertilizers that were being introduced when he first started working with his father's vineyards:

> I remember, at the beginning of the sixties, those trucks arriving from Porto Marghera [where Italy's chemical industries are based]. It was like manna from heaven. We harvested 200 quintals of grapes per hectare, while until then we could barely get to 50. For millions of years, the vine drew its nourishment only from organic material, and with the arrival of these fertilizers it was like someone becoming addicted to cocaine. I stopped using pesticides in 1979, but we are now short of stable manure.

Today, environmentally conscious winegrowers are eager to abandon pesticides altogether and return to traditional fertilizers, such as cow manure. But manure has become almost impossible to find: the traditional stable with its oxen and cows has been replaced by gigantic tractors. Altare himself has long dreamed of creating a community stable that could supply manure for the vines. Some years ago, he founded a group of nine winegrowers who were dedicated to this project. In their initial conception, the stable would have thirty or so cows and be operated by a single family. A book, titled *L'Insieme* after the name the group took for themselves, narrates their story. In the foreword, Petrini notes:

I remember clearly the beginnings of the wine producers who are the main characters in this book. Especially, I remember the first time I met Elio Altare in the mid-eighties. It was a difficult period of transition: the wine producers of the Alba hills were torn between feelings of resignation and a will to redeem themselves. The memory of the methyl scandal was still fresh and was raising unsettling questions about the future of their little world. I discussed at length with Elio the need to change direction, to re-found the whole system on a new basis that could take into consideration the potential of this generous and proud region. . . . Each of us went his own way, and our paths (first with Arci Gola, then with Slow Food) passed many more times by those vines that finally began to vibrate with new sap and new confidence.

Likewise, the Arci Gola movement was getting an infusion of new blood from the group of "arch-gourmets" that had met at the Fontanafredda estate. In a short time, their ranks had swelled from a few hundred members to thousands. These people did not conform to the common stereotype of the gourmet: that of a more or less cultivated person interested in talking about culinary traditions. That type was represented by the members of the Accademia italiana della cucina, founded in 1953 by Orio Vergani, whose motto was "Italian cuisine is dying." Members of the Accademia tended to be doctors, lawyers, journalists, and bombastic gourmets. However, the gatherings of the newly born Arci Gola had a more informal atmosphere: the focus was on enjoying the traditions of the farmhouse, trading the stories and knowledge of the older generation, and eating well. The organization's first journal, soon followed by other magazines, periodicals, newsletters, and books, was called *Rosmarino* (Rosemary), and its editor in chief was Elio Archimede. In the first issue, from February 1987, Enrico Menduni, who was no longer the Arci president but still a spiritual father to the gang from Bra, wrote: "Today the Left wants to eat well, even at the cost of running up debts. Wisely enough, it prefers to eat a banana rather than having a bad meal in a pretentious restaurant; even better, though, is investing in an excellent dinner in the right place at the next opportunity. Quality, service, technique, sensitive combinations of flavors, creativity, fantasy. 'At noon something changed,' would go a title of the *Unità. Buon appetito*."

MILITANT GASTRONOMIC CRITICISM:
GAMBERO ROSSO

They walked, and walked, and walked, until at last, towards evening, they arrived dead tired at the Inn of the Red Crayfish. "Let us stop here a little," said the Fox, "that we may have something to eat and rest ourselves for an hour or two. We will start again at midnight so as to arrive at the Field of Miracles by dawn to-morrow morning."

Thus begins chapter thirteen of *Pinocchio*, the masterpiece of Carlo Lorenzini (better known under the pseudonym of Carlo Collodi), one of the most famous children's novels of all time, written in 1883 and adapted for the screen by Walt Disney in 1940. The puppet invented by Collodi is arguably the most popular national stock character in Italy: he is the archetype of the bourgeois citizen, but he also has a light streak of the protester. This is the reason why the name of the tavern where the Cat and the Fox take their victim, the "Red Crayfish," or "Gambero Rosso," was chosen to represent the publishing activities of the new nonelitist, regionally based gastronomy organization. Only months after the formal inauguration of Arci Gola, Petrini and his associates launched a nationwide platform from which to communicate their views on food: the *Gambero Rosso*. *Gambero Rosso* was an eight-page insert that appeared on a monthly basis in the leftist newspaper *Il Manifesto*; it came out on the second Tuesday of each month. The masthead of the first issue, which appeared on December 16, 1986, read: "Edited by Arci Gola. Editor in Chief: Stefano Bonilli."

Petrini and Bonilli came up with the idea for this publication, which was to combine a vade mecum, a ready reference, for experienced gourmets with criticism of the big food conglomerates. Bonilli was at the time in charge of news reports for *Di tasca nostra* (Out of our pockets), a program on consumer protection that appeared on the television station Rai Due, and he had gone to northern Italy to report on the methyl alcohol scandal. Petrini and Bonilli talked a lot about food, consumer protection measures, and the need to take action: these conversations were the origin of the plan to convince the newspaper of the "radical-chic" Left to publish a monthly insert dedicated to "insatiable and curious consumers."

Bonilli had a house in Tuscany and regularly went to the restaurant Gambero Rosso in San Vincenzo, where Fulvio Pierangelini, now one of the top restaurateurs in Italy, had prepared seafood delicacies since 1980. Various meetings between Bonilli's "Romans" and Petrini's "Piedmontese" took place over a meal of fish at the Gambero Rosso. Taking the inspiration for the name partly from Collodi and partly from Pierangelini, the two groups committed their ideas to paper and circulated the insert every month to a readership of eighty thousand. Arci Gola had never had so much freedom to spread its ideas. Simultaneously, these ideas began to circulate throughout the peninsula by means of local groups or chapters that were called "Condotte" (literally, "behaviors"), a term whose use was intended to connote the sense the word has in a medical context in Italy: "the practice of duties in the public interest in a certain context and territory" (the closest term in English medical terminology would be "protocols"). Once the Slow Food movement began to spread abroad, these local chapters were called "Convivia," a word drawn from Latin, suggestive of both gathering and conviviality.

A title on the front page of the *Gambero Rosso* triumphantly reported that Arci Gola, with "twenty-two thousand members, is the largest oeno-gastronomical association." It was signed Carlo Petrini.

I have the great luck of having been born and living in an extraordinary part of southern Piedmont, the Langhe, which borders on the end of the Ligurian Appennin foothills and is surrounded by the slow and sinuous course of the Tanaro River. In this sub-alpine part of our beautiful country, we grow up having conversations and discussions about good wine, the typical dishes of our tradition, and about food as a redemption from our ancient misery. Fenoglio, Pavese, Lajolo, and Nuto Revelli are our literary legends; in their works we can read our story, our way of being, and also the extraordinary development of the local wine industry, once poor and dispossessed. Similarly, it was my good luck to have been active in the early seventies among those intelligent people on the Left who gravitated around *Il Manifesto* and later the PDUP. Well, one day, while I was having a lengthy chat about gastronomy with a well-known comrade, I was hastily interrupted by this statement: "You *langaroli* [inhabitants of the Langhe] constantly talk about eating, you're like country priests." Later on I learned that that famous comrade spent his vacation in France systematically visiting the good transalpine restaurateurs; he was particularly appreciative of their cuisine, service, and extraordinary wine selection. I recall this detail because it effectively summarizes the odd relationship that the Italian Left has had with gastronomy: a private, almost secretive enjoyment of good food and its delicacies, but also, generally, detachment and indifference when it comes to the role of food in public life, which, incidentally, if understood to include food production and food sales, involves more than a quarter of our population.... Here are the coordinates within which I think the work of Arci Gola should situate itself and grow: environmental protection and consumer protection, with the right amount of conviviality, good living, enjoyment, and pleasure that such issues require.

Only many years later would Petrini be called the first "eco-gastronome." What is often overlooked, however, is that the ecological theme was already present in his discourse, as this article shows, at the dawn of Arci Gola. In the first issue of *Gambero Rosso,* sarcasm coexisted with a concern about food, consumer protection, and food criticism. One could, for instance, read a learned article on the therapeutic qualities of the truffle, or the report of an editor in Turin who had gone to eat at the cafeteria of the Fiat Mirafiori car factory at Christmastime with a committee of food critics to evaluate the sandwiches and *spumanti* (sparkling wine). The subjects covered included just about anything related to food, from wine to restaurants.

For three years, the eight pages of the *Gambero Rosso* confronted all the issues that are still of concern to Slow Food philosophy, and they helped Arci Gola to grow. Soon, the group was starting to plan courses on the knowledge of wine, alongside their usual roster of cultural happenings in the Langhe. The insert was such a success that, in 1989, it became a magazine with a color front cover, though it was still distributed through *Il Manifesto* until 1992, when it began to come out on its own. Bonilli transformed his experiment on food culture into an autonomous publishing enterprise, Gambero Rosso Editore, which through the years has continued to issue an elegant magazine. Gambero Rosso went on to launch a satellite television channel devoted to gastronomy—RaiSat Gambero Rosso Channel was born in 1997—and the group has now created an enormous forum for food and cooking in Rome, the Città del

Gusto, offering cooking classes, cooking "performances" by visiting chefs, wine tastings, and other events. Bonilli's group has developed in a different direction from that of Slow Food, and the only collaboration today between Gambero Rosso Edizioni and Slow Food is the *Vini d'Italia* guide.

GOOD FOOD FOR THE LEFT

Ever since his visit to Montalcino, which had convinced him to focus in a more systematic way on food rather than on popular music and social tourism, Carlo Petrini had dreamed of changing the attitudes of the Left toward food, which were halfway between an abstemiousness worthy of a Franciscan friar, and an eager commercialism that was illustrated by the Communist Party's annual Feste dell'Unità. The Feste was Italy's biggest popular banquet, organized to finance the party's newspaper, *L'Unità*. Every summer these feasts attracted thirty million participants, and they constituted part of the worldview of the Italian Left.

While Petrini continued his personal battle against the lamb chops that were the most popular food during those parties—they were usually charbroiled and enveloped in clouds of smoke and the nauseating smell of fat—Arci Gola worked on reaching a wider audience. The *Gambero Rosso* magazine, with just a few tens of thousands of readers, was not enough. At *L'Unità* (which on Sundays sold close to a million copies, and, on weekdays, 250,000 copies), there was a new editor in chief, an amicable senator from Naples who was interested in the joys of life, Gerardo Chiaromonte. He began by updating the newspaper, first with a satirical insert, followed, between April 1987 and December 1988, by the insert *A/R* (meaning *andata e ritorno*, or roundtrip) devoted to "vacation, travel, adventure, and slight diversions," which appeared every Thursday.

The closing page of *A/R* was devoted to gourmandism, with a report from Arci Gola. Petrini wrote some twenty articles. In the summer of 1987, he established an unusual gastronomic competition. "More than thirty inspectors of Arci Gola will visit and taste, incognito, those restaurants participating in the Feste dell'Unità who wish to compete. These inspectors will be asked to judge, evaluate, and comment, grading the quality of the cooking, the wines, the ingredients, the originality of the dishes, the cordiality and attentiveness of the service, and the fairness of the prices. Consistent criteria and parameters will be used to award scores of up to five hundred points."

The competition was a great success, and Petrini had to retract his earlier negative statements: he wrote openly about it in *A/R*, in July 1987, after a first visit. The article was titled "At the Pinerolo Festival the food was sublime":

> I had a great dinner on the evening of July 1 at the Festa dell'Unità in Pinerolo [a small town near Turin, in northern Piedmont], thanks to chefs who passed on their passion and love for cooking. Perfectly cooked rice was served with a tasty eggplant sauce, the green salad was excellent and dressed with extra-virgin olive oil, the vegetable purée soup was perfect, and the desserts were simple but stunning. I recall the classic Piedmontese *bonet* [a kind of pudding] that one can find only in some farmhouses in the Langhe and in Monferrato, and an excellent buckwheat cake. I cannot express the same enthusiasm for the wines that were on sale there: they were all average in quality, and the refills were too small.

A restaurant of a Communist branch in Bologna won the first competition. Petrini commented: "There's a place at the table for the Left as well." The competition led to a conference, held in Montalcino naturally, that was given the appealing title: "At the table with the PCI." It took place on November 28, 1987, at the Casa del Popolo. The conference consisted of a big luncheon for one hundred guests; the food had been prepared by the restaurants on the podium: truffle appetizers, *trofie* (pasta twists) with pesto, venison in a sauce made from Brunello wine. In *L'Unità*, a witty article reported: "Once upon a time, as we all know, the Communists ate little kids. But then, partly because the main ingredient became scarce, partly because it was necessary to switch from craftsmanship to an industrial scale, the season of sausages (or *salamelle*, according to the Emilian school of thought) began. We are now at a turning point, it's the 'Copernican revolution.' The Communists have discovered the culture of good living."

Many executives of the PCI arrived from Rome, and Folco Portinari, the poet and critic who was one of the first intellectuals to join Petrini's association, was there. In his speech he exalted the culture of honesty and authenticity at the table, what he called the "slow food approach" of eating well and slowly, and he spoke out against the ideology of "fast food" and against the constant rush to make a profit. It was the very beginning of the "revolution of the snail."

The collaboration with *L'Unità* ended, and a number of years passed during which the movement no longer had a newspaper to spread its ideas. During this period, Arcigola and Slow Food consolidated at the international level and maintained their visibility by appearances at wine conventions, exhibits, and other events. Only in October 1998 did Petrini resume writing for a national newspaper, *La Stampa*, based in Turin and owned by the Agnelli family and the Fiat corporation.

VINI D'ITALIA:
CELEBRATING WINE WITH "THREE GLASSES"

Cesare Pavese wrote in *Il compagno* (*The Comrade*): "You are young ... and do not know that one needs three noses to drink Barolo." Bonilli and Petrini may have been thinking of these lines from the Piedmontese writer, or perhaps also of the three stars of the Michelin guide, when they developed another interesting publication for their most devoted consumers: the annual *Vini d'Italia* wine guide. *Vini d'Italia* was different from all existing Italian wine guides: it used accessible language, rather than the jargon of the wine critic, in its accounts of producers and their vintages; it contained recommendations of little-known but highly rated labels; and the reviews were specific to the wines released that year. The first edition of *Vini d'Italia* came out for the year 1988. The research that had gone into this publication included "blind" tastings of 1,500 wines of the year, made by five hundred different producers. It also offered a critical selection of the year's wines, as no publication had previously attempted, focusing on the best of the best of Italian wine production. Thirty-two bottles, ten from Piedmont, eight from Tuscany, three from Friuli, and the other eleven from regions all over the peninsula, were given a special mention next to the label, a symbol of three wineglasses, or "tre bicchieri" (pronounced "tray bee-kee-air-ee"). When today a restaurant sommelier proposes a special wine, he often specifies: "I suggest this one, it is a 'tre bicchieri.'" The symbol is now synonymous with quality for Italian wines.

Vini d'Italia, produced jointly by Gambero Rosso and Slow Food, was an overnight success, a best seller, and it came to be regarded as a reliable reference tool for wine lovers, restaurateurs, wineshop owners, importers, and distributors of high-quality Italian wine. With the passing years, the numbers have been impressive: the 2006 edition examined 2,126 wine producers, tested 15,476 different labels, and awarded 246 "tre bicchieri." But in the first edition of 1988 the editors, Daniele Cernilli and Petrini, did not fail to mention the methyl scandal that had once seemed like a dark sign of the decline of the Italian wine industry:

> Still today most of Italian wine is sold in bulk, unbottled, and there are few laws governing its production. There is no law that limits production, which is very excessive (the surplus is approximately 25 to 30 percent), or provides consumers with a guarantee of the integrity of wine production. Not even the recent DOCG, the guarantee of origin, which according to law, is given only to "especially prestigious wines," serves to resolve this question, because it has been assigned to wines that already had the DOC and fails to take into consideration other new high-quality vintages. Several wines that achieve the maximum score in our guide are officially classified as "table wines," which confirms the fact that the legislation is outdated and absurd, since it neither protects consumers from fraud nor promotes wines of the highest quality. And yet, with the exception of a few hundred gems, the overall picture of these "table wines" is discouraging. This is the area in which frauds such as the methyl scandal are perpetrated; in fact, compared to them, the infamous *zuccheraggio* [sugarization] hoax looks like an elementary school prank.

There are many surprises among the wines receiving the honor of "tre bicchieri" in the guide's first edition. There were four different bottlings of Barolo-Ceretto (Prapò 1983), Luciano Sandrone (1983), Elio Altare (Vigna Arborina 1982), and Aldo Conterno (Vigna del Colonnello 1982). The list also included Angelo Gaja's legendary Sorì San Lorenzo Barbaresco 1983; the Moscato d'Asti Bricco Quaglia 1986 by Giuseppe Rivetti of Castagnole Lanze; and the Pigato 1986 Massarotti by Parodi of Albenga. The guide featured several fabled Tuscan wines and, from Sicily, the Marsala Superiore Vecchio Samperi by De Bartoli. An article in the *Gambero Rosso* was more specific: "All of this has not cost the wine producers more than the wine tasted in the wine cellar; we have made a point of not asking for contributions or offering publicity; we really wanted to maintain our independence of judgment."

Publishing *Vini d'Italia* was a big risk, as Gigi Piumatti, the guidebook's current editor, acknowledges: "We went out on a limb by giving space in the book to some relatively unknown labels, by telling the stories of the winegrowers and of the people working alongside them in the wine cellar, and by giving awards to innovators who were experimenting with winemaking techniques that had been used before in Napa Valley and in Burgundy, but not here in Italy. I still have no idea how we managed to publish that first guide in 1988, since it all started at a summer dinner at the Gambero Rosso in San Vincenzo, when we met with the Piedmontese and the Romans."

Andrea Gabbrielli, one of the "Romans," who at that time was already a member of the *enoteca* Cavour 313 and who later served for many years as editor of *Gambero Rosso* magazine, adds: "Wine was what held us together. In the wake of the methyl crisis, we felt we were playing a vital role by teaching people about the quality of Italian wines. Our idea to award scores and to classify wine producers into four main categories (those that are simply mentioned and those that are awarded either one, two, or three glasses) was also a reaction to the crisis in the field. Although we knew that our opinions were not likely to be shared by everyone, we thought it was necessary to establish a scale of values." The critics, however, received the *Vini d'Italia* guide with enthusiasm. Petrini goes back to those early years:

> Wine was still the focus of our attention. Once I read the texts by Renato Ratti and Gino Veronelli and learned about wine tasting, my world became one with the one of wine producers, vineyards, and wine cellars. It was a world full of human warmth, of great stories to tell, of labels to discover. With respect to where we started out: it was an exciting period of rapid change, we had learned a lot and now it was time to allow our ideas to bloom and mature. We wandered through the Langhe looking for inns and new restaurants, but there was not an awful lot (apart from some good restaurateurs who were already in the guides):

very often they just recited the menu for you, there was no wine list, and the Dolcetto was the one and only wine the innkeeper would serve you. Hardly anyone served Barolo. So it was inevitable that we developed the gastronomic project before the environmental one, although we had the basic idea for it.

One evening when the members of Arci Gola were sitting around doing some blind wine tests, we invented the *gioco del piacere* [game of pleasure]. We judged the wines based on how enjoyable they were and we compared wines from different regions. Everybody could vote for one, and then the votes were tallied to pick a winner. The first game (twenty-three more followed, with increasing success) took place on April 29, 1988, and 852 people in thirty-eight different restaurants participated. The same night, the scores were telephoned to Via Mendicità, and after the tallies, the headquarters declared the winner "live." It certainly was a unique initiative; the internet and instant messaging were still in the future. In the first game, we compared austere red wines, and a Chateau Clark Bordeaux 1985 won, followed by a D'Angelo Aglianico del Vulture 1982, an Allegrini Amarone 1981, and a Clerico Ghemme 1982.

Then we started thinking that it might be possible to build a new model for the development of the *terroir*, with a more integrated production, marketing, and distribution system, similar to the one we had seen in France. At that point we called a general oeno-gastronomical assembly of the Langhe in Alba. It was July 4, 1988, and there was a lively discussion on the topic: "Is the Langhe to Piedmont what Côte d'Or is to Burgundy?" Two years later, following the French model, we called "agrarian councils."

At that point, Arcigola was using wine to gain recognition and gather support throughout Italy. From July 10 to July 13, 1988, the first National Congress of Arcigola (by that time the two words had been fused) took place in San Gimignano, Montalcino, and Siena. In two years, the Condotte of gourmands had enabled Arcigola to extend its hold over the entire nation; it had started a didactic program with cooking courses, wine tastings, and historical research. The association's stated objectives were to "safeguard food quality from environmental degradation, from disreputable counterfeiters, and from speculators who care more for the promotion than for the authenticity of a product."

ANGELO GAJA AND THE
"DIRTY DOZEN" OF CALIFORNIA

As they drank wine, Angelo showed that he too was a poet. When you drink a wine before its time, it was, according to him, like committing infanticide. "Infanticide?" said Angelo, "No, this is a perfectly healthy baby." Sorì San Lorenzo '89 was certainly not a *vin nouveau*.

This is a passage from a book by Edward Steinberg, an American who moved to Italy, fell in love with Italian wine, and followed each and every production phase of the most famous label by Angelo Gaja, the winemaker of Barbaresco, the great standard-bearer for the Langhe's reds. The volume, first published in the United States in 1992 and then in Italy in 1996, is titled *The Making of a Great Wine: Gaja and Sorì San Lorenzo*. Under the entry for May 4, 1992, this pleasantly discursive diary tells about the magic moment in which Guido Rivella, the company's oenologist, and Gaja taste the product of their grape harvest of 1989 for the first time.

Gaja is another legendary figure whom Petrini had met during his years of apprenticeship. In February 1988, they were together in Napa Valley, perhaps the most famous wine region in California. Their trip has gone down in Slow Food history as the voyage of the "dirty dozen," a reference to the number of participants in the trip. As a wine producer, Gaja had organized a tour of U.S. wine cellars, which were generally unknown to Italians, with the idea of importing the best labels to Italy. The group was composed of three journalists linked to the wine world: Carlo Petrini; Davide Paolini, a writer for *Il Sole 24 ore* who was known as a "gastronaut"; and Gigi Piumatti, today the editor of *Vini d'Italia*; four agents of the Gaja wine company; and four restaurateurs—Mastrantonio Coriolano from Rome, Mario Stoppani from Milan, Guido Alciati from Piedmont, and Gianfranco Vissani from Umbria. Coriolano had a voice that was notoriously hoarse due to his irrepressible enthusiasm for his city's soccer team. Every three months he came to the Langhe to look for wines for his restaurant in Rome; located in the Parioli quarter, it was then one of the most highly regarded restaurants in the city. In the nineties, his specialty was *coda alla vaccinara* (stewed oxtail) and handmade pasta. Mario Stoppani, along with his brothers Angelo and Remo, was the owner of

Peck in Milan, the excellent store and restaurant catering to gourmands of all stripes. It was founded in 1883 by a sausage maker from Prague named Francesco Peck, and eventually it passed down to the Stoppani brothers in the seventies. In the late eighties, Peck's specialties were international dishes like walnut and lobster mousse, and regional ones like osso buco *cremolato* (glazed veal shank). Alciati, who died prematurely in 1997, was the owner of the famous restaurant Guido, a temple of Piedmontese cuisine, which consistently ranked at the top in gastronomic guides from the end of the seventies through the eighties. It was located in Costigliole d'Asti and was family-run: Lidia, his wife, was at the stove in the kitchen, and his sons Ugo, Piero, and Andrea in the dining room. In the nineties, his specialties were ravioli, an unbeatable traditional dish, and such innovative dishes as a parmesan flan with a pea sauce. Vissani, who was born in 1951 in Civitella del Lago in Umbria, has been among the top-ranked Italian restaurateurs since 1982 when the *Guida dell'Espresso* (comparable to the Michelin guide) started giving him "three hats." He learned to cook from his father, also a chef, and by visiting the best restaurants in Italy and Europe. In the nineties, his creative specialties included his tagliolini with fava beans, flounder, and curry sauce and clams.

Gaja, who was born in 1940, is unanimously considered the standard-bearer of the Italian winegrowing and wine-producing renaissance. Possibly the best-known Italian wine producer in the world, he has always been a leader. He has a degree in economics, and, since 1961, he has run the family business that was founded by his great grandfather in 1859 on the Barbaresco hills overlooking the Tanaro River. To his Piedmont estate, he has added properties in Tuscany, in Castagneto Carducci (Ca' Marcanda), and in Montalcino (Pieve Santa Restituta). In the *Vini d'Italia* guide of 2006, the Gaja of Barbaresco company has nine wine labels receiving "three glasses," and Gaja has thirty-seven labels with "tre bicchieri," making it the premier wine cellar in Italy. In addition to Sorì San Lorenzo, Gaja has all along produced another specialty, Sorì Tildin, named after the nickname of Angelo's grandmother, Clotilde Rey.

Gaja, who was the leader of the American expedition, tells it this way:

> In 1987, I started including some wines from California on my list, the
> Mondavi and others, and I wanted Italy to know about these wines, so I

organized a trip with twelve people. I believe it was on that occasion that Petrini and Paolini talked for the first time about doing something related to food, some selection of regional products that would be available alongside the wines at Vinitaly. Carlin found those ten days in the States a useful way of getting to know all those famous cooks he traveled with. The strong personality of Vissani, who could be a little eccentric sometimes, obviously stood out, while Alciati proved to be an attentive observer.

Americans had by that time proved their ability in promoting their "premium wines," and had impressed all of us. The "premium wines" were different from table wines: they were products of extraordinary quality, with an added high "imaginative" value, linked to the region, the history, and the producer. This type of wine is classified as popular-premium, premium, super-premium, or extra-premium. Petrini was particularly struck by the fact that a nation so far removed from our rich oenological history was so devoted to the production of premium wines and neglected table wines. We asked ourselves: is it only a matter of profit? This was certainly one reason, but not a sufficient one. We realized that a producer could focus on producing premium wines of higher quality because consumers were willing to pay for them. It was a new approach, still relatively rare in Italy. The production of table wine prevailed in our country, and there was a surplus with respect to the demand. Furthermore, our export was substantially based on that product.

In the dozen or so wine companies we visited in our trip, we noticed a high degree of technology: first of all, in the use of the *barriques*, which in Italy have been the source of so many ideologically charged disagreements; and then in the use of temperature-controlled containers, and how accurate the temperature controls are during the production.

One day we went to a big Safeway store in San Francisco (the Safeway chain has 1,800 stores in the United States): we were surprised to find out that every Friday night a section of the store was assigned to singles only. There was also a big space for fresh fruit and vegetables of extraordinary quality, with much higher prices for organic products; everything appeared wrapped in a faint fog, because they were spraying the vegetables and the pyramids of peaches and strawberries with water to keep them fresh. We realized that the American consumer strove for quality, in food as well as in wine. This recent development showed that we now had fellow travelers on our adventure. Since 2000, in the area of the docks in San Francisco, there have been farmers' markets for organic products that are run directly by the farmers themselves. It has been twenty-two years since a great chef, Alice Waters, spurred Californian farmers to achieve a higher level of quality with her restaurant Chez Panisse in Berkeley, in the same way Guido Alciati did in Piedmont. The situation in America was already very advanced in 1988. It's not by coincidence that Slow Food is today a success in the U.S.: Alice has become the international vice president of the movement, and I am sure that it's only a matter of time before the United States will be the country with the largest number of members. All the intelligentsia supports our association, particularly on the West Coast.

In a country that, from the Italian standpoint, had no gastronomic history whatsoever, the "dirty dozen" members of Gaja's trip were impressed to discover how welcoming the American winemakers could be. The Americans wanted to make the whole culture of wine more broadly familiar, hence it was essential to them to open up to visitors: wineries were ready to welcome tourists, with annexed restaurants and gift shops of all kinds. Gaja continues:

In the United States, wine producers knew they had to deal with people, possibly of different ethnicity, drinking only Coca-Cola and milk—the wineries knew they had to educate people. Often I hear Europeans looking down on the culture of wine in the United States. And yet, with magazines like *Wine Spectator*, and the power of their media, they are able to influence the production of the entire world. When there are companies capable of distributing millions and millions of bottles to, potentially, 260 million consumers, many of whom are ready to spend between $80 and $100 a bottle, it's easy to influence the market. We had a different perspective, we thought of wine as a food beverage that had to be cheap, like olive oil or bread. You also have to remember that, in the years after the scandal of methyl, our exports had collapsed. Luckily, within the domestic market consumers were beginning to look attentively not just for the name of the wine—Barbera or Barbaresco or

Soave—but also for the DOC and the names on the label. We got the message: Italy had to work hard to produce premium wines instead of table wine.

Before it began to center on food, the Slow Food movement was focused mainly on wine for several years. After the trips to Burgundy and the visits to the Vinexpo Fair in Bordeaux, the leaders of the movement introduced interesting new ideas from California. Upon their return to Italy, Petrini and Piumatti presented these ideas to the wine producers of the Langhe. Since then, Gaja and Petrini have established a real, lasting tie, based on mutual admiration. As Gaja says of Petrini:

> He is capable of inflaming us; he can ignite the passions each of us has inside and makes them come out. He inspires his collaborators to work at a low salary to carry out his mission, and at the same time he has instilled farmers and winegrowers with professional self-esteem. If you have a valuable product, he convinces you to obtain just compensation. This reasoning is the more powerful since it comes from somebody who has never sought to line his own pockets and who has been able to involve public institutions in his project. Wine producers have acknowledged how much Slow Food has done for them and have supported the movement through the University [of Gastronomic Sciences]. I see a similarity between Carlo Petrini and Gino Veronelli. The latter fought for the dignity of the vineyard workers, but with the approach of an anarchist, a loner. He was a Don Quixote who attacked the powerful, so that he was sued dozens of times. Carlin has always fought for the importance of acknowledging agricultural work, and through the association he leads, he has also given us the instruments to consolidate the working dignity of farmers and producers.

A MANIFESTO AGAINST FAST FOOD

Even before José Bové, the French leader of the antiglobalization movement among farmers, attacked a McDonald's restaurant in Millau, the French sociologist Paul Ariès had written of the restaurant chain's significance in his book *Les Fils de McDo: La McDonalisation du Monde* (McDonald's Children: The McDonaldization of the World, 1997). As

Ariès explained, the hamburger cannot simply be described as a food that is typically American; rather, it represents the first ageless and cultureless food. It is "neither national nor international, but cosmopolitan, and is based on the negation of all the pre-existent culinary cultures."

The biggest fast-food chain in the world started with the encounter between the McDonald brothers, owners of a small restaurant in San Bernardino, California, on the legendary Route 66, and Ray Kroc, a dealer of electric mixers, who in 1955 became the licensing agent of the McDonald brothers' restaurant model. Through franchising, Kroc soon started opening other restaurants identical to the first McDonald's in the United States and all over the world. The first one opened in Des Plaines, Illinois, on April 15, 1955: it was called McDonald's Speedee Service System. As Ariès notes, "His objective was to serve a complete meal in less than a minute." Half a century later, there are twenty-nine thousand McDonald's worldwide, of which thirteen thousand are in the United States, with a million and a half employees who serve forty-three million customers a day (these are data obtained from the website: www.mcdonalds.it). With Kroc's fast food (in 1961, he bought out the McDonald brothers and obtained rights to the use of their name), a new concept shows up in food preparation: standardization. Taking its impetus from industry rather than the centuries-old traditions of food preparation, standardization also ushered in another tendency in food consumption—that of the "global palate," as the Italian sociologist Vanni Codeluppi defined it in his essay on business marketing, "*Il potere della marca.*" For the first time, taste is becoming standardized on a global level. "The binary structure (sweet/salty, raw/cooked, hard/soft, etc.) that our traditional taste structure has always been based upon . . . is tending more and more to merge into a single synthesis that pleases every palate." Codeluppi is referring here to a fundamental text of modern anthropology, *The Raw and the Cooked* by the French ethnologist Claude Lévi-Strauss. Lévi-Strauss studied the indigenous myths of Latin America and identified fire as an element of mediation between the human being and nature, thus introducing for the first time a sort of equation between "cooked" and "socialized." Referring to the human capability to use the five senses, Lévi-Strauss writes: "We begin to understand the essential place occupied by cooking in this indigenous philosophy. Not only does fire mark the passage from nature to culture: thanks to it, the human condition defines itself with all its attributes, even those (like ethics) which could seem more arguably natural." This text by Lévi-Strauss, which has deeply influenced Petrini's cultural outlook, is fundamental to the Slow Food philosophy.

The first McDonald's in Italy (today there are 330, fewer than the 1,000 in Germany, the 880 in England, and the 790 in France) opened discreetly in the town of Bolzano on October 15, 1985, and closed in 1999 due to problems relating to the lease. However, the second, in Rome, which at 1,200 square meters was said to be the largest in the world, generated disagreements and bitter reactions among Italian intellectuals, who were more worried about the scar that the "golden arches" might inflict on the façades of the old buildings in Piazza di Spagna than the quality of the food. On March 20, 1986, the day it opened, at least twenty thousand *"paninari,"* or "sandwich eaters"—a synonym for young people who eat on the go—stepped up to the 30-meter-long counter amid fake mosaics of classical Rome, little water fountains, and wicker chairs. In the April 13, 1986, issue of *L'Espresso*, Gianni Riotta reported from the United States on the way fast-food chains and shopping malls had transformed the cities of the United States: "The architects Paolo Portoghesi and Costantino Dardi are scandalized. 'It's as if a bomb had hit the city center,' Portoghesi has written." The former representative of the Communist Party, Antonello Trombadori, asked McDonald's to move its restaurant somewhere else, while the sociologist Franco Ferrarotti issued warnings against further colonization by the United States. The critic and urban planner Bruno Zevi added: "Will Piazza di Spagna become a garbage dump identifiable by the nauseating smell of fried food? The scandal should be ascribed to the authorities responsible for the ruin of Rome." Zevi concluded by saying that "the city authorities, not McDonald's, are guilty of inappropriate zoning."

The arrival of fast food was a significant event in Italy, and in Rome in particular, where it was impossible not to notice the large restaurant in Piazza di Spagna. The municipality took up the case, and the mayor, the Christian Democrat Nicola Signorello, decided that McDonald's should be allowed to stay on its site but at the same time was obliged to remove the big "M" from its façade. The fast-food phenomenon could not simply be waved away with a decision of city planning, though. Italian commercial television quickly caught on to the new fast-food habit and soon launched a program with a *"paninaro"* as the main charac-ter: the program took American culture, fast food, and drive-in theaters as its frame of reference.

One evening, while having dinner at the Osteria dell'Unione in Treiso, in the Langhe, the members of Arcigola sat around grumbling about how Italy had become consumed with television and con-sumerism. Between a glass of Dolcetto and a *tajarin* made by Pina Bongiovanni, a plan was hatched to fight back. Folco Portinari, who was then a television executive in Milan, was there and recalls:

> Some historic Italian restaurants, even in Florence, had transformed themselves into fast-food joints. Hearing about this kind of thing drove us to come up with the idea of containing this barbaric invasion by means of slow food: it was intended as a defensive maneuver. Carlin asked me to write a manifesto with our philosophy. I tried to explain that behind fast food there was a new civilization and a new culture with one and only one motive: profit. Pleasure is totally incompatible with productivity, for the time one spends pursuing it is deducted from productivity: in this perspective, even to make love is a useless and sinful activity. I set down to work, even acknowledging to myself that a manifesto against fast food had already been written by Charlie Chaplin in his film *Modern Times*. We wanted to reclaim the value of pleasure and of the body. I came up with the expression "fast life," which seemed to sum up all the daily rituals of which fast food was a part. As a subtitle for the manifesto I wrote "International Movement for the Defense of and the Right to Pleasure." What prepared me for the task was my experience writing for the periodical *La Gola*, which had dealt with food culture long before it became popular to do so; a number of intellectuals from *Alfabeta* and from Nanni Balestrini's *Gruppo '63* also wrote for it. Writing for *La Gola* was a slightly elitist experience: we had our special rituals, such as our endless discussions during the editorial meetings with no editor in chief. Culturally, this contributed to the birth of the Slow Food movement. Our target was not exclusively food: we wanted to bring back the tango, the umbrella, and to celebrate a leisurely daily pace. I fought for the name Arcigola for the association, with the superlative connotation in mind (i.e., arch-gourmand), and not Arci Gola.

Portinari, who was the author of various critical essays on Italian literature, did indeed write the text of the manifesto, and on November 3, 1987, Petrini, wth his disciples gathered around him, witnessed the appearance of the manifesto on the first page of *Gambero Rosso* (year II, issue no. 11). The signatures of Portinari and Petrini came first, followed by those of Stefano Bonilli, the founder of Gambero Rosso, and Valentino Parlato, who signed for *Il Manifesto*. There were then the names of Gerardo Chiaromonte, the Communist senator and editor of *L'Unità*, and various intellectuals and well-known artists: Dario Fo, Francesco Guccini, Gina Lagorio, Enrico Menduni, Antonio Porta, Ermete Realacci, Gianni Sassi, and Sergio Staino. The original document was much longer than the final official one. Here is the unabridged version:

The culture of our times rests on a false interpretation of industrial civilization: in the name of dynamism and acceleration, man invents machines to find relief from work but at the same time adopts the machine as a model of how to live his life. This leads to self-destruction; *Homo sapiens* is now so consumed by the cycle of production, consumption, and overconsumption that he has been reduced to the status of an endangered species. Since the dawn of the century, many manifestos have been churned out and declaimed, with speed being the main ideology.[1] The fast life has been systematically proposed for or actually imposed on every kind of form and every attitude, as if in a risky attempt to culturally and genetically remodel the human animal. Suitable to this kind of existence, whether we are talking life in the commercial arena or the emotional sphere, are intimidating slogans rather than rational critical considerations. At the end of the century, we cannot say things have changed much, far from it, since the fast life finally now subsists on fast food.

More than two centuries after Edward Jenner's discovery of vaccination, vaccines have become the only reliable weapon against

---

1. Filippo Tommaso Marinetti published the Futurist Manifesto in the French newspaper *Le Figaro* on February 20, 1909. In addition to glorifying war and expressing contempt for women, the Futurist Manifesto declared the Futurists' objective: "We want to chant the love of danger, the habit of energy and fearlessness. We declare that the splendor of the world has been enriched by a new beauty: the beauty of speed."

endemic and epidemic diseases.[2] Why don't we therefore follow and support science in its methodological lesson? We have to prevent the fast virus with all its side effects. We therefore propose to replace the dynamic lifestyle with a relaxed one. Against those, and they are the majority, who can't see the difference between efficiency and frenzy, we propose a healthy dose of sensual pleasures to be followed up with prolonged enjoyment. Starting from today, fast food is to be avoided and replaced by slow food, that is to say by centers of enjoyed pleasure. In other terms, the table should be given back to taste, and to the pleasure of the gourmand.

This then is the proposition for a progressive and progressionist recovery of the human being, both as an individual and as a species while he awaits a restoration of environmental balance, in order to make life livable again from the standpoint of his basic desires. This implies eating slowly and reinstating the *Regimen Sanitatis Salernitanum* (the Salernitan Regimen of Health, composed at the famous medieval medical school of Salerno in the twelfth or thirteenth century) which is unjustly considered to be obsolete, setting aside time for its highest purpose, namely, pleasure (and not intensive production, as the owners of machines and the proponents of things fast would have us believe). The alternative, a hyper-efficient lifestyle, is just stupid and sad: one need only observe it to see that.

If forced by the prevailing barbaric mode of communication to adopt slogans, we've got plenty. "You won't grow old at the dinner table," for instance, a slogan that contains wisdom and common sense that has been proven over centuries. Alternatively: "Slow Food is *allegria* [cheerfulness]; Fast Food is *isteria* [hysteria]." Yes, Slow Food is cheerful!

Besides, thousands of years of experience have taught us that fast-footed Achilles never reaches the turtle, who in fact wins the race: it's an important lesson, both mathematical and ethical. That sums it up: we are on the side of the turtle, or rather, the side of the common snail, which we have chosen to be the emblem of this project. Under the sign of the snail, we will welcome lovers of food culture and those who still love the enjoyment of easygoing, slow pleasures. The snail *is* slow.

---

2. The English doctor Edward Jenner introduced the vaccine against smallpox in 1796.

The manifesto appeared in issue number 11 of *La Gola* in November 1987. Antonio Porta wrote a very ironic article titled "Fear of the quickie": "The Slow Food manifesto is after all the dream of holding the old kitchen stove in our arms, our chest against its knobs, in a slow embrace." The poet concluded with a more practical warning: "But aside from inciting demonstrations, the Slow Food organization should offer tools to be used for knowledge and orientation. We hope that the new guide, *Vini d'Italia,* edited by Arcigola and by Gambero Rosso, will help to achieve this goal. Can you imagine how much fun it will be to compare the meager (often inexistent) wine lists that you find in restaurants with the pages of the guide? There's no question that Slow Food will lead to an improvement in the manner of drinking."

The founding manifesto of the movement was laid out on the cover of *Gambero Rosso* over the drawing of an enormous snail, with the announcement that in 1988 the association's membership card would carry the snail as a symbol. "The manifesto will assert itself as a life proposal. Under the sign of the snail," the first page concluded. From that moment on, the lovely little animal stylized by Gianni Sassi became the logo on all communication materials that issued from Via Mendicità Istruita. Petrini and his associates from Bra knew the little animal well: the town of Cherasco, the gastronomic capital of the *Helix pomatia* (the edible snail) and an important center of Baroque art, was only a few kilometers away. The snail had also been an important item in French cuisine since the mid-nineteenth century—two of the most popular forms of serving it are *à la bourguignonne* (with butter, garlic, and parsley) and *à l'alsacienne* (with a beef broth aspic).

First came the Slow Food concept, which then slowly morphed into a plan of action, which in turn gave birth to an international slow movement, with two years of discussions, conferences, articles, and meetings along the way. The choice to keep the phrase "Slow Food" in its English-language form in Italy was an ingenious twist. Those two words, a reaction to the Big Mac phenomenon, became the best way to spread the group's philosophy. Another kind of food could exist, another way to eat, another way to comprehend the pleasures of life.

SLOW FOOD HAS A FEAST IN PARIS

Petrini and his associates decided to present the newly born movement to the world and to swear to the manifesto, now in a much simplified version and translated in many languages, not just on French soil but in Paris itself. Leading up to the event, on November 10, 1989, some thirty press conferences had taken place simultaneously on five continents. There were articles in all the Italian newspapers. The *New York Times* defined the movement as "a faintly amused answer to fast food." A Japanese TV crew from the NHK network showed up in Bra. In France, even *Le Monde* and *Le Nouvel Observateur* reported on the movement. In Bra, Petrini and his colleagues received enthusiastic support from the intellectual, political, journalistic, and artistic worlds. The Arcigola members' magazine, now called *Prezzemolo* (Parsley), published many of these appreciative letters on October 15 and November 15, 1989. Here are some excerpts from the most significant ones:

> In a world that's always in a hurry, it's beautiful to stop and listen to a song, sipping a glass of *ratafià*.
>
> —Paolo Conte (songwriter)

> A bright idea, that of Slow Food. The elegy of pleasure is fundamental. One can say: man does not live by bread alone, but has to live especially by pleasure.
>
> —Dario Fo (writer, actor, Nobel Prize winner for Literature)

> Slow Food is not only a hygienic norm; it is a civilized choice. Food is a cultural expression; it requires love and art in its preparation and is a source of pleasure, hence it has to be respected.
>
> —Massimo D'Alema
> (President of the Democrats of the Left
> and former prime minister of Italy)

> In big cities, the fast food business is pursued at the expense of the young. When I was a young man in Trieste, there were places where you could eat at any time. From today's perspective, these were fast food restaurants: but they served traditional cuisine, genuine and well made, like at home. And we stayed at the table for hours enjoying each other's

company. The table is the pleasure of eating, drinking, and being with friends: it has to be a pause to relax, to meet others.

—Ottavio Missoni (fashion designer)

Intent now on turning Slow Food into an international movement, Petrini and his colleagues organized a second major event for the press in Paris on December 7 to 9, 1989, at the Hotel Méridien in Boulevard Gouvion St Cyr. At a cost per person of 720,000 Italian lire (approximately $750 today), members of the media were given access to a troupe of 250 Italian Slow Food associates. At the opening on December 7, a fabulous dinner was prepared by a team of Italian and French chefs. The appetizer was entrusted to a rising star in the world of catering, Igles Corelli of the Trigabolo in Argenta, who prepared a flan of sturgeon with black cabbage sauce, potatoes, and thyme. This was followed by *agnolotti al plin* (pasta stuffed with veal) with white truffles from Alba, created by Pina Bongiovanni from Treiso. The main course was the *filet d'agneau au café* (lamb tenderloin with coffee) prepared by Jean-Marie Meulien from the restaurant Clos-Longchamps in Paris. Then there were slivers of Grana Padano cheese sprinkled with balsamic vinegar, and finally a dessert by the great French chef Michel Trama (Trama and his wife, Maryse, own the Château Relais l'Aubergade in Puymirol, Aquitaine), who presented a *gelée de miel au vinaigre balsamique traditionnel de Modène et au fraise du bois* (honey jelly with balsamic vinegar and wild strawberries). All the cooks made an effort to create dishes using Italian products. Italy was also present in the wine list for the 460 guests: Nebbiolo, Chianti, and Moscato d'Asti.

The participants also celebrated the bicentennial of the French Revolution, which had "liberated" the chefs of the aristocracy, who went on to open modern restaurants to serve the bourgeoisie. Additionally, the dinner was the occasion for the launch of the *Almanacco dei golosi* (the gourmand's almanac). At the Opéra Comique, on Sunday, December 10, 1989, for the inauguration, there were four hundred members from eighteen countries with a specific message: "We refuse to be labeled an association of gluttons: there are already so many of them, nobody needs another one." The French Minister of Culture, Jack Lang, sent a message of support. The newspapers commented: "The objective is to establish some sort of United Nations for gourmets."

The final version of the Slow Food Manifesto, which was translated into eight languages and signed in Paris at the Opéra Comique in November 1989 by representatives from fifteen countries, reads as follows:

Our century, which began and has developed under the insignia of industrial civilization, first invented the machine, and then took it as a life model.

We are enslaved by speed and have all succumbed to the same insidious virus: Fast Life, which disrupts our habits, pervades the privacy of our homes, and forces us to eat Fast Foods.

To be worthy of the name, *Homo sapiens* should rid himself of speed before it reduces him to a species in danger of extinction.

A firm defense of quiet material pleasure is the only way to oppose the universal folly of Fast Life.

May suitable doses of guaranteed sensual pleasure and slow, long-lasting enjoyment preserve us from the contagion of the multitude who mistake frenzy for efficiency.

Our defense should begin at the table with Slow Food. Let us rediscover the flavors and savors of regional cooking and banish the degrading effects of Fast Food.

In the name of productivity, Fast Life has changed our way of being and threatens our environment and our landscapes. So Slow Food is now the only truly progressive answer.

That is what real culture is all about: developing taste rather than demeaning it. And what better way to set about this than an international exchange of experiences, knowledge, projects?

Slow Food guarantees a better future. Slow Food is an idea that needs plenty of qualified supporters who can help turn this (slow) motion into an international movement, with the little snail as its symbol.

chapter 4

THE SOWING: 1990–1996

When connoisseurs of good cooking hear the name Baschi (a small town between Rome and Orvieto), they immediately think of Gianfranco Vissani, the most televised and famous chef in Italy. Likewise, when they hear Erbusco (a town not far from Milan), they are transported to Franciacorta, the haven created by Gualtiero Marchesi, the father of innovative cuisine in Italy. However, only a very knowledgeable gourmet with solid cultural roots might be moved at the sound of two other toponyms for Italian taste, Argenta and Samboseto. Argenta and Samboseto are two little towns in the Po Valley that no longer appear on the map of good food but that belong to the historical memory of Italian cooking and represent two milestones of Slow Food history.

Argenta, some 30 kilometers south of Ferrara near the Comacchio Valley, was home to a flourishing restaurant in the nineties, driven by a team of innovative chefs. The restaurant was called Trigabolo (after an ancient local Celtic community), and Igles Corelli, then thirty-five years old, performed his rites there. In the 1990 restaurant guide published by the Italian magazine *L'Espresso,* Trigabolo was ranked second in Italy, right after the three restaurants that shared first place: the Antica Osteria del Ponte di Cassinetta in Lugagnano, the Enoteca Pinchiorri in Florence, and Gianfranco Vissani in Baschi. Corelli, a great friend to Petrini and his colleagues since the eighties, is now a familiar face on Italian television and owner of the Locanda delle Tamerici in Ostellato, north of Argenta.

Corelli was the creator of the sturgeon flan that was presented at the official inauguration dinner of Slow Food in Paris: "At the time, no one was proposing that kind of dish: to eat fish using a spoon was a completely new thing. The preparation was very peculiar: you had to mash and sift the fish and steam it in the oven, at a temperature of 68 degrees Celsius. We were the first to introduce that kind of cuisine, which involved this new technique of making dishes that had a consistency not generally associated with their taste. Beginning in 1986, we were offering a meat foam and an ice-cream made from the balsamic vinegar of Modena." Cooking for the gala dinner for the formal debut of Slow Food was an emotional experience: "I have happy memories of that night in Paris: in the kitchen with us were Pina Bongiovanni from the Langhe, and Michel Trama, from the Aubergade in Puymirol. Pina had brought her *plin* ravioli for 460 guests and wanted to cook them in a pot for twenty; we convinced her she had to use bigger ones. I also remember there were some incredible truffles from Alba, each of them as big as a fist."

Da Cantarelli, another famous restaurant that has now disappeared, was located in Samboseto, near Parma. From 1953 to 1982, it occupied the back of a simple village store where they sold tobacco, wine, cold cuts, soaps, and detergents. It was a cozy place, with brick walls, a nice fireplace, and a series of distinguished wine bottles up on the shelves. This was not innovative, but it was great traditional cuisine. Peppino and Mirella Cantarelli ran the place, and in the sixties it hit the headlines of gastronomical criticism with two Michelin stars.

Da Cantarelli was notable for its simple food. The cured meats that were served as appetizers were renowned: *culatello di Zibello*, made from the best part of the pig's thigh, cured like prosciutto; and Felino salame, which is seasoned for thirty to thirty-six months. And then there was *strolghino* salami, which is made from the scraps left over after making *culatello* and is available for only a few months a year. (It turns out that some great food products come from leftovers. In the dialect of Parma, the verb *strolgher* means "to invent something"; one day, presumably, somebody working as a butcher thought there had to be a way to make good use of the *culatello* scraps, and so the *strolghino* was born.) After the appetizers, the choices for the first course and main course included items like *tortelli* (stuffed pasta similar to ravioli) with fresh herbs and parmesan, or a *sformato di riso* (baked timbale of rice) with saffron, veal ragout, and peas. There was also the legendary rice *savarin*, a *sformato* with mushrooms, and meat ragout wrapped in pickled tongue. In the mid-seventies, the crew of the director Bernardo Bertolucci, who was shooting his film *1900*, ate there regularly, transforming it into their company dining room. Burt Lancaster, Gérard Depardieu, and Robert De Niro could be found there frequently, wearing their period costumes, eating, and drinking great French wines.

The Cantarellis were overwhelmed by the success, but to the dismay of their clients, they decided to retire at the age of sixty. Since 1992, all that has remained of that legendary trattoria is a wine bar, or *enoteca*, run by their son Fernando. He recalls: "Guests came to us after having experienced nouvelle cuisine and said: 'Finally, some real food'; then they drank either the chilled whites or the Antico Bruscone [a Lambrusco mixed with Barbera to reduce its effervescence] and left happy."

Cantarelli was a place for the soul, a hidden-away spot in the Po lowlands that represented the archetype of the old-fashioned tavern. It was one of those places threatened by the homogenization of taste, by fast food, by sandwich shops, and by nouvelle cuisine. That restaurant was offered a tribute in the first gastronomical guide to Italian taverns and inns, the "primer" published by Arcigola and dedicated to simple restaurants. As the first page announced, the handbook had been conceived in Samboseto, "where Mirella and Peppino Cantarelli showed us how to reach the highest levels in cooking while maintaining a strong bond with tradition and the warm atmosphere of the country inn." This was the first edition of *Osterie d'Italia,* which listed 712 inns all over Italy and was published in 1990. The book grouped these establishments together as *osterie,* or "inns," rather than restaurants, because they were generally small, family-owned businesses that shared a sense of hospitality and offered local cuisine and good wine at a good price.

In his preface, Folco Portinari explained that Arcigola chose to publish the book out of a commitment to break with the tired custom of giving grades, stars, hats, and suns to the same familiar list of great restaurants. "The word '*osteria*' (inn or tavern) makes you think of when, in adventure stories and in movies set in the Renaissance, a door opens wide to let somebody burst into a smoky inn. Additionally, the word has a variety of subtly differing associations, from *hospes,* 'guest,' to *hostis,* 'foreigner,' and also 'enemy.' Today, the '*osterie*' are practically archeological finds, the evidence of an overwhelmed civilization—a human civilization overwhelmed by a mechanical one."

Today, Portinari remembers: "I persuaded Carlin not to put even the word 'guide' on the book cover: it was supposed to be a manual as in the elementary schools, a primer of dining and drinking, with an index to make it easy to find exactly the dish you wanted. I was crazy about the Piedmontese *finanziera* [a typical dish with sweetbreads, mushrooms, and giblets]. Well, then, turning the pages of the *Osterie d'Italia*, I wanted to be able find out where to go to eat it."

The manual was divided into regions, and every gastronomical area had an author to introduce it. The Piedmontese writer Gina Lagorio recalled the Piedmontese trattorias, which are locally called *tampe*, or *piole*: "I recall their names, all so beautiful, so full of cheerfulness, and so different from today's, which are unfamiliar and make me want to laugh and cry at the same time because they have so little to do with this region and its history. What is a 'pub' doing in the Langhe, or a 'spaghetteria'? And a McDonald's? Never mind a pizzeria. These days not even the monks on Mount Tabor are immune from it, but then what about 'hamburgers' in the region that has the most tender meat in the world, please!"

About Lombardy, the journalist and writer Gianni Brera wrote: "All the precocious adolescence, and the youth interrupted by the war like an undue amplexus, have a mournful revival regretting the *osteria* that is no more, with its formica, its neon light. The children of the owner show off university degrees in engineering, or excellent marriages. The *osterie* pass from hand to hand, and change into disgustingly inhospitable bars." The Sicilian writer Vincenzo Consolo ended a series of memories with a beautiful anecdote about a trattoria in Palermo called Patria, which is set in a maze of narrow streets, in the neighborhood called La Kalsa. It's a cooking course in a few lines: "A short, chubby boy wearing glasses and a pedantic and ironic expression immediately shows up and, in a bored and monotonous tone of voice, recites, in a single breath, a litany of dishes: 'Appetizers: *panelle* [fritters made from chickpea flour], *cazzilli* [small potato croquettes], olives, eggplants, anchovies; first courses: *rigatoni alla Disgraziata* [rigatoni with eggplant and breadcrumbs], *rigatoni alla Norma* [rigatoni with fried eggplant and ricotta], tagliatelle with spinach and ricotta cheese, spaghetti or rice with black squid ink, pasta with sardines, pasta with breadcrumbs; main courses:

stuffed calamari, swordfish rolls, meat rolls, *merluzzo a linguata* [fried cod flavored with vinegar], sardines with capers and orange, *polpette di neonata* [baby fish cakes]...' "

Osterie d'Italia was a success beyond all expectations. After the *Almanacco dei golosi*, which Arcigola co-published with Gambero Rosso and presented in Paris in 1989, Petrini and his colleagues started thinking about the association's potential as a publisher. Mavi Negro, who was part of Petrini's office staff, got down to work with Gigi Piumatti and Corrado Trevisan to give birth to their own publishing house, Slow Food Editore.

> The Romans of *Gambero Rosso* wanted to come out with their own guide, modeled on the one published by *L'Espresso*. However, we decided to emphasize the idea of food as part of Italy's natural and cultural resources, like its landscape or its works of art. We wanted our readers to know about places where respect for cooking, for tradition, for local and seasonal products was still vigorous. After all, the inns were our first Presidia: later, our attention turned to the products of the Ark of Taste. *Osterie d'Italia* remains our best seller, with steady annual sales of around one hundred thousand copies. Thanks to its success, our publishing house took off: today, it has a "live" catalogue of more than a hundred titles, comes out with a dozen new books a year, has four hundred collaborators, and some twenty associates.

The most recent editions of this so-called manual for dining and drinking have gotten considerably larger and now include about 1,700 addresses. The editor, Paola Gho, in the preface to the 2005 edition explains, however, that the main philosophy of the manual has not changed:

> Fifteen years after the summer of 1990, when, despite many difficulties, we assembled the seven hundred entries for the guide, which was received by some critics rather coldly but by the public with considerable favor, we are still here to preach against homogenization and bad taste at the table. To be honest, our adversaries have changed a bit since then. Nouvelle cuisine is dead and buried, but everyone now makes too much fun of it or doesn't give it much credit; after all, we used to condemn it only when it looked fraudulent or perverse. The other enemy,

American-style fast food, is now on life support and marginalized even at its home, where it is accused of being the root of all nutritional evil. Still, if an enemy dies, another comes to take his place.

According to the guide's editor, the real danger now is that the book will lose its edge: because of the *Osterie d'Italia,* the idea of regional cooking has become trendy, and as a result one now sees the same specialties on menus and the same wine lists from Trentino to Sicily.

IN THE NAME OF WINE: BOOKS AND CONVENTIONS

The organization, after the big meeting in Paris, began to change its skin, using its publishing house, Slow Food Editore, to establish roots in Italy and to develop its international profile. Above all, it became more proactive: organizing events became the organization's core business.

In Via Mendicità Istruita, the years between 1990 and 1996, when the first Salone del Gusto, Slow Food's great trade fair devoted to food, opened in Turin, are remembered as a period of frantic work. Everywhere, the world was being shaken by major events: the Gulf War, the tragedy of the Balkans, and the end of the Soviet Union. In Italy, the First Republic was dying, as the leaders of the big parties were brought to justice in the influence-peddling scandal known as Tangentopoli (Bribesville).

"Strong" ideologies were replaced by special interests—expressions of "weak thought," according to the term coined by the philosopher Gianni Vattimo—that defended interests related to a specific problem: civil rights (with the Radical Party of Marco Pannella and Emma Bonino), the environment (with the Green Party), and fiscal autonomy and territorial identity (with the Northern League, founded by Umberto Bossi who then participated in Berlusconi's administration). Slow Food's priorities were now to defend the quality of food, save endangered products, and increase the value of *terroir.* Carlo Petrini remembers that period as a whirlwind of initiatives and proposals. The seed planted between 1986 and 1989 was bearing its first fruit:

When we came back from Paris, where the value of the term "Slow" as a global marketing tool became clear, we realized that we had to consolidate our image and build a truly international movement. We started with wine, strengthening the ties among wine producers, who were just beginning to acknowledge how much influence we could wield, and the consumers and our members, who counted on us for information about a culture that until then was not widely known. It is clear from the names of those who signed the manifesto at the Opéra Comique that many of our first contacts were Italian expatriates. In fact, the launch in Paris was really all about the support that was out there for the "made in Italy" brand. But that was not our main interest. In the first years, in fact, we made the mistake of defining ourselves too much as a movement devoted to promoting the Italian approach to living well. As a consequence of that, in Germany and in Switzerland, where our wines and our cuisine were much appreciated, we had a fairly easy time of it, and the Convivia (the name used outside Italy for the local chapters, the Condotte) started coming to life. But it was different in France, where they did not completely understand what *les Italiens,*" as they called us, really wanted, and they rejected the English term "Slow" that had opened so many doors for us. Between 1990 and 1992, we took important steps toward establishing the foundations of eco-gastronomy, although this was only fully developed after the 1996 Salone del Gusto.

The first step was in April 1990 in Alba where the first in a series of *comizi agrari* (agrarian councils) took place. They were conceived after the French model of the *comices agricoles*, free associations of farmers, breeders, and landowners that spread widely in the nineteenth century. Petrini continues: "We organized a series of thirteen meetings; they took place at the congress hall and lasted until July. All the most influential wine experts in the world were there. The meetings were coordinated by winemaker Giacomo Tachis, technical director at Marchese Antinori for the past thirty years and the creator of such landmark wines as Sassicaia and Tignanello."

The second important step was the International Convention on the Wines of Piedmont. During the convention, 250 of Piedmont's most prestigious winemakers met with the leading players in world oeno-gastronomy and with the top journalists in the field. The third step was the publication of the *Atlante dei grandi vini di Langa* (Atlas of the great wines of the Langhe), an extraordinary enterprise that offered a comprehensive introduction to every vineyard in Barolo.

Finally, the fourth step was to enhance the organization's international reputation. For a year, the same team that had been involved in carrying out *Vini d'Italia* worked on the first *Guida ai vini del mondo* (Guide to the Wines of the World), with report cards on 1,900 cellars and 5,000 labels. These meetings and publications represented a great success for Petrini and his colleagues from Bra, who for the first time were facing some of the same challenges as those faced by big national and international enterprises—coordination, marketing, and name recognition.

BUREAUCRACY AND EDUCATION

In Italy, the membership and the executive branch of Arcigola Slow Food were both growing rapidly. By the early nineties, there were almost two hundred Condotte, with twenty thousand members, and a vast web of officers and "fiduciaries" (leaders of local Condotte or Convivia who are nominated by the Via Mendicità Istruita headquarters). These people were volunteers who came from all walks of life: they were lawyers, professors, retired union workers, and others—and, unlike wine journalists, merchants, or importers, they did not have social ties to the oeno-gastronomical world. Upon enrolling, one was first a "learned member" of the association; gradually one became what was jokingly called a "neo-fork" or an "arch-gourmand," and eventually, in parallel to the development of the organization as a whole, one came to embrace the entire philosophy of the eco-gastronomist.

The movement began to have an extensive bureaucracy and to conduct all the typical rituals of a large organization: officers' assemblies, board meetings, and conventions. After the first pioneering meeting in Siena, there were two pivotal moments in the development of the organization: the World Congress of the International Slow Food Movement, which took place in Venice from November 29 to December 1, 1990, and ended with the launch of a statute and a Council of Ten; and the second international congress of Arcigola, from June 13 to 16, 1991, in Perugia, where it was decided to add the expression "Slow Food" to the original name, Arcigola.

Roaming around the streets of Venice, between a taste of *sepie aroste* (roasted cuttle fish) at the Trattoria Ca'd'Oro, and a *cicheto* (appetizer) at the Aciugheta in campo Santi Filippo e Giacomo, the delegates of

twenty-two nations decided to create an international magazine in several languages. This was to be the quarterly magazine *Slow*, the first issue
of which appeared in April 1996 in Italian, English, French, and German.
And, after two days of discussions, the Venice delegates also promulgated their first statute. Among its thirty-two articles, point 2 indicates
the main task of the association: "Slow Food operates for the safeguard
of and the right to pleasure, for the respect of the rhythm of life of the
human being, and for a harmonious relation between the human being
and nature." In addition, it was established that Slow Food had to fight
to improve food culture, to teach children to have an awareness of tastes
and smells, to "safeguard and defend the food heritage of culinary
practices of every country," and finally, to "promote the distribution of
quality products."

Slow Food—what could have appeared to be just a pun was becoming serious business. The conference of Arcigola in Perugia in 1991
launched new ideas, with different possibilities for the development of
regional issues, consumer protection, taste education for schoolchild-
ren, and, not to be forgotten, the concept of pleasure as a right, which
had started it all ten years earlier. Among other proposals, there was one
advanced by Giovanni Ruffa in the June *Newsletter* for "a school of
advanced gastronomical studies, a kind of university whose goal would
be to train young professionals for the oeno-gastronomical sector. We
have to educate the future chefs, restaurant managers, journalists to be
really competent in this field, which is now overpopulated with people
who have plenty of attitude but doubtful competence." To the school of
taste, this was the secret code. Speaking at the conference in Perugia,
Carlo Petrini reaffirmed the point:

> New eating patterns; new methods of distribution, preservation, and
> sale; new dietary models; the steep increase in prices, at the market
> and in restaurants; the decline of lunch at noon: they are all radically
> transforming the food culture of our nation. Styles, manners, processes,
> and languages are changing fast, along with the hours, rhythms and
> pauses, cooking times, techniques, and the taste of the people who
> work in the kitchen. The country of bread and wine is no more; gone too
> (if it ever existed) is a true geography of food. In the big imaginary map
> of Italy's eating habits, the smaller-scale maps that represent regional

and municipal varieties tend to get blurred or to blend into one another. This is the great contradiction in which Arcigola immersed itself when we decided to cover a severely jeopardized territorial cuisine: we were perfectly aware of the fact that the *osteria* of our memories had disappeared long ago. It has been a long time since the Italy of olive oil has become confused and indistinct from the Italy of butter and the Italy of lard. On this map of transformation even the ancient boundaries between the area of *pastasciutta*, broth, rice, and soups; the area of polenta; and the area of spaghetti have become unclear—they seem like surreal symbols of a past that has been overwhelmed by the irresistible march of homogenization and leveling. Yet, our work has only just begun: we don't mean to follow the model of the archeologists, looking for the lost dishes of ancient peasant civilizations, but to contribute to the creation and sustainability of the places where these cuisines can be offered with simplicity using locally obtained raw materials, with respect for taste, the environment, conviviality, and last but not least, the consumers' wallet.

It is clear that beginning in 1991, Slow Food had begun pursuing the goal that would finally be accomplished in 2004: the creation of a university. Petrini continues:

New ideas about professionalism are taking root: competent, enthusiastic young people with energy and new approaches are taking over kitchens, cellars, and wineries, giving life to a generation of key players who are updating this field. Arcigola wants to support this movement, first of all by providing information about it. In a time when many new masters are preaching the gospel of lightness, advertising the aesthetics of being thin, and fighting their battles with weapons like calories, cholesterol, metabolism, and any pseudo-scientific blather they can lay their hands on, it is not easy to make good choices. The time has come to reaffirm the still valuable fundamentals of our traditional values in food: simplicity, variety, seasonal changes, and sense of proportion. . . . In the years ahead we should work on three different levels: first, we have to make our courses in wine tasting, cooking, and nutrition science available throughout the entire country. . . . Second, we have to provide every Condotta (Convivium) with a permanent tasting commission, constantly active and open to explore scientifically the world that tastes open up for us. . . . The third objective, the most ambitious one, is the institution of a school of advanced gastronomical studies, an expression of Arcigola, that could outfit young graduates to operate in this sector with just two years of coursework. The food sector has a vital need for responsible professionals who have a strong cultural background: a large variety of jobs now require new forces, with specific expertise and, at the same time, a large vision of food issues. Along with chemists, analysts, wine technicians, cooks, and scholars in marketing and in the study of marketable products, there is a need today for people capable of interpreting the complexity of the world of gastronomy. They would have an excellent chance of finding a job either in journalism, in the tourist-hotel sector, or, in numerous consortia devoted to conservation.

VINITALY NEWS AND THE TASTE WORKSHOPS

When, in Verona in 1967, Vinitaly, now the best-known international wine show in Italy, sprang from the rib of the Agricultural Fair, Italian wine was emerging from a period of low-quality mass production. The story of Arcigola is closely tied to this show: in part because it was the first site of a wine tasting sponsored by the organization's guidebook, *Vini d'Italia*, and also because it marked the debut of Petrini and his colleagues from Via Mendicità Istruita as both event organizers and eclectic journalists. In 1991, for the first time, Arcigola Slow Food went to Vinitaly with its own exhibition booth, which featured cooks from restaurants that had been favorably reviewed in *Osterie d'Italia*. In festive procession, wine producers brought along their bottles, while the Condotte of Arcigola Slow Food offered bread, cured meats, local cheeses, honey, sweets, and preserved foods. There were only six tables available, and only the members of the association could eat and drink for free. This was not the way things were usually done at Vinitaly, as one can infer from the review of the event that appeared in Vinitaly's newsletter (no. 3, 1991): "The cellar of the *Osteria* was literally bursting with excellent bottles, all at the visitors' disposal. It was a sort of bottomless well of food specialties: every thirty minutes a new display appeared, and one could find more new goodies."

Very pleased with this result, the Vinitaly team devoted twice as much space to Arcigola Slow Food in 1992. Petrini and his associates were also called upon to write a daily journal for the show. It came out every day and was available in Italian or in English at every stand; afterwards, it was published for six more years, until 1998.

All of this happened thanks to the general secretary of the Fair of Verona, Umberto Benezzoli, who held the position until 1998; since January 2003, he has been the general director of the Lingotto exhibition center in Turin, where the Salone del Gusto takes place. Having finally met the pleasant, bearded fellows from Bra he had heard so much about, Benezzoli viewed them with a combination of suspicion and admiration:

Vinitaly was subjected to a very critical analysis by experts in the field — they constantly compared it with the Bordeaux Vinexpo — and we were looking for an initiative that would revitalize it. So I decided to go to Bra and meet with Carlo Petrini, Roberto Burdese, and Piero Sardo. Despite his demure look, Carlin made an extraordinary impression on me: his capacity for keen criticism, his intelligence, and his way of expressing himself were all really special. At the time, the Fair's daily journal resembled *Pravda*, so it occurred to me to ask them to put together a bilingual daily newspaper for the following year's fair. I wanted something with a more objective, journalistic approach that would report on new projects, talk about various problems in wine production, and confront issues of larger interest than the merely technical ones. I suggested that they create a proper editorial office like a newspaper's, so that they could print it at night and distribute it the next day to visitors for free. It was a difficult project to carry out, but Carlin was undeterred. Naturally, he came back with a counterproposal, namely to have his space doubled for free and placed in a better position. I accepted right away.

The newspaper was distributed at the exhibition booths for the first time on the morning of Friday, April 3, 1992. It was called *Vinitaly News* and its editorial board was composed of Petrini and his associates from Bra, and a few qualified external collaborators. On the five days that followed, the newspaper reported on all the news and views of those attending the fair, including a poll that asked participants to name the best label. The 1990 Sauvignon Gastaldi won, followed by the 1988 Barolo Cannubi Boschi by Sandrone, and by the 1990 Chardonnay Gaja & Rey by Gaja.

Over the course of the six days of Vinitaly, the eating and drinking continued at the Osteria of the Arcigola Slow Food exhibition booth: eighteen restaurants and trattorie took turns in the kitchen, every day there were one thousand place settings, for a total of six thousand meals, and more than one hundred Condotte working at collecting products for donation from dozens and dozens of producers. This was Petrini's conclusion in his article in *Vinitaly News*:

We owe the success of our participation in Vinitaly to the generosity as well as the selflessness of the directors of the Condotte, to the members, and to the very many friends who have sacrificed a week of their vacation to come help us. This was a success not just for the few who actually attended Vinitaly. It was a success not just for the Slow Food organization. Sharing in the cheerful atmosphere at the Osteria, and engaging in serious and not so serious chats, songs, jokes, and merry-making have been the best way to show how wine brings people together and how it can stimulate conversation and nurture relaxation and friendship. Sipping a glass of really good wine in good company is always the best way to promote wine.

Devoting itself to the new objective of improving local products, Slow Food launched a new initiative, the "Grand Menu," at the 1994 Vinitaly, with five days of tastings; and it also issued a book on food production titled *Il buon paese* (The good country), published with the support of the Verona trade fair and edited by Piero Sardo with the collaboration of Mavi Negro and Cinzia Scaffidi.

From that point on, Via Mendicità Istruita devoted itself to covering the best products of both the wine and food sectors. The book inspired the Taste Workshops, which were part of the Grand Menu event that had been successfully piloted at Vinitaly in 1994. The Taste Workshops were a new kind of didactic food exhibition. Three rooms of delicacies were arranged to welcome visitors: one for wines, including some internationally famous labels such as Château Margaux, Château Pétrus, Penfolds,

Cloudy Bay, and Mondavi; one for artisanal food products, such as canned fish, bread, cheese, goose liver, chocolate, coffee, salami, oils, and salmon; and a third for food and wine pairings.

After their debut in Verona, the Taste Workshops constituted one of the distinctive traits of the Salone del Gusto, the biennial "salon of taste" that was inaugurated in Turin in 1996 and still attracts hordes of gourmets from all over the world. The workshops are "a concrete and deliberate sensorial experience; an opportunity to know the techniques and the context which determine a certain food product, a wine, a dish; a moment to learn (or process) the language of taste." This phrase is taken from *Il Dizionario di Slow Food* (The Slow Food dictionary, 2002), a small handbook summarizing the movement's philosophy, with separate entries on key Slow Food ventures. The goal of the workshops is not just to sample different products, but to get to know the history and manufacturing of a given product—often presented by the producers themselves. Less an evaluation than an education in taste, the workshops are straightfoward presentations that seek to stimulate the participants' relationship with food through curiosity and comparison. The workshop entrance fee is used to compensate the producers presenting their products (which are often rare and brought from far away). The approach is both playful and pedagogical, for it makes its participants aware of the necessity to safeguard these rarities.

The natural next step after these experiments was the exhibition called Milano Golosa (Gourmand Milan), which took place between December 1 and 4, 1994. Participating gourmands could choose from a variety of workshops: a sampling of nine great Angelo Gaja wines; a comparison among five prosciuttos; mozzarella from small producers in the South; and the noble pleasure of the Sacher torte. Milano Golosa was the final rehearsal for a big leap: a show entirely handled by Via Mendicità Istruita.

THE ARK OF TASTE SETS SAIL FROM THE LINGOTTO

The Lingotto building (the historical Fiat car factory) in Turin is part of Italian collective memory because both the city's working class and a group of its Left-leaning executives were trained there. One could actually say that the Lingotto is part of national history: it was the first really big Italian factory, with thirty thousand people working there. Built by Senator Giovanni Agnelli, the car factory covered 126,000 square feet and was inaugurated by King Victor Emmanuel III in 1923. In 1982, the assembly plant stopped producing vehicles; it remained vacant until the nineties when it was remodeled by the architect Renzo Piano. Today, the Lingotto houses an auditorium, a hotel, a commercial center, and a cineplex.

These days, the name Lingotto also has an international resonance thanks to Slow Food: every two years the exhibition hall underneath the former car testing track, which is on the roof of the building, provides the setting for rituals dedicated to traditional tastes and for workshops that promote the rarest and most refined food products. Where once the walls echoed with the sound of engines and assembly lines, the first international Salone del Gusto took place from November 29 to December 2, 1996. The show was then confined to only one pavilion, just a fifth of the Lingotto's interior space: at its center was the Market, filled with stalls presenting every conceivable delicacy and thousands of wines, cured meats, cheeses, and sweets. The show was besieged from the very beginning, so much so that the organizers had to restrict entry to a maximum of eight thousand people a day, all of whom had made reservations long in advance. In the 7,000 square meters assigned to the exhibit, there were seventy Taste Workshops modeled after the arrangement used at Vinitaly and at Milano Golosa. Many famous restaurateurs "performed" in the Theater of Taste, demonstrating the preparation of a special dish. But the greatest diplomatic coup was an evening celebration in honor of the great Barolo producer Aldo Conterno. For the "vertical" (chronological) tasting of his vintages, from 1970 to 1990, other producers of great Piedmontese wines, from Elio Altare and Domenico Clerico to Franco Martinetti and Angelo Gaja, took turns serving at the tables in dinner jackets to offer a tribute to their colleague. It was an homage that would have been completely out of the question in the fashion world: try to imagine Armani and Valentino presenting the shows of Missoni or Dolce & Gabbana.

The preparation of the Salone del Gusto was made possible by an agreement between Slow Food and the region of Piedmont. The new president of the region of Piedmont was Enzo Ghigo, a former executive of Publitalia, who was recruited by Silvio Berlusconi, the former prime minister, for parliament. Ghigo foresaw the possibilities of development for Turin and the Piedmont region in the idea that Petrini had proposed to him. The two of them, through ten years of collaboration, have become friends despite their different political perspectives, and the "snail movement" has always found a strong supporter in the region: the Salone del Gusto trademark is a property shared equally by the region and by Via Mendicità Istruita.

Roberto Burdese, the vice president of Slow Food, says:

We had already understood at that point that we had to broaden our perspective beyond the world of wine to the entire universe of food. Outside the oenological sector, it was rare to meet producers, crafts-men, and farmers. Grand Menu in Verona and Milano Golosa were already commercial fairs. From the beginning, we decided not to renounce the commercial aspect, because potential exhibitors had specifically asked us to have their own exhibition booths, something they could not find in other fairs. The first objective was to offer "visibil-ity" and protection to these little producers; the second was to remain faithful to our strong educational mission by giving consumers the keys to understanding the characteristics of the specialties at the fair.

Thus, the Salone del Gusto not only laid out a cornucopia of foods, but also—in the manner of Noah's ark—promised to rescue those on the verge of extinction. The concept of the ark was the winning idea of Petrini, and at the end of the Salone of 1996, he presented his project for an Ark of Taste. It would be a kind of a "planet of tastes." Today Petrini remembers:

The pressure produced by the combination of the big food industries and health regulations that are threatening local, traditional craftsman-ship could provoke, I have said, a flood capable of sweeping away our country's food culture. But with that meeting [the Salone del Gusto] and our password ["Slow Food"] we tried to object. We realized that market pressures and the loss of biodiversity, i.e. the wealth of various species, would lead to a reduction of Italy's gastronomic heritage. During a dinner in the Asti province, we also realized that the renowned bell pepper of the Motta in Costigliole was giving way to fat cousins that are grown in greenhouses and imported from Holland. To be able to eat a soup made with the Badalucco beans, you now need a letter of recommendation. The Salone of 1996 revealed an embryonic market. Someone at the time defined it as a "niche" market, a term I do not like. The consumers who want to know what they eat are very numerous. Over the years it has been demonstrated that the "niche" is getting larger and larger.

We were obviously aware that the concept of an ark might be interpreted as a form of conservatism. I immediately stated that it would have been reductive to value and support, in an absolute way, small-scale craftsmanship, without looking at industries, which do exist, that are honest and take an entrepreneurial approach that respects the environment. We could not possibly lock ourselves in a small, ancient world and not look beyond that.

Since the flood was imminent, as I said at the meeting, our ark could be the only salvation. The incoming storms threatened to inflict genocide. Neither marketing, nor community politics, nor sharp intuitions would have been sufficient. We had to build an ark, I said, based on information and knowing that anybody who worked in this sector was a cultural actor.

I ended my talk by saying that, once the flood was over, we would come down from the ark, back to earth, like Noah. That is what we did later with Terra Madre, in 2004.

chapter 5

THE HARVEST: 1997–2003

AN ARK OF TASTE IN THE FLOOD OF GMOS

Maso replied that they were chiefly to be found in Nomansland, the territory of the Basques, in a region called Cornucopia, where the vines are tied up with sausages, and you could buy a goose for a penny, with a gosling thrown in for good measure. And in those parts there was a mountain made entirely of grated parmesan cheese, on whose slopes there were people who spent their whole time making macaroni and ravioli, which they cooked in chicken broth and then cast it to the four winds, and the faster you could pick it up, the more you got of it. And not far away, there was a stream of Vernaccia wine, the finest that was ever drunk, without a single drop of water in it.

This fictional land of plenty is to be found in Boccaccio's *Decameron*, a classic of Italian literature written in the mid-fourteenth century. The trickster, Maso, is having a joke at the expense of a certain Calandrino, whom he has duped with his description of "Bengodi" ("cornucopia," or literally, "enjoywell"). Synonymous with outrageous abundance, Bengodi has earned a comic—though much-loved—standing in the Italian collective consciousness. It would be no surprise, then, if Italians entering the halls of the Lingotto exhibition center in Turin during the Salone del Gusto were to laugh out loud and declare it Bengodi: piles of sausages, hundreds of different cheeses, rows of wine bottles, casks of olive oil, arrays of sumptuous delicacies. It's the Italian way of saying one has "died and gone to Heaven!"

But was this the future of Slow Food? In bringing Bengodi to life, were Carlo Petrini and the Arcigolosi—not to mention the fair's visitors—losing sight of the underlying politics of their mission? As the success of the Salone del Gusto made clear, that was a danger to be avoided. As Petrini explains:

Until World War II, the Italian family spent 60 percent of its budget to buy food, the diet was low in calories, and there was a strong bond with the world of farming. Today, buying groceries consumes only 17 percent of family income. With the end of rural civilization and the rise of the industrial age, the umbilical cord between country and city has been severed. New consumer habits have been established. In the mid-eighties, when Arcigola was taking its first steps, only the rich were looking for quality products, but farmers and producers could not make enough profit from selling them. At the same time, most Italians were consuming low-priced food, the product of intensive agriculture and livestock farming by rich landowners, whose great economic strength enabled them to influence the market. It was a paradox: food for the rich produced by poor farmers, and mass food products produced by rich farmers. In the view of the Slow Food leadership, it was a trend that had to be turned around. Growing an endangered species of bean, raising a particular kind of free-range chicken, producing cheeses made from raw rather than industrially pasteurized milk had to become profitable. It wasn't a question of providing charity to poor exploited farmers, but rather assisting them to obtain proper recognition for their work from discriminating consumers who were willing to spend a bit more in exchange for wholesome, better-tasting food. And it wasn't just an Italian problem; it was a global one.

Some Italian laws, following European Community guidelines, had begun to defend this heritage through the rigorous DOP [*Denominazione di Origine Protetta,* or designation of protected origin], which was enforced particularly on cheeses, and the IGP [*Indicazione Geografica Protetta,* or protected geographical indication], which was less restrictive because the certification process required only one of the stages in a food item's production to have a specific geographical origin. Slow Food judged those rules either too generic or too little understood by consumers and in 1997 began working at drafting some new rules.

That was also the year of Dolly, the first cloned sheep. On February 21, 1997, researchers at the Roslin Institute in Edinburgh announced that they had successfully transferred the genetic data from one animal to another and thereby had constructed a "photocopy" of the former. A cell was placed in a denucleated ovum, the two cells fused, and an embryo was formed; the animal that grew from that embryo was an identical copy of the provider of the original cell. As an experiment, it provoked unsettling questions: To what extent was it possible to clone an adult mammal? Could a human being be cloned? Could humans be cloned to produce spare parts?

The rush toward the manipulation of DNA for commercial purposes had begun in 1980 when the U.S. Supreme Court declared a researcher's patented invention of a genetically modified bacterium to be legitimate. The year 1982 saw the advent of genetically modified food. From 1986 on, GMOs (genetically modified organisms) flooded the market. In California in 1994, Calgene Inc. created the Flavr Savr, a tomato that could keep for months after it was picked: fortunately, its taste was so bad that it was withdrawn from the market. Around the world, the public was deeply shocked by the birth of Dolly and worried about the marketing of genetically modified soy. The latter was being touted as a miracle product by multinational conglomerates, who had invested heavily into their own biotechnology research. Meanwhile, farmers, rather than joining forces with consumers to form a united opposition against GMOs, soon found themselves cultivating plants that had been designed to kill their own parasites by generating toxins. Of course, no one was able to provide a precise, long-term forecast of the consequences of GMOs for the environment.

Environmentalists have long made the preservation of indigenous species a core goal of their movement. In the face of vanishing indigenous food products, Slow Food likewise took up the cause of protection and preservation, and this theme became central to the expanding conceptual make-up of the Slow Food movement. In June 1997, a conference was held at the Fontanafredda estate in Serralunga d'Alba, attended by representatives from the world of agriculture and oeno-gastronomy, scientific researchers, journalists, and politicians. It was at this meeting that Petrini, in the name of Slow Food, officially launched the "Ark of Taste to save the planet of tastes." With the Ark came a mission statement that articulated the movement's commitment to serving both a scholarly and a general audience:

> To the general public, we commit ourselves to:
>
> Accounting for and publicizing a list of the best-known and most symbolically significant endangered products so that the battle for their protection can be the more engaged;
>
> Analyzing these products from the sensory perspective, giving names and addresses of the most recent producers, and disseminating the information through media and specialized publications so that the concepts of protection and economic gratification can be successfully and tightly linked to each other;
>
> Encouraging consumers to buy and eat these products, because it is only through their reintroduction into the commercial food circuit that they can be saved from extinction;
>
> In every region, identifying and giving awards to a series of restaurants that effectively promote products of the Ark within their own region, while using them on a daily basis in the preparation of proposed dishes;
>
> Inviting the most distinguished restaurateurs to adopt one product of the Ark as their own "core product," thus becoming its protector and integrating it in their own dishes.

SAY "CHEESE!"

Still, there was much to do before these concepts could be put into practice efficiently, and a committee immediately started working on the program. One of the first concrete ideas related to the new goal of protecting indigenous products was the plan to hold a fair devoted to milk in all its forms. To lend the event an international flavor, it was called "Cheese," rather than the Italian, "*formaggio*." With the support of the Italian Ministry of Agriculture and the European Union, the fair took place in Bra, just a few hundred meters from Via Mendicità Istruita, from September 19 to 22, 1997. The first edition of Cheese: Milk in All Its Shapes and Forms consisted of a series of tastings held throughout the city's historical center in the courtyards of buildings decorated for the occasion.

Slow Food's leadership used their experience in organizing festive wine events to create a similarly festive atmosphere around these rare and vanishing dairy products. "Cheese trains" arrived from the Milan railway station, while even more visitors arrived by bus or car from all over Italy and Europe. In the end, the first edition of Cheese was a great success: approximately fifteen thousand visitors were on hand to sample 127 cheese varieties from eleven countries of the European Union, in addition to Swiss, Turkish, and Maghrebi products. Since then, the event has taken place every other year, alternating with the Salone del Gusto. In recent years, Cheese has reached significant figures: almost two hundred exhibitors from some twenty countries, for a total of 155,000 visitors.

ORVIETO: THE SECOND INTERNATIONAL CONGRESS

At the second international congress of the Slow Food movement, which took place in the Umbrian town of Orvieto from October 16 to 19, 1997, there were 650 delegates representing thirty-five countries and forty thousand members from all over the world, figures that clearly marked a qualitative leap forward. Many politicians of the Left came to pay their respects to the "Noah from Bra," as journalists were now calling Carlo Petrini. The cartoonist Sergio Staino told a newspaper:

> The Left is exhibiting an inclination to hedonism relatively unknown in its history. And it seems like the Right also likes to see this, the forging of bonds between regions and their traditions, doesn't it? But that is only a part of the Slow Food culture. The other part is made of curiosity, of international exchanges, and of comparisons. For example, I joined Arcigola as a result of a process of self-examination. I belong to a Florentine family that thought of being Tuscan as a founding value. Then, gradually, I discovered that with the exception of Brunello, we had a lot to learn from others. As far as the Ark project is concerned, I can say that I worked hard to save one particular local specialty: the *lardo di Colonnata* [a special type of cured pork fat]. As Italo Calvino writes in his *Six Memos for the Next Millennium*, aromas and flavors are the elements of a place that can neither be transmitted vicariously nor sent electronically.

There was no shortage of events that lent themselves to flattering media coverage. Gianfranco Vissani, the celebrity chef internationally known for his TV appearances, prepared a special meal for the soldiers who were rescuing the victims of the terrible earthquake that had struck the region just a month earlier; two chefs, one Palestinian and one Israeli, cooked a "peace menu" that consisted of almond soup, dry figs with warm foie gras, mint sorbet, smoked stuffed pigeon with garlic and chilled sauce, *mahlabia* (a pudding made from milk and rice), baklava, and coffee with cardamom. There was also a pyramid of glasses filled with Champagne. Additionally, 20 million Italian Lire (roughly the equivalent of $12,000) were donated to the cheese factory of Colfiorito, which had been hit by the earthquake. Government officials of the Left participated in the congress.

Petrini acknowledges that he was very pleased by the event:

> That congress marked the flawless merging of two movements: one, Arcigola, was Italian; the other, which we had founded in Paris, was international. Still, before the congress, someone had asked me: "Is this going to be the fourth National Congress of Arcigola, or the second International Congress of Slow Food?" I answered that for the first time it was going to be both. At that point, the international nature of our movement was coming into its own. This was also due to our new trilingual magazine, *Slow*, the earliest issues of which were appearing just at that time. After the Salone del Gusto in Turin and the conference of the Ark, we kept emphasizing the biblical metaphor of the deluge: the deluge represented the tendency toward homogenization that was about to hit Italy and Europe and overwhelm the culture of food. In Italy alone, we had noted the existence of more than 1,500 types of cheese, 660 salamis and sausages, and a thousand varieties of fruit and vegetables. But many of these products were disappearing, because they did not yield enough profit to enable them to compete with intensive agriculture. In other cases, the cost of marketing a local specialty made it too expensive to produce. These are the kinds of calculations you make when you are producing on a massive scale. In Orvieto, I said that we had finally reached a striking paradox: in rich countries, a lot of money was spent with the aim of not eating, rather than eating. I was

referring to the diets, pills, doctors, and quacks who manage the big business of losing weight, a business whose success has more to do with aesthetics than with health. At the congress in Orvieto, we coined a slogan for restaurateurs: "Adopt endangered food." In the meantime, amongst ourselves we began theorizing the Ark. I did not feel like some Noah, ready to embrace everybody. But we wanted to make a selection, establish some criteria, and adopt them in order to protect biodiversity. The Ark was our first instrument.

In 1998, the second Salone del Gusto, which consisted of 203 Taste Workshops and three huge tasting halls, gave the project even more momentum. Slow Food employees accepted reservations by phone, mail, fax, or email, and many workshops were sold out two months before the doors of the Salone opened. From November 5 to 9, Turin hosted more than eighty thousand visitors who had come to sample all the flavors of the world. Gianni Agnelli, then the president of Fiat, attended the opening of the Salone and asked to be introduced to Petrini. Even the *New York Times* covered the story: "Launched by a group of leftist intellectuals who are in love with politics and disgusted at the success of fast food, this event has recently become very popular in Italy and in Europe. English people may kill to protect animals and the French become militant in defense of the purity of their language, but Italians get indignant only when food is concerned."

CITTÀ SLOW, SLOW CITIES

After my meeting with Carlo Petrini, I set off on a walking tour of Bra. Even on a normal workday, the headquarter city of Slow Food seems like the perfect place to get away from it all. Locals linger over coffee at sidewalk tables, gossiping with friends or watching the world drift by. In the shady, tree-lined squares, where the air smells of lilac and lavender, old men sit like statues on the stone benches. Everyone has time to say a warm *"buon giorno."*

And no wonder. By local decree, *la dolce vita* is now the law of the land here. Inspired by Slow Food, Bra and three other Italian towns signed a pledge in 1999 to transform themselves into havens from the high-speed frenzy of the modern world. Every aspect of urban life is now recast in line with the Petrini principles—pleasure before profit, human beings before head office, Slowness before speed. The movement was christened Città Slow, or Slow Cities, and now has more than thirty member towns in Italy and beyond.

The London-based Canadian journalist Carl Honoré is perhaps just a tad optimistic in his book *In Praise of Slowness*, when he describes the little capital of the Slow Food movement. Yet, the ideas of Petrini and Company were clearly contagious, and it hadn't taken long for the notion of "slowness" to make its way to other cities. In 1999, a group of Italian mayors founded an association of small cities that all shared a special quality of life and were centers for artisanal food production. The idea originated with Paolo Saturnini. At the time, he was the mayor of Greve in Chianti, a town with a population of about ten thousand set among some of the finest vineyards in Tuscany, about 30 kilometers from Florence. Saturnini sent a letter dated November 17, 1997, to Via Mendicità in which he proposed to Petrini to launch a "slow city" movement. The basic assumption was that the Ark project involved not only consumers, food craftsmen, and restaurateurs, but also institutions. For the Ark to be effective, Saturnini argued, there had to be leadership from city mayors. Saturnini succeeded in obtaining commitments from the towns of Orvieto, Positano, and Bra. From this agreement, a manifesto on "urban sustainability" ensued, along with the launch of Città Slow, the Slow City Association. The association was formally introduced on July 20, 2000, in Rome at the meeting of the National Association of Italian Cities.

If the "slow" slogan worked for food, it could easily work for urban development, too. Stefano Cimicchi, the mayor of Orvieto, has been among the most enthusiastic supporters of the Slow City movement, and with good reason: the town of Orvieto is well known for being the "capital of slowness." As mayor, Cimicchi set lifestyle regulations prohibiting fast food and sex shops in Orvieto; today, he also serves as president of Città Slow. Just as a winegrower would seek to preserve his vineyards even as he extracts from them the best possible wine, so these provincial leaders hope to enhance their cities by reasserting the value of their local traditions with regard to agriculture, craftsmanship, and the historic fabric of the city. New technology is not rejected but rather used to advance humanistic ends, as in the promotion of hydrogen fuels and telecommunications. Predictably, it is easier to improve the quality of life in a small town than in a big city. Mayors who subscribe to Città Slow's ideals have made a threefold commitment: first, to create environmental policies designed to preserve and develop the characteristics of the town and its urban fabric; second, to create economic incentives to spur production of foods obtained with natural methods and minimize production of genetically altered ones; and, third, to create opportunities and spaces favorable to the direct exchange between consumers and producers.

The journalist Pier Giorgio Oliveti, a leader of Città Slow and director of the Palazzo del Gusto in Orvieto, explains: "These cities have decided to bet on values that thwart alienation. We want to limit the spread of 'non-places,' like suburbs, fast-food restaurants that are identical everywhere you go, and shopping malls filled with families on Saturday afternoons. We want to prevent what the World Watch Institute defines as 'unnatural catastrophes,' that is, those caused by the environmentally destabilizing actions of humans."

This topic has been explored in various essays, among them architect Emanuel Lancerini's recent Ph.D. dissertation on urban planning for the University Iuav of Venice. Lancerini analyzed the distinctive sense of quiet that characterizes Italian towns in certain regions. His study used the Bresciana lowlands, east of Milan, the Langhe hills in Piedmont, and the Marche in central Italy as examples. From these regions, he was able to formulate a viable idea of "slow" development. The research proposes the mingling of agricultural and tourist areas, with a moderate expansion of residential and industrial development, held in check by a respect for local tradition and the landscape. Lancerini warns that "slow territories," as he calls them, cannot possibly be conceived as a new model for development, but should rather be considered a metaphor to pursue new hypotheses in urban planning. Indeed, Italy has a network of small rural towns that together have a population of slightly over four million inhabitants and an area of almost 6 million hectares, a quarter of the entire national landmass. In these areas, agriculture, industry, and services for tourists are all integrated. Inspired by Slow Food's success, Lancerini recommends establishing Presidia (projects to preserve endangered products) in these areas in an effort to support small manufacturers of high-quality products, whose existence has been threatened by contemporary market pressures.

This combination of agriculture and tourism makes the establishment of slow regions an appealing idea. According to Lancerini's study, the success of the Langhe is due precisely to the fact that it has presented the local landscape as inseparable from the local wines and the local cuisine. Lancerini explains:

> Actually, as one surrenders to the sweetness of the landscape of the Langhe, one has the impression of living in a region where tradition and innovation happily blend and where the tone and rhythm of life are, in consequence, friendly. This impression permeates cottages, farmhouses, historical centers, production and leisure places where elements of the past and the present are constantly combined. The ways of production, the relationships and connections among social agents, are far more important than the products themselves. The Barolo producer Ceretto, for example, had the artist Sol LeWitt restore an ancient chapel in his vineyards, in exchange for the promise to send LeWitt a bottle of his wine each week for as long as he lives.
>
> The only way to protect and defend slow regions is to slow down growth and enhance quality-oriented development. The concept of a slow life can be applied not only to a region but also to many aspects of our society—indeed, the use of the term "slow" has grown exponentially, as if "slow" could be used as a broadly applicable concept to identify styles of life in which quality plays a substantial role. We now have slow-fitness at the gym, slow-cinemas that offer wholesome snacks instead of popcorn, and slow-smoke after the law against smoking. Neologisms like these seem to indicate the success of a philosophy of life, and in Via Mendicità they are regarded with both suspicion and satisfaction.

DARIO FO: SPEAKING OUT AGAINST GMOS IN EUROPE

"To Dario Fo, who emulates the jesters of the Middle Ages in scourging authority and upholding the dignity of the downtrodden." With this, the members of the Swedish Academy assigned the Nobel Prize for Literature to the Italian playwright in 1997. Fo, author of the political farce *Mistero Buffo,* among other comedies, chose to attack the genetic manipulation of food in his award lecture at the Stockholm Concert Hall. At the time, he and his wife, Franca Rame, happened to be touring Europe to denounce the birth of a "human pig"—a product, in Fo's opinion, of the European guidelines to allow patent rights on biotechnologies. This is a part of his Nobel lecture:

> At another university we spoofed the project—alas well underway—to manipulate genetic material, or more specifically, the proposal by the European Parliament to allow patent rights on living organisms. We could feel how the subject sent a chill through the audience. Franca and I explained how our Eurocrats, kindled by powerful and ubiquitous multinationals, are preparing a scheme worthy of the plot of a sci-fi/horror movie entitled "Frankenstein's pig brother." They're trying to get the approval of a directive which (and get this!) would authorize industries to take patents on living beings, or on parts of them, created with techniques of genetic manipulation that seem taken straight out of "The Sorcerer's Apprentice."
>
> This is how it would work: by manipulating the genetic makeup of a pig, a scientist succeeds in making the pig more humanlike. By this arrangement it becomes much easier to remove from the pig the organ of your choice—a liver, a kidney—and to transplant it in a human. But to assure that the transplanted pig-organs aren't rejected, it's also necessary to transfer certain pieces of genetic information from the pig to the human. The result: a human pig (even though you will say that there are already plenty of those). And every part of this new creature, this humanized pig, will be subject to patent laws; and whosoever wishes a part of it will have to pay copyright fees to the company that "invented" it. Secondary illnesses, monstrous deformations, infectious diseases— all are optional, included in the price.
>
> The Pope [John Paul II] has forcefully condemned this monstrous genetic witchcraft. He has called it an offence against humanity, against the dignity of man, and has gone to pains to underscore the project's total and irrefutable lack of moral value.

Fo's campaign continued at the European Parliament two months later, in February 1998. The Green Party, with the support of the World

Wildlife Foundation and Greenpeace, was circulating a photo of Fo in which he appeared with a pair of pig feet in place of his hands. But Fo's opposition to the proposed measure met with little success. To be precise, the European Union guidelines were also aimed at safeguarding European research from the United States. The law passed with a vast majority, and the Socialist Left split up from the environmentalists. In May 1998, after the measure received the definitive approval of the assembly of European deputies, the playwright commented: "Multinational conglomerates win." In an article in the newspaper *La Stampa* dated October 28, 1998, he added: "The vote of the European parliament in favor of the licensing of living organisms is an insult to ethics, to intelligence, and to logic."

That year, Fo attended the opening of the Salone del Gusto in Turin, where there was a panel on biotechnology and new frontiers in eating. Fo wanted to support his friend Carlo Petrini, twenty years after their battles in support of Radio Bra Red Waves. He declared to the journalists that although not a gourmet himself, he nevertheless wanted to participate in the panel "to express support and friendship to those who fight for the safety of taste and against the extinction of many, too many indigenous products."

Genetically manipulated food and the consequences of GMOs on nutrition were about to become one of the most controversial battles in which Slow Food engaged. Some rationalists accused the movement of being anti-science and of assuming an obscurantist perspective toward research. This perspective drew Slow Food closer to certain conservative political parties, like the Alleanza Nazionale (National Alliance) in Italy and the Green Party in Germany, who defended tradition.

In fact, Petrini did sometimes reveal himself to have anti-technology attitudes. During the 1998 Salone del Gusto, to journalists complaining that it was impossible to reach him by mobile phone, he said: "I do not have one. In fact, I'd like to see the installation of special boxes for cellular phones in restaurant entrances, like in some Wild West saloons where the customers' guns had to be left at the entrance, to be picked up again on the way out." According to the same logic, only a few months earlier, he had opposed the introduction of a label on wine bottles that would state, "Drinking wine may seriously compromise your health." Petrini made his point: "Aside from any scientific proof, wines and liquors deserve respect because they are cultural products, and represent the labor, tradition, and economy of a country."

Slow Food also fought against some "hygienic" norms the movement's leaders believed would jeopardize the production of raw milk cheeses. Similarly, the movement led the opposition to the excessive zeal of the HACCP (Hazard Analysis and Control of Critical Points) norms. HACCP is a system of food-production guidelines introduced by NASA in 1959 to guarantee the integrity of the food used in their space programs; the guidelines were adopted in Europe in 1994 and affirmed by Italian law in 1997. When applied, those norms would have compromised the quality and distinctiveness of many locally produced foods. Slow Food argued that the craftsmen of these specialized products should not be prohibited from using their traditional manufacturing techniques. The argument held sway with local health authorities and municipalities, and as a result of these efforts, many typical and traditional products were exempted from HACCP norms and saved.

On February 14, 2002, the European Union issued guidelines that set the stage for the introduction of genetically modified grapevines. Slow Food marshaled support against this important innovation in wine production, while making it clear that the movement was not reflexively anti-science. The Slow Food leadership issued a document that affirmed the movement's favorable view of research in this field in Europe, but requested that the research on winegrowing be confined to long-term experiments within a particular region. In addition, Slow Food requested that equal research be carried out on a variety of topics, including eco-friendly farming.

In every anti-establishment situation, Slow Food stood up for the weak in the food business. And yet, denouncing the status quo was not enough.

THE BIRTH OF THE PRESIDIA

The land is rough and mountainous between Sestri Levante and La Spezia in the Cinque Terre region of Italy's western coast. Dry terraces go down to the sea, with olive trees and grapevines that have somehow managed to survive despite the rocks and the wind. Even with the dilapidated state of the centuries-old vineyard walls, the *cian* (vineyards) of the

Cinque Terre still produce a noble and ancient passito wine made from sun-dried grapes. Produced in very small quantities, this sweet dessert wine, Sciacchetrà (the name comes from the words *sciacca*, "tread," and *trà*, "set aside," in the local dialect) was gradually becoming scarcer and scarcer. After a visit to Pisa and the Apuane Alps to observe the production of *larda di Colonnata* (so dear to the cartoonist Sergio Staino), Petrini found himself walking around the ancient and dwindling vineyards of Sciacchetrà. Here, too, was a product on the brink of extinction. Petrini decided it was time to do something more conspicuous to save all these products. The manifesto of the Ark had just been issued, and the Salone del Gusto in Turin had been a positive experience. In the late fall of 1998, Carlin took a vacation in Castelnuovo Magra, a small town between Tuscany and Liguria, staying with his friend Salvatore Marchese, a journalist and food culture enthusiast who wrote for *Slow* magazine and other publications. Marchese recalled: "Carlin had never visited the Cinque Terre. He took an excursion and was impressed by the spectacular beauty of the landscape. The previous year, UNESCO had declared the area a World Heritage Site. We took one of the tiny private trains that descends from Riomaggiore dramatically down to the Serra River. It looked as if the sea wanted to swallow us, running toward us through dense heather and vines. We stopped in a small clearing which fell sheer into the sea. A few meters from us, terraces had crumbled apart because of a landslide. A walk through these impracticable paths made Petrini aware of the consequences for the region of human neglect. On the way back, he seemed somebody else: only silence accompanied us."

The group then stopped in the cellar of a winemaker who offered everybody his precious Sciacchetrà. He described the hard labor he had to endure on the terraces to make it. That evening, while Petrini and his friends were having dinner at the Trattoria Armanda in Castelnuovo Magra, eating the famous stuffed lettuce in broth, they thought back to the long, leisurely walk that had served to acquaint them with an endangered heritage. That heritage had to be saved, but how?

The idea came after another visit, which took place near the end of the year in the plain of the Cuneo province in Piedmont. In December, almost in conjunction with the Fiera del Bue Grasso (Fair of the Fat Ox) in Carrù, there is the Fiera del Cappone (Fair of the Capon), which is held in the small township of Morozzo, widely known for its particularly tasty breed of chicken. According to tradition, the roosters were castrated by the town women in August—a process that would naturally make them sweet and tender—before being granted another four more months to fatten up. The Morozzo capon was a traditional Christmas dish among the gentry and other traditional, food-loving Piedmontese families. Yet, in Morozzo the breed was close to extinction. In the year that Petrini made his visit, only three hundred Morozzo capons were left, because of the declining demand for them.

Upon learning of the imminent demise of the precious breed, the leaders of Slow Food rushed to Morozzo. Petrini joked: "We have to stage a military occupation of the grounds where the capons are bred, we have to prevent them from being destroyed by advancing globalization." The idea of a "presidium," a military term meaning garrison, worked. In Via Mendicità they decided to use it to define the products that were being taken into the Ark. The first gesture was vaguely reminiscent of a famous scene in the nineteenth-century Italian novel *The Betrothed* by Alessandro Manzoni: Slow Food bought a bunch of capons and sent them as Christmas gifts to the administration of the then prime minister, Massimo D'Alema. They also put in a reservation for a good quantity of capons, which were sold by subscription in the Condotte.

After practice, there comes theory. The concept of the Ark needed to be better clarified and contextualized. In 1999, a scientific board was established; it sampled 450 products to judge whether they met adequate standards regarding their place of origin, use of traditional material and techniques, and gastronomic excellence. Public institutions— and especially the media—began to take note. After many years during which public debate over agriculture had focused mainly on the question of maximizing production, expressions like "locally produced," "bio-sustainable agriculture," "organo-leptic quality," and "traditional techniques" began to be widely used. Nevertheless, many food delicacies continued to be endangered.

Piero Sardo, the current president of the Slow Food Foundation for Biodiversity, explains: "We decided to start thinking on a grander scale. Perhaps it was a wild idea, but an appealing one. We obviously had several discussions about it, because until then Slow Food had stayed out of economics. Still, we could not just sit there and wait, doing nothing. So the Slow Food trustees at their meeting in Bologna in November 1999 gave us the green light to start working on our project. The word "presidio" itself caused skepticism: to some it sounded too pugnacious, almost like the occupation of a territory. However, the verb form "to garrison" means also "to subsidize" and "to defend": to us it had positive connotations. In any case, after we started using the term [Presidia], we realized little by little that it worked."

Slow Food was appealing to consumers to let their consciences lead them and to adjust to paying more for these locally produced delicacies. To grow the cardoons of Nizza Monferrato in Piedmont—the essential ingredient of a sauce for bread and vegetables with olive oil, butter, anchovy, and garlic—the cardoon plant has to be bent while still underground so that it stays white and tender, a technique that young cardoon pickers can learn only by working side by side with experienced farmers. It was against the background of considerations such as this that the "Island of the Presidia" debuted at the 2000 Salone del Gusto in Turin. The event marked the official debut of 91 endangered delicacies, including the purple asparagus from Albenga (Liguria), the buckwheat of Valtellina (Lombardy), the Puzzone cheese from Moena (Veneto), the true thin-skinned San Marzano tomato from Campania, the *caciocavallo* Podolico cheese of the Basilicata region, and the famous pistachios from Bronte (Sicily).

A research commission had defined in detail the categories of products that were to be included in the Ark: vinegars, grains and cereals, vegetable preserves (such as sauces and marmalade), preserved fish (*bottarga*, anchovies, tuna), prepared meats (paté), sweets, aromatic herbs and spices, cheeses and other dairy products, dried and fresh fruit, legumes, honey and beekeeping products, must, wine beverages, fermented beverages, olive oil, mechanically pressed seed oil (walnut and hazelnut oils), vegetables, bread, pasta, oven products, wild products (only if picked or transformed with traditional procedures), edible animal breeds, salt, sausages and cold meats, wine, and vines.

Above all, there were precise criteria according to which a Presidium could be instituted:

1. Products have to be of a particular quality (meaning they must have excellent flavor). Quality is defined by local customs and traditions.

2. Products should be linked to the memory or the identity of a group; they may be species, varieties, or vegetable ecotypes and animal populations that are indigenous to a given region. The main raw material of manufactured products has to be of local origin. It may have external origins only if it comes from a place that has been a traditional supplier. Complementary ingredients (spices, condiments, et cetera) may come from any source, provided that they are handled according to a traditional process.

3. The relationship with a region has to be proved: the products have to be linked to a specific area historically, environmentally, and socioeconomically.

4. The products have to be made in limited quantity by small farms or producers.

5. The products have to be actually or potentially endangered.

To organize a Presidium requires long and attentive work. Through its network, which today extends to the entire world, Slow Food tries to find endangered, high-quality products. When Slow Food singles out farmers or fishermen who display a special interest in the production process, it works with them to develop a means of rescuing and safeguarding these products. Local institutions and people specialized in various fields participate in the process as well. Then, production guidelines that will protect the quality and honor the history of the product take shape. Through a comparative tasting system, the differences in flavors between comparable products made in different areas and by different producers are subsequently identified, and suggestions for correcting possible flaws in the product are offered.

Slow Food actively participates in every step of the process. First, it encourages the composition of a committee to promote a Presidium, then it helps to form an association, like a co-op or a consortium of small-scale producers. The final step is communication: all over the world, consumers are told about some extraordinary product that has been made following strict rules and is identifiable by a trademark that appears on the packaging of the product itself. Without an economy able to support the Presidia and increase their production, preserving good, traditional flavors would be unthinkable.

THE PRESIDIA: DISTRIBUTION IS THE KEY

With the launch of the Presidia, Slow Food gambled on being able to find a market for each of the Presidia products, thus enabling numerous small, local economies to improve. Such a program could succeed only with the participation of people living in the region, and it banked on consumers being willing to pay a little more to have higher quality food.

In addition to Slow Food's own research, a survey conducted in 2002 by Bocconi University in Milan, a prestigious institution specializing in economics and business studies, confirmed that the Presidia strategy could be successful and could meet with a positive economic response. Over the course of five years, the different Slow Food Presidia had together generated a yearly revenue of €30 million, with approximately three thousand people involved. Between 2000 and 2002, the Presidia registered annual growth of approximately 30 percent, and the number of people involved almost doubled.

The Bocconi report gives as examples of this growth the fact that in two years the number of workers in citrus groves in Puglia jumped from nine to approximately one hundred. The cheese of Montebore, a village in the Tortonese area between Liguria and Piedmont, had all but disappeared and was now being successfully produced again at a rate of two hundred cheeses per week. An increase in the average price of Presidia food products was also noted: from €4 to €6.2 per kilogram.

Research conducted by Slow Food in 2004 examined forty-five Presidia in three regions: Piedmont, with sixteen Presidia; Veneto, with nine; and Sicily, with twenty. In Piedmont, the number of participating companies doubled in four years, with an 81 percent overall increase in the number of employees. Two hundred and twenty-five new jobs were created: the Piedmont Presidia companies saw an increase from a total of 277 employees to 502. There was a 429 percent increase in business as well. For example, production of a goat's milk cheese called Cevrin di Coazze, made in the Alps north of Turin, grew from a little more than 150 to 4,700 cheeses per year.

Data coming from Veneto also were encouraging: there was a 24 percent increase in the number of participating companies, a 23 percent increase in employees, and a 231 percent increase in sales. In Sicily, the trend was similarly positive, albeit less dramatic. In four years, the number of companies grew from 377 to 405, mainly due to trade in the winter melons of Alcamo and the capers of Salina. The report concludes: "In two years, thanks to promotion and a new production and commercial organization, the Presidia companies have established themselves as successful new producers, with sales to consumers and particularly to specialized stores and restaurants having dramatically increased."

Another report came out in 2005. The data referred to 1,450 companies with approximately four thousand employees, including the temporary ones. In four years, 864 jobs had been created, and there had been a 93 percent increase in producers' profits with respect to the prices before the creation of the Presidia. Overall production had increased 643 percent. A particularly striking case was that of the Cicerchia di Serra de' Conti, a legume similar to the chickpea that is grown in the region of Ancona, production of which went from a mere 30 kilograms (66 pounds) per year to 100 quintals (11 tons).

To achieve results like these, Slow Food needed a national distribution network. In April 2001, among other options, Slow Food chose to experiment with one of the biggest distribution chains in the country, Coop Italia. With sixty-five hypermarkets and 1,250 supermarkets, Coop Italia controlled 17 percent of the mass-distribution market, with annual sales of €10.5 billion. Petrini and his associates also felt encouraged by the history of this great chain, which opened its first store in Turin in 1854 in an attempt to curb inflation.

This was one of the first steps taken to commercialize endangered foods. The Coop, with its five million consumers, began to support the Presidia. The results of the various efforts to promote Presidia products stunned even the Coop managers: there was soon business of €1.5 million, not including wines. In effect, each day of promotion generated a profit of €26,000. Surprisingly, the supermarket sales staff, who received instructions from Slow Food personnel in the promotion of these almost unknown products, felt motivated and transformed themselves into consumer "counselors" in the style of the old "mom-and-pop" retailers of the past.

Besides the agreement with Coop Italia, Slow Food embarked on a new adventure: through the Condotte, it sought to create retail centers similar to American farmers' markets. Ideally, both consumers and producers would profit from this initiative, the former because they would find better prices and better quality, and the latter because their work would be better remunerated. Slow Food President Roberto Burdese announced the new initiative at the Salone del Gusto in Turin in 2004, with the purpose of "better connecting supply and demand."

BIODIVERSITY:
SAVING AGRICULTURE FOR THE FUTURE

May Thou be praised, my Lord, for our sister, mother earth, who sustains us and governs, and produces various fruits with colored flowers and green plants.

The *Canticle of Brother Sun*, written by St. Francis of Assisi around 1224, is the first celebration of biodiversity in the Italian language. Eight centuries later, "Mother Earth" is endangered. It has never been so scorned, mortified, and corrupted. Only recently has attention been devoted to safeguarding the organisms of the planet. Carlo Petrini had the wisdom to see that food and gastronomy, hunger and taste, consciousness and pleasure could not be considered separate entities anymore. After many years spent discovering and tasting the best products, Petrini knew it was no longer acceptable simply to eat delicacies without knowing what raw materials they were made of. But what does biodiversity exactly mean? But what does biodiversity exactly mean? In his *Life on Earth*, an encyclopedia dedicated to this topic, the biologist Niles Eldredge explains that the term "biological diversity" is a complex one and has a variety of meanings. Biodiversity is defined as "the variety of life on earth at all levels, from the genus to the ecosystem," and as the whole of "ecological and evolutionary processes that sustain it." The word "biodiversity" was used for the first time in the United States in 1986, at the Biodiversity National Forum. For a long time, the term was found primarily in scientific studies, but in the last few years, thanks to the work of environmentalists, both the media and political figures have started to use it frequently. Eldredge's encyclopedia describes eight types of biodiversity: genetic biodiversity; biodiversity of organisms, linked to the variables of anatomical characteristics; population biodiversity, also with reference to geographical distribution; intraspecific biodiversity, through the evolutionary perspective in a certain area; community biodiversity, which pertains to relationships among organisms and species which live in the same environment; ecosystem biodiversity, which signals the interdependence of living creatures and the nonbiological aspects of the environment; terrestrial and aquatic biodiversity; and biogeographic biodiversity, which is correlated to the geological or geographic and climatological history of a certain area.

In three billion years, evolution has disseminated millions of biological species. Before the human being appeared on earth, it has been estimated that each of these species flourished for a period of between one and ten million years. Currently, extinction rates range from one hundred to one thousand times faster. In the span of a century, we have lost three hundred thousand varieties of plants, and others keep dying out, one every six hours. A third of the bovine, ovine, and swine species are either extinguished or on their way to extinction. The sea is endangered as well: 75 percent of the planet's fish reserves are endangered.

Reports of the rate at which humans are consuming natural resources are also startling, suggesting that humanity is headed toward a planetary disaster. Today, for example, we consume approximately twice the energy that was consumed in 1970, and in 2020, there will be a further increase of 60 percent.

Energy and the possible exhaustion of oil fields are much talked about, and yet, shortages of food and water are possibly the most worrisome albeit undervalued problems now facing human beings. According to Eldredge, for example, "the earth could feed 10 billion people eating the way Indians do; 5 billion who follow the Italian diet, and only 2.5 billion with the eating habits of North Americans." (The current population of the earth is 6.1 billion.) This is because cereals and water are mainly used to feed the animals we eat: today, 45 percent of farming production is used for this purpose, whereas in 1900, the ratio was only 10 percent.

In this context, with 820 million people in the world now suffering from hunger, intensive and industrial agriculture does not look like a good solution at all. Rather, it seems a way to further impoverish the planet. There was a time when humans fed themselves on twelve thousand different species of plants; now they subsist on about thirty. There are 235 varieties of potatoes, but only seven of them are cultivated. Still, for thousands of years, crop rotation, the complex interaction between animals and plants, and seed selection were the best insurance policy for traditional agriculture. Industrial farming, which became widespread in the late 1980s, especially after the "green revolution" of the 1950s and '60s in developing countries, has led to the loss of biodiversity. One of several consequences of this development is the creation of monocultures that require extensive use of pesticides: now, only three species—rice, wheat, and corn—supply 60 percent of the world's nutritional intake from plants. Furthermore, the transport of food also consumes huge amounts of natural resources: in the United States alone, the distance traveled by a food from its point of production to a supermarket can be hundreds and hundreds of miles.

Defenders of biodiversity, seeking to stress the importance of a change in our eating habits, have imparted a few rules, paraphrased here from Eldredge:

Eat food made from organisms at the lower level of the food chain.
Choose organic products.
Buy locally grown products.
Buy seasonal products.
Buy products with little packaging material (or none).
Avoid consuming food obtained by biological species submitted to
    excessive exploitation.
Broaden our diet so that it may comprehend a larger variety of food.
Buy groceries using reusable canvas bags rather than disposable
    plastic ones.
Minimize the waste of food.

In a world where consumers may choose between being victims of the system and becoming conscious and active citizens, these common-sense recommendations constitute an agenda not to be forgotten.

Slow Food has two further additions to the agenda: Remember the pursuit of pleasure; and, Give everyone the right to choose. However, this is an option only for certain consumers. Economics, far more than taste, remains one of the most powerful determinants of what people eat, and hunger remains an issue in many countries around the world. *Food Wars*, written by Tim Lang, a professor of food policy at London's City University, and researcher Michael Heasman, examines the impact of free trade policies on public health in the context of food. Lang and Heasman note the negative consequences of the modern diet of fast food and packaged foods—illnesses such as obesity, heart disease, and diabetes—while adding that the same problems have begun to occur in developing countries as well. Alongside persistent food shortages, developing countries have seen the arrival of the global "fast" diet, with its concomitant health problems. *Food Wars* underscores the inherent contradiction between free trade policies that seek to offer a global market for the corporate food industry, and public health policies that must address the damage wrought by that industry's products, both in developed nations and, now, in developing nations.

The products of the food industry, then, would seem to be a poor solution to the myriad problems facing a nation, be it public health, environmental preservation, management of natural resources, or the eradication of hunger. Biodiversity, by contrast, presents a new perspective on all of these issues, one that stands to be far less destructive in its ends and means. The advocates of biodiversity believe it could be a key to the battle against hunger, and not surprisingly, many institutions, including the United Nations' Food and Agriculture Organization (FAO), which is based in Rome, are passionately devoted to it. The FAO is a leader in the fight against hunger, and its reports predict that in the year 2030 there will be 8.3 billion people to feed. For many years, the principal goal of the FAO has been to save people from hunger, by whatever means possible. Now, thanks to an exchange between researchers at the FAO and Slow Food, even the FAO has begun to recognize the importance of pleasure in food, and the organization has shown a willingness to rethink the food traditions that hold communities together. On February 27, 2004, a letter signed by FAO Director Jacques Diouf officially acknowledged Slow Food as a nonprofit organization with a program similar in perspective, goals, and range to that of the FAO. Fittingly, the representatives of the "snail movement" can now participate in FAO events and have access to FAO documents and information when the two organizations work together on projects.

Vandana Shiva, founder and executive director of the Research Foundation for Science, Technology, and Ecology in India, is a highly trained physicist and philosopher who decided to devote her considerable talents to the battle against globalization in the name of biodiversity. She now serves on the board of the International Forum on Globalization and the Slow Food International Council. One of her favorite aphorisms is from a sacred Indian text: "The person who gives food, gives life."

Petrini stresses this point: "An environmentalist who is not a gastronomist is sad; a gastronomist who is not an environmentalist is silly. We changed our point of view with the idea of defending good food in a healthy environment. This move ratified our transformation into an eco-gastronomic movement. From this new perspective, we are trying to keep the concept of pleasure alive: we set it in a wider context, which includes the environment where food is created. This has allowed us to overcome the real taboo of every gastronomist: hunger." As Petrini has pointed out, those who battle hunger have often turned to the fastest, easiest, and cheapest solutions, frequently with negative results. He cites as an example the introduction of corn and potatoes from the New World, both of which were cheap and easy to produce. But potatoes were initially unpopular, and corn was served without beans, its traditional accompaniment in Latin American cooking, thus making it an inadequate protein. Petrini says, "It produced an ephemeral sense of fulfillment, but was one of the causes of death by malnutrition." The potato, on the other hand, led to an even worse crisis. In the seventeenth century, many European governments actively promoted the potato among the peasant populations. As explained by Alan Davidson in his prodigious encyclopedia on food, *The Oxford Companion to Food*, the crop enjoyed tremendous success in Ireland and was probably connected to a population boom that occurred in the first half of the nineteenth century. But production increasingly concentrated on a single, high-yielding variety, the Lumper, despite its poor taste and cooking qualities. When the potato blight came to Ireland in the mid-1840s, this variety proved extremely vulnerable and entire harvests were wiped out, leading to a famine of devastating proportions and sparking much of the Irish diaspora. As Davidson states, "The tragedy gave the world one of the clearest lessons it has ever had in the necessity to maintain diversity of crops and of genes."

A FOUNDATION AGAINST *PRÊT-À-PORTER* FOOD

In his most recent book, *Il cibo come cultura* (Food as culture), the historian Massimo Montanari examines the history of food and observes that the now popular relationship between food and local culture has been a neglected one. During the Roman era and the Middle Ages, the rich tried not to allow their local surroundings to determine their diet. Rome was a celebrated emporium of food from all over the world, as were Bologna and Milan in the Middle Ages. Montanari explains that a "taste of geography" became apparent in the kitchen only after the industrial revolution. "It seems like a paradox, but it is not: rather, it is the beginning of a validation process and the internationalization of markets and eating patterns that caused, along with a new interest in local cultures, the invention of systems that we now like to call regional cuisines. That is not to say that these cuisines appeared out of nowhere, because local differences have always existed. But regionalism as a positive notion is a new invention."

Montanari's thesis is especially valid in the Western world. It may well be applied to Pellegrino Artusi's influential book codifying Italian cooking, *La scienza in cucina e l'arte di mangiar bene* (1891) and, similarly, to its French counterpart, *Almanach des gourmands* (1803) by Grimod de la Reynière. But it will soon be clear, with the horizon opening up to the entire world, that food expresses cultural differences everywhere and is the first marker of a people's identity. This is one of the reasons why it is necessary to protect the heritage of food from globalization. This is the message that began circulating at the 2000 Salone del Gusto, where Frenchman José Bové and his anti-globalization movement, protesters from Seattle's 1999 World Trade Organization meeting, and Tuscan farmers defending the zolfino bean, could all find an unprecedented but constructive synergy. An interesting article by the Spanish writer Manuel Vásquez Montalbán, "Prêt-à-porter food does not feed the world," appeared in the Italian newspaper *La Repubblica* on July 30, 2000, and it captured the mood well:

> All of a sudden, a choir of scientists and gourmets feels obliged to give its opinion of genetically modified products. Nutritional engineering has in fact already become a topic that has been globalized through the Food and Agriculture Organization and the Internet. Sociologists have

become possessed by the topic and are asking themselves if transgenic food research should be used to eradicate world hunger. I do not think so. Such research ... does not intend to eradicate world hunger, but would create new prêt-à-porter products mostly made from chemicals.

There is a new strategic and philosophic front for people who intend to establish the logic of a universal process that responds to the real needs of the poor: for the first time in the history of hunger, the critics of food inequality stand to find themselves on common ground with socially conscious gourmands. The meeting of these two groups may produce results in time for the exposition in Turin in October, where the extremely interesting Salone del Gusto will provide the extraordinary occasion to talk about hunger and the desire for food.

To reach this goal, Slow Food put together a "catalogue" of hundreds of endangered Italian products, working from the products selected for the original Ark in 1999. The organizers used the Presidia to get directly involved in the production world. Pilot projects were launched in Piedmont, with the capons of Morozzo, and in Tuscany, with the zolfino bean. At the Salone del Gusto of 2000, the Island of the Presidia was the area most visited, most talked about by the media, and most appreciated by politicians.

Petrini describes what happened at the Salone of 2000 in these terms:

In 1999, the Fair of the Capon in Morozzo was, thanks to our work, a hit. It lead to the greater appreciation of traditional products. With the Presidia, we did not limit ourselves to denouncing the possible extinction of this or that product. Instead, we started working at a project to give a new momentum to the country's rural economy.

We realized that farmers felt deprived, despoiled by mass production and by genetically modified organisms. Unfortunately, for many years in Italy they had been victimized by the unions, which had pushed them into living on subsidies, rather than pursuing quality and ancient, traditional farming. At the same time, we realized that there were certain ways of approaching the problem that were just too radical to be practical. I went to meet Bové in France when he came out of jail. I wanted to express Slow Food's support for what he had done. He asked me if I wanted Slow Food to be the "sutler for the people who were planning the protests in Seattle." I replied that we had chosen a different path from that of the antiglobalization groups, they were too oriented toward youth and the urban context and had lost the farmers on the way.

We had never been a particularly chauvinist organization, and we felt that the time had come to change a little and to broaden our perspective. We realized the idea of the Ark had great potential, but we hadn't found a practical application for it yet. After the first experimental phase, we started working at two different projects at the same time. On the one hand, we decided to develop the international Presidia, modeled on the ones that had been tested in Italy. To do this, we asked for the support and help of our collaborators and associates all over the world. We also established an international award to be given to a farmer, shepherd, or fisherman who had opposed globalization and defended biodiversity through scientific research and production of an endangered food. For us, these heroes of taste and flavor were guardians of the past who also understood how to safeguard the future.

The first ceremony of the Slow Food Award for the Defense of Biodiversity took place in Bologna in October 2000. Bologna then was the European Capital of Culture, and we received support from both Mayor Giorgio Guazzaloca, who represented the center-right, and the president of the Emilia-Romagna region, the leftist Vasco Errani. We brought about five hundred jurors from all over the world to the city: they were journalists, experts, and producers. Thirteen exemplary persons were chosen as award recipients. Subsequent Biodiversity Award ceremonies took place in Porto, Portugal, in 2001; at the Salone del Gusto in Turin in 2002; and at our world convention in Naples in 2003. The Naples event led us to hold the Terra Madre of 2004—an extraordinary assembly that brought together food communities from all levels, from poor farmers of the Southern Hemisphere to craftsmen from North America and Europe.

In Bologna, the awards honored stories of labor and dedication in the protection of endangered biological species and flavors. There were thirteen finalists, selected by more than five hundred experts from forty nations. A jury composed of four hundred members subsequently voted on October 24, 2000, and elected five champions. The awards went to Russian biologist Marija Mikhailovna Girenko; Spanish shepherd Jesus

Garzón; Turkish beekeeper Velic Gulas; Mexican vanilla grower Raul Manuel Antonio; and Nancy Jones, a British citizen who had created a dairy farm in Mauritania.

Serena Milano is a thirty-something member of the new generation of Slow Food executives who is especially passionate about the third-world solidarity projects. She has followed the development of the Ark and is involved in the international Presidia. Milano remembers that the first nineteen international Presidia were presented at the Salone del Gusto of 2002.

> On the whole, the European Presidia were and are philosophically similar to the Italian ones. However, the others have developed new ways of involving themselves in food issues. In certain cases, we have realized that we had to take into account totally different kinds of food traditions: in the United States for example, cooking and food are the result of influences from various countries. In the States, a Presidium was founded that did not promote one particular "historical" cheese, but rather, defended the raw milk-processing technique, which had been maintained by a heterogeneous group of cheesemakers. Other realities have urged us to question our concepts of taste and quality and have compelled us to compare tastes, histories, and flavors that are very distant from one another. We have launched some Presidia in the Southern Hemisphere, taking into consideration for the first time not only the production process, but also its social factors, such as the direct involvement of women and the education of the producers' children, and environmental aspects. In such cases, the Presidium does not limit itself to preserving a food tradition; it also intervenes to improve a product by offering technical assistance, or by purchasing manufacturing instruments.

THE INTERNATIONAL PRESIDIA ARE LAUNCHED

The year 2001 was a difficult one for Carlo Petrini. While in Porto for the Slow Food Award for the Defense of Biodiversity (where he met Vandana Shiva for the first time), he had the early symptoms of an illness that was to keep him out of public life for almost a year. The first cures were inadequate, and he got worse. He felt increasingly tired and was eventually diagnosed with a virus that had seriously compromised his liver: he suffered for months, between his home and hospital. The liver affliction forced Petrini to change his lifestyle and eating habits for a while, but today he has finally recovered. For a gourmet with his physique—around 6 feet, 3 inches, and 220 pounds—adjusting to a new life was not easy, but in the end, when he reappeared at the fifth national congress of Slow Food in Riva del Garda in June 2002, he was definitely back on track. The Italian delegates found him thinner ("After losing 20 kilograms, I am back," he said) but still ready to lead the movement again. On that occasion, Petrini had a special audience: Luigi Veronelli, the wine critic; Folco Portinari, the food writer; Enzo Ghigo, the president of the Piedmont region; and the Minister for Agricultural Policies Gianni Alemanno. Ghigo, Alemanno, and Petrini shared the same views on genetically modified organisms, because, as Petrini said "the problems of poverty, hunger, and mass agriculture as practiced by big conglomerates belong neither to the Left nor to the Right." He kept a distance from the anti-globalization movement led by Vittorio Agnoletto, which was about to march against the FAO in Rome: he explained that Slow Food was open to a dialogue with the U.N. organization, in the interests of finding a way to make a virtue of globalization.

That strategy took shape a few months later, on October 25, 2002, when the double project involving the international Presidia and the Slow Food Foundation for Biodiversity was presented at the fourth Salone del Gusto in Turin. For the first time, Slow Food introduced the concept of relativity applied to the excellence of products: to expect Mediterranean populations to dress salad with Indian mustard oil was unrealistic, as it was to expect Muslims to appreciate *sanguinaccio* (sausage made from pork blood). At the inauguration speech, Petrini was explicit: "We need to go back to nature, to the raw material. With the international Presidia we will offer concrete support, teaching how to fish instead of bringing fish, as my old friend Mao Zedong said. We also need to stop believing in the myth of the rich countries that are autonomous and independent. It's a fake myth. Happiness is in interdependence."

The Salone del Gusto of 2002 was a record event, with 138,000 visitors and media coverage that exceeded all expectations. This success made consolidation of Slow Food philosophy possible. Important roles were also played by the province of Tuscany, which supported the Slow Food

Foundation for Biodiversity; the Piedmont region, which adopted the Argentine Presidia, and other Italian winegrowing and wine-producing companies that came out in support of Slow Food's international plans.

THE MANIFESTO ON THE FUTURE OF FOOD
In the summer of 2003, Claudio Martini, president of the region of Tuscany, and other Tuscan officials organized the International Commission on the Future of Food in San Rossore, an estate formerly owned by the president of the republic. Participants in the meeting came from all over the world, including a number of executives of the International Forum on Globalization. Carlo Petrini participated on behalf of Slow Food, alongside Martini and Vandana Shiva (who co-chaired the meeting), and nutrition was the main topic on the agenda.

For Petrini, this was his international debut in front of the political and intellectual group who led the anti-global environmentalist movement. One of his assistants, Carlo Bogliotti, recalls:

> The first meeting of the Committee on the Future of Food marked a symbolic moment. Our eco-gastronomic philosophy was officially introduced to the top activists of international environmentalism. I was one of the few people who attended the roundtable, and I have to say that among the many people who participated in the meeting, Vandana Shiva was possibly the only one who had ever heard of Slow Food before. Carlin's intervention stressed the concept of safeguarding and affirming the right to pleasure. The enjoyment of food as a human right: this was the golden rule in any food policy, both in the rich Western world and in the Southern Hemisphere. "Pleasure is physio-logical, one may feel it either eating a steak in Paris, or a *feijoada* [Brazilian national dish, made from pork and beans] in a favela in Rio." I am certain that none of the participants had ever before listened to a discussion of the pleasure of food, in all the hundreds of symposia and conventions on food and the environment they had attended. After all, even the Food and Agriculture Organization considered it taboo, a mis-take that would later be acknowledged. The reactions to Carlin's speech were initially cold, but soon there was a heated discussion of the topic, and finally Vandana Shiva convinced everybody of the validity of

the eco-gastronomic philosophy. On that occasion, it became clear she shared many ideas with Petrini. In the end, the right to the pleasure of food was proclaimed in the Manifesto on the Future of Food. As often happens after one of Petrini's passionate speeches, a number of people—including Vandana Shiva; Wendell Berry, the American novelist known for championing agrarian ideals; Tim Lang, professor of food policy at London's City University; and Edward Goldsmith, author and founder of the Ecology Party in Britain—ended up becoming very good friends and partners of Carlin and me.

At the end of the meeting, the commission produced the Manifesto on the Future of Food, edited by Jerry Mander, president of the Board of the International Forum on Globalization. As stated in the manifesto, the goal was to achieve "a more decentralized, democratic and cooperative, non-corporate, small-scale organic farming as practiced by traditional farming communities, agroecologists, and indigenous peoples for millennia." Eco-sustainable agriculture, then, needed to be defended from industrialization, which cannot reduce world hunger because it "drives farmers from their lands, brings abhorrent external costs to the environment and to farming communities, and is itself highly susceptible to pests and a myriad of other intrinsic problems. Also, by most standards of measurement, small-scale biodiverse farms have proven at least as productive as large industrial farms."

In the Italian context, the regional government of Tuscany stands out as one of the most advanced institutions as far as Slow Food and its food policy are concerned. Indeed, the Manifesto on the Future of Food, which went on to be promulgated at the meeting of the World Trade Organization in Cancún in September 2004, owed its existence in part to Tuscan officials who had made the meeting in San Rossore possible. Before a regional law against genetically modified organisms was approved in Italy in November 2004, Tuscany had already launched measures to safeguard certain regional seeds as a defense against those patented by multinational conglomerates.

"Food and Commitment" were the themes of the October 2004 issue of the Italian cultural and political magazine *Micromega*. Piero Sardo, president of the Slow Food Foundation for Biodiversity, has described in that issue the itinerary from the Presidia to the foundation: "Slow Food is an international association, represented in thirty countries, with organizational structures of different effectiveness. In the United States, in Germany, in the United Kingdom, in Switzerland, in France, Slow Food is strong, so it has been relatively easy to transfer to each of them the experience of the Presidia. The issue of biodiversity is most fraught, however, in the developing countries and disadvantaged areas. There, the risk posed by big food conglomerates to local productions is the most severe. Nevertheless, one can still find unique plant varieties, animal breeds, and products in these countries. To create Presidia in those countries has inevitably meant making small investments and transferring needed resources.... We went to Tibet, for instance, to evaluate the possibility of producing a yak's milk cheese in a dairy farm run by monks. We went to Madagascar to find out how to improve the quality of the local red rice. We went to Guatemala to convince producers to invest in optimum growing areas, as the only way out from a market that is suffocating all the coffee growers in the world. We went to Ecuador to draw attention to a special kind of cocoa, called the *Nacional,* that has been found only there. All in all, we went a long way, always following our special compass: we think that farmers, to free themselves from the ill effects of globalization, have to strive for quality, have to gamble on their own tradition and their specific cultures. We have not transformed ourselves into one of those NGOs [nongovernmental organizations] that cannot treat weak countries as well as they do strong countries."

FROM SNAIL TO SLOW FISH

For centuries, the Mediterranean Sea and Genoa have cast a dark and bewitching spell over the Piedmont hills. The songwriter Paolo Conte has captured that feeling in one of his most celebrated songs dedicated to the city: "The fear we have of that dark sea / that moves even at night / and never stays still." For years, the executives of Slow Food had kept Genoa at a distance, as if fearing they might be swallowed by the waves. But in 2004, they could no longer resist the call of the squids, crabs, sea bass, and tuna that dominate the meals of this ancient port city. The halls of Genoa's trade fair center, the Fiera di Genova, are directly at the waterfront and have helped reestablish the old relationship between the city and the sea; every year the Genoa Aquarium attracts hundreds of thousands of visitors. It was here that Slow Food decided to launch their next development event, this time devoted to the world of the ocean. The "Slow Fish" fair debuted in 2004 with a big fish market, Taste Workshops, and conferences on sustainable and responsible fishing. After the Salone del Gusto in Turin, and Cheese: Milk in All Its Forms in Bra, Slow Fish has become the third trade show bearing the logo of the snail.

Restaurants, bistros, and cafés today are ready to offer you fish from almost anywhere, in a globalized world where even the most distant places are now just a flight apart. Yet, the sea is not a bottomless well. The FAO has frequently warned that fish stocks are endangered. Food historians explain that seafaring communities have never been big fish consumers, except in times of food emergencies. Today, populations around the world are demanding sea bass, lobster, and sea bream, and there are countries such as China, Japan, and Peru where fishing represents one of the most important elements in the national budget. For this reason, it is difficult to make these countries accept norms of responsible conduct. Similarly, the Mediterranean situation is not at all encouraging. A century ago, for example, during the tuna-fishing season in Sicily, it was easy to catch thousands of tuna, each weighing approximately 300 kilograms. Today, there are only a few dozen tuna that weigh more than 100 kilograms. The anchovy from Liguria is about to disappear altogether: this fish, a traditional staple among the poor, has reached incredibly high prices. And this is not even to mention the African seas, which are on the verge of leaving fishermen's nets empty.

Thanks in part to Slow Fish, the first gastronomic exposition entirely dedicated to fish, attention is finally being devoted to the protection of small fishing communities that are still respectful of marine ecosystems. Efforts are being made to get consumers to cook and eat lesser-known varieties of fish and to promote aquaculture, a technique that may offer a valuable solution to the shortage of marine resources, provided the methods are environmentally friendly.

Petrini explains:

The sea, even if many people may think otherwise, is not an inexhaustible source of food. When we talk about fish, the praise goes to its nutritional values and to its taste, only rarely does one talk about the problems that afflict the delicate marine ecosystem. Sushi bars, taverns, and restaurants keep seducing their clientele with seafood dishes (even as the quantity of fish consumed by households decreases), but in the meantime there are marine species that are endangered because of fishing. Every day, new forms of pollution hit the sea and the coasts, while the consumption of good and inexpensive species is declining because no one remembers how to cook them.

We envisioned an event that could focus on defending endangered species; on the quality of the species that are forgotten and thrown back into the sea; on sustainable fishing practices to oppose methods that exterminate entire shoals despite the sophistication of the technologies used; on small-scale fishing, which keeps alive coastal micro-economics and ecosystems; and finally on farming practices that take into account consumer health along with the quality level of the product.

Even a simple gesture like eating or not eating a shrimp may reveal an attitude toward nature and food communities. If not for the destruction of their coastal mangrove forests, which would have served as a buffer against the waves, and the massive development of tourist resorts along coasts that had never previously had large structures, India and Sri Lanka would have suffered less damage from the tsunami of December 2004. And what was the reason for the destruction of the mangrove forests? To create space for the intensive cultivation of shrimp for export to the United States and Japan. These farms had been built with funds from the World Bank. This was an example of an acquacultural plan with no respect for the environment, a plan against which Indian women had fought for years, thinking that the farms were responsible for the effects of sea desalinization. Battles such as this were what ultimately convinced Vandana Shiva, having earned degrees in physics and philosophy of science, to put aside her academic career and take up the cause of those who were seeking to establish sustainable agriculture. Is it really so difficult to see a connection between little shrimps and the tsunami's destruction?

A COMMUNITY OF TERRESTRIAL DESTINY

At the Suor Orsola Benincasa Institute in Naples, in July 2003, Carlo Petrini gave an articulate lecture in which he summarized Slow Food's twenty-year struggle:

International communities are facing some important choices regarding food and food security: coming at the beginning of a new century, these choices are really complex and controversial. Colossal economic interests are advancing competing models of development, and the result of this conflict will determine the agricultural policies of the sovereign states as well as the destiny of millions of men and women....

The peaks of scientific and economic absurdity that agriculture has reached in our time are clear. Industrial agriculture and genetically modified farming consume massive quantities of water. In France, it has been reported that 50 percent of the nitrates in the soil have been washed away by water, contaminating groundwater and threatening serious consequences for the health of animals and human beings. This is not a simple hypothesis from an environmentalist association, but a scientific analysis conducted by the National Institute of Agronomic Research. Worldwide, the consumption of water has increased 350 percent from 1950 to the present, with 73 percent of what is currently being consumed going to agriculture. So water is becoming a precious resource, of both our present and our future....

Faced with these uncontrollable forces, the so-called international community has established new institutions to guarantee free trade. The Codex Alimentarius (a food code established by the FAO and the World Health Organization) and the World Trade Organization [WTO] are the institutions that control trade and food safety. Created in 1963, the Codex Alimentarius establishes health norms "to protect consumer health and to guarantee the legality of practices adopted in the production of and trade in food." The European Union and the United States have 60 percent of the delegates, while representing 15 percent of the world population. Needless to say, the lobby of the food industry has a primary role within this institution. Suffice it to say that in 1997, the United States had a proposal to forbid the production of raw milk products placed on the Codex Alimentarius agenda. The very bases of the WTO are remarkably antidemocratic and iniquitous. The dogma of free trade is the antithesis of sustainable development: it is in fact based on the erroneous assumption that the whole planet and its future generations may consume resources in the same way as the richest countries do without leading to an economic collapse.

By confusing development with growth, one confuses quality of life with material accumulation and the frantic pursuit of greater profits, which do not necessarily produce improvement in quality. . . .

We thus need to strongly support the rights of every population to provide its own nutrition and to choose freely and democratically the kind of agriculture they prefer. Rural agriculture is fundamental both in the battle against GMOs and the big conglomerates of agrichemistry and agrifood and in the defense of biodiversity and the sovereignty of food and farmers. . . .

The coexistence of these two approaches to agriculture is not possible, since GMOs are infesting adjacent fields. Our lands are too small to guarantee the coexistence of biological agriculture and GMOs. The Piedmont region rightly destroyed the illegal transgenic cornfields, and common sense requires other regions to act accordingly and to be more careful in their controls.

From the mountains to the desert areas in the Maghreb, from the Amazon rain forest to the great plains of Siberia, the humble work of humanity has convinced us of the immense value of the heritage of these communities.

Through intervention in the Southern Hemisphere in particular, it is possible to emphasize the complexity of the economic and social issues that need to be confronted in countries where colonization has nullified agronomic practices. Wherever the quest for colonization ran into strong civilizations, many indigenous food products and raw materials were adopted by the colonizers into their daily life. One need think only of curry, which became an ingredient of British cooking, or of the famous Worcestershire sauce, whose origin is also Indian. . . . Once again, the community's freedom to choose farming practices, equal trade, and food sovereignty are the only values upon which to base development policies. It will be a long journey, and there are no shortcuts for these rural communities that have been forgotten by God and the saints. . . .

The rural community, with its rituals, its celebrations, its social relationships, its agronomic practices, and its beliefs is not only a good topic for an anthropological analysis, it can also have a real impact on politics, economics, and science, with unexpected and extraordinary results. . . .

I believe that when we commit ourselves to a comparison with different cultures, we must critically examine the dark and aggressive side of our culture, and in so doing, we must reject ethnocentrism. Mutual respect, comparing ourselves through diverse experiences, the exchange of knowledge among different communities of farmers, fishermen, craftsmen of good food, home cooks, and innkeepers will, I am sure, help to enrich a cultural heritage of something that Edgar Morin, a Slow Food emeritus member, has aptly called our "community of terrestrial destiny."

Four months later, Slow Food returned to Naples for its fourth International Congress, which took place in the Royal Palace from November 6 to 9, 2003. Piazza del Plebiscito, in the very heart of Naples, transformed itself in a wonderful display of typical products coming from 120 Presidia. It was the most important event yet held in southern Italy by Slow Food: in attendance were ministers, politicians, members of the regional administration for agriculture, six hundred delegates from thirty-six countries, eight hundred guests, and more than three hundred jurors for the Biodiversity Award. On November 7, the newspaper *La Repubblica* bore witness to "the birth of the first world eco-gastronomic association." Slow Food took the occasion to reintroduce some little-known kinds of street food: this was the fare of the "*magnamaccheroni* (spaghetti eaters), *tarallari* (cookie sellers), *acquaioli* (water sellers), and *spigaioli* (wheat sellers)," as Lucian Pignataro wrote, on the same day, in the Neapolitan newspaper *Il Mattino*. At that point, the government of the region of Campania became an official supporter of Slow Food, with the approval of the governor, Antonio Bassolino. The Neapolitan festival ended with the writing of a statute, the formation of a new international executive committee, and the creation of a document establishing the copyright for the use of the little snail logo. Slow Food wanted to prevent the erroneous use of it by the nearly one thousand Convivia scattered all over the world.

THE CORPORATION OF SLOW FOOD

In the twenty years following the foundation of the movement, the "little snail" had traveled far. By the year 2005, there were approximately eighty-three thousand Slow Food members scattered around the world. Italy was first, with thirty-eight thousand members; the United States came in second, with almost fifteen thousand members. Third was Germany, where a national association was established in 1992, with approximately 7,500 members. Switzerland joined the movement in 1994 and had 3,800 members. Following, in terms of membership, were Japan, which joined in 1998; France, which joined in 1995; the United Kingdom, Australia, and many more countries. In 2005, Slow Food was represented in 122 nations, with membership subdivided as follows: 61,253 in Europe; 15,910 in the Americas; 5,510 in Asia and Oceania, and 484 in Africa.

The association is now led by an international executive committee and an international council. In addition, there are national executive committees that are autonomous and have their own headquarters and full-time managerial staffs. Since 1995, the international office has been based in Bra, in Via Mendicità Istruita: it keeps track of Slow Food activities around the world, as well as of the initiatives of the 850 Convivia. The Convivia, or Condotte, as they are known in Italy, are run by volunteers, who organize dinners and tastings and other kinds of convivial and cultural meetings. They often have their own web sites and manage the contacts with the Presidia of the region.

Currently, in addition to Italy, there are six national associations with autonomous offices: the United States, Germany, Switzerland, France, Japan, and the United Kingdom. Each of these publishes its own local newsletter, in addition to the other bulletins and periodicals, whether in print or online, published by different branches of the Slow Food association.

The Slow Food universe may be described as a relatively complex corporate structure. The various components include the Slow Food International Association; the seven national associations with some thirty permanent employees; the Slow Food Foundation for Biodiversity; the Terra Madre committee with some forty full- and part-time employees; Slow Food Promotion, a commercial entity whose forty-five employees organize events like the Salone del Gusto; and Slow Food Editore, a commercial publisher with approximately thirty permanent employees and two hundred contributors. To this list, one might add the hospitality and catering sections, which are managed by the I Tarocchi cooperative; these are the restaurants Osteria dell'Arco in Alba and Il Boccondivino in Bra (roughly twenty employees and €1 million in business per year); the Albergo (twenty-one employees) of the Agenzia di Pollenzo at the University of Gastronomic Sciences; and the Enoteca, or Wine Bank. The little snail today employs almost two hundred people, with overall revenues of about €20 million.

The total income is provided by sponsors and public institutions and by membership fees ($60 per year for a single membership, $75 for a couple, and $30 for a student), a portion of which is allocated to financing the movement's growth in developing countries. Slow Food today is reaching out for new memberships from developing areas, areas which are linked to the food communities with whom Slow Food works toward a sustainable agriculture. The employees at Slow Food headquarters in Italy are a motivated group of individuals, most of them degree-holders in their thirties or forties, who earn a salary that ranges from €1,100 to a maximum of €1,900 a month.

In her master's thesis in corporate economics for the Bocconi University in Milan, Elena Schneider analyzed the corporate culture of Slow Food, a culture she finds to be characterized by open communication and especially by a budget review process "capable of evaluating and communicating not only economic achievements, but also accomplished facts." Dr. Schneider's study shows how Slow Food has grown, having become an international entity with many foreign branches and significant internal diversification, including the publishing and promotional division, environmental advocacy, and other sections all sharing the same mission. In the thesis, we read that growth problems can generate two types of issues. There is a strategic aspect, in which the executive board redefines the mission, and an organizational aspect, due to an ever-expanding structure whose management is complex. Schneider explains: "The Slow Food organization is relatively articulate, because the areas of activity of the different structures are very diversified, and also because there are many functions and staff bodies. Resources are scarce and shared by many areas and projects simultaneously, and the remarkable intercorrelation among the organizational entities generates constant need for coordination."

In Via Mendicità Istruita, the roughly 120 people who work daily at projects, initiatives, and contacts with the world operate in "organized chaos," at once feverishly active and serene, taking breaks to think or have a chat with Petrini. The president welcomes everyone in his study overflowing with books, papers, and snails of all sorts. His door is invariably open, and his second-floor window looks out from the same palazzo where, twenty years before, the main office of the factory workers' union shared a space with Bra's first cultural club of the Left.

chapter 6

A SNAIL IN THE WORLD

LUNCH FOR THE INTERNATIONAL EXECUTIVE COMMITTEE

It's a beautiful, sunny morning and the plain of Cuneo is already beginning to bake in the heat. On the horizon, the skyline of Cherasco, with
its churches and aristocratic houses perched atop a rocky outcrop, is
outlined against the distant peaks of the Maritime Alps, still covered
with gleaming white snow. In the hamlet of Pollenzo, near Bra, people
are coming and going at the campus of the freshly minted University of
Gastronomic Sciences. Opened by Slow Food in May 2004, the university is housed at the Agenzia di Pollenzo, a former agricultural complex
once belonging to the House of Savoy, Italy's former royal family. In a
small, tastefully decorated sitting room within the Agenzia's elegant new
restaurant, some twenty-odd people have gathered around a massive
wooden table. Light filters in from the gothic windows, but someone has
switched on the modern halogen lamps. Documents, folders, and glasses
of fruit juice are scattered over the table, and the guests' headphones
crackle with the sound of simultaneous translation in English or Italian.
The atmosphere is relaxed—more university seminar than corporate
board meeting. Carlo Petrini is at the center of the table, and facing him,
the two vice presidents: Alice Waters and Giulio Colomba. Flanking
them on either side are young people in their thirties or forties, many
wearing the golden snail clipped to their lapels.

This is a meeting of the international executive committee of Slow
Food. From the topics under discussion, it is apparent how much the
movement has changed in the almost twenty years since the first
Arcigola convention took place. The participants have changed, too:

American journalists, French professors, Swiss and German managers now sit side-by-side around the meeting table. Wrapped in an orange-and-red silk sari, the Indian scientist and Slow Food International Council member Vandana Shiva smiles luminously as she participates in the proceedings.

The committee tackles various issues through a free exchange of ideas—a brainstorming session of the kind favored by advertising firms and communications experts. Among the topics are the Slow Food International Congress of 2007 in Mexico, the world campaign to mark the 250th birthday of Anthelme Brillat-Savarin in 2005, and the possibility of offering summer courses for foreign Slow Food members in Pollenzo. Some of the board members are holding the galleys of a brochure in English that summarizes the movement's philosophy. It quotes a famous phrase of the French gourmet: "The pleasures of the table are for every man, of every land, of every place in history or society; they can be a part of all our other pleasures and they last the longest, to console us when we have outlived the rest." The brochure also addresses the use of the Slow Food trademark on products being sponspored by the various Slow Food outlets. Some members perceive the danger of losing control over a network that extends across five continents, and Petrini intervenes by saying that it's important to avoid becoming a "BINGO [a big, international nongovernmental organization]." This trendy acronym refers to such multinational nonprofits as Greenpeace and the World Wildlife Fund. Shiva adds that there is a need to institute a system of universities.

Vice president Colomba, an Italian who was elected to the Slow Food executive committee in 2002 after many years as Slow Food governor of the province of Friuli-Venezia Giulia, is perhaps the only person in the room with experience in politics. He began as a Communist Party representative from 1976 to 1983 and then served as mayor in his hometown, Bordano, near Udine. He shares the other board members' skepticism: "In recent years, we have grown very fast, therefore we must think carefully about how we are perceived around the world. We know the snail brand should not be used merely for commercial purposes. There are countries with whom we are already encountering communication and exchange difficulties, in part because of linguistic reasons. We should improve our network and better outline our future."

After this, everyone sits down for lunch. Halfway through the meal, the chef, Daniele Sandri, appears: he has been called into the dining room to be congratulated on his sturdy *tajarin,* a north-Italian style of homemade pasta. Petrini says: "Daniele, do you remember February 1989, in Caracas, during one of our first trips abroad with Arcigola? At that time, the connoisseurship of food and wine was a totally different thing. You cooked the same dishes as you have today. We were staying in a deluxe hotel frequented by the Kennedys and President Andrés Perez, and your job was to introduce Piedmontese cuisine to the haute bourgeoisie of Venezuela."

Sandri nods. "How could I possibly forget that adventure? We brought all our own ingredients: eggs for the *tajarin,* parmesan cheese to top it, and rabbits from the Langhe to cook in the oven. We had our wines, everything had been shipped over the ocean in a container. Carlin, I think you also remember that we were held up inside the hotel because there was curfew."

"You're right; the 'bread rebellion' had broken out," Petrini replies. "Thousands and thousands of poor people were in the streets to protest the most recent rise in the price of food. In Caracas, they were attacking stores, the government had declared martial law, and the armed enforcement by the military had caused dozens of deaths. And there we were, devoting a week to the traditional dishes of Piedmont. Edoardo Raspelli, the famous food critic, was there too. We were socializing with the well-to-do, the only ones who could afford those meals, while the general population was starving. We would have been better off discussing *pobellón,* the national dish of beans and meat. Fortunately, we were able to get back to Italy, but only just before they closed the airport. The whole experience exposed an immense contradiction: eco-gastronomy had acquired an elitist dimension, in some places representing no more than an haute-bourgeois amusement. A few months later, when we founded Slow Food in Paris, we drew on that experience."

THE UNITED STATES: CSAS AND FARMERS' MARKETS
Corby Kummer, the American journalist and well-known food writer for *Boston Magazine* and the *Atlantic Monthly,* is also present at the meeting in Pollenzo. When he was in Italy in 1998, he fell in love with the style and ideas circulating in the Salone del Gusto. In his book *The Pleasures of*

Slow Food, Kummer praises food craftsmen from every part of the world, introduces recipes, and tells the story of the people of Via Mendicità Istruita, always encouraging readers to look for the most local and genuine food possible. He calls the Salone del Gusto the "Mecca of food" and says that there is no other place in the world where a cook from Caracas can run into a Turkish farmer, or a vanilla grower from Chiapas can talk to a pastry chef from Athens.

Kummer is a thorough connoisseur of Italy and its products, a member of the board of directors of Slow Food USA, and a witness to the movement's success in the United States. He notes:

> In my book, I talk about my discovery of the Salone del Gusto in 1998 and the encounter with Petrini. It was Petrini who first explained to me clearly something I had previously suggested in my articles for American readers about old-time country cooking, which is so simple and flavorful: the upper class is happy to pay a lot of money just to eat like the poor people of long ago. The latter, by contrast, can only afford junk food at the supermarket. Petrini saw the need to narrow this gap. In Turin, I met a lot of people who shared my views: I had no idea that a perspective linking gastronomy and socio-economic analysis could be so interesting. At that point, I had to decide whether to go on working as a journalist or to join the group. I chose to join the movement.
>
> Both pragmatic and political, Petrini succeeded in organizing several major events in Italy. Americans would like to do the same thing, but are just now beginning to get institutional backing. In Italy, Petrini could convince the public and private sectors to support his ideas, but in the United States, it is much more difficult to obtain government funding for similar projects because of the influence of the big food corporations on the government. The American administration has no interest in promoting a different way of living and eating, a style which follows the rhythm of life and the origin of the earth. In Rome, it is easy to see how the Department of Agriculture could have nationalistic reasons for supporting Slow Food, to build a kind of barrier against genetically modified foods, protect Italian products, and hence sustain the domestic and export markets. In the USA, there are no such interests. In recent years, environmentalists and university professors, more than the gastronomes, drove the movement.

According to Kummer, the American model has nonetheless yielded some innovative new relationships between consumers and producers, particularly on the East and West coasts. Quirky and homegrown, these relationships offer promise for European agriculture as well. In Massachusetts, for example, where Kummer lives, there has been a steady loss of farmland to residential and other types of development, which offer far greater profits. In response, the State Department of Agriculture, in the absence of federal initiatives, has provided financial assistance to growers. Additionally, the Department of Agricultural Resources now has an office that strictly regulates and supports the growth of farmers' markets, which have become popular throughout New England. Kummer notes: "Today, rich people are not the only ones to shop at farmers' markets. The Department of Public Assistance provides needy people with food stamps that are accepted at all the farmers' markets. This way, in the last three years, farmers' stalls have reached areas outside Boston's richest neighborhoods. Generally speaking, in low-income areas of the city you cannot find fresh vegetables in supermarkets."

There are now dozens of organizations in North America that are trying to break down the cellophane-and-styrofoam barrier that divides cities from their sources of food. One very popular strategy is called Community Supported Agriculture (CSA). An individual consumer joins a CSA program in his or her region by purchasing a share of a farmer's harvest in advance of the growing season. This reduces the farmer's financial risks and bypasses the waste of national and global food distribution networks. Every week during the growing season, each shareholder receives a share of the crops.

But in many cities, the "fast food nation" darkly described in Eric Schlosser's fascinating book, *Fast Food Nation*, still prevails: whereas only a generation ago Americans spent their money to prepare homemade meals, today, according to Schlosser, half of this money is spent in fast-food franchises. Nevertheless, positive experiences like the ones described by Kummer are gaining momentum: in markets everywhere you can see signs, often supported by local Slow Food Convivia, with the slogan "Buy fresh, Buy local," and many schools now offer courses in food literacy and up-to-date gardening methods.

In California, in New England, in New York state something is changing, as reflected by the big success of Slow Food, with 150

Convivia (local groups) located throughout the fifty states, its national headquarters in Brooklyn, and its official bulletin, the newsletter "The Snail." In 2000, when Patrick Martins, the author of *The Slow Food Guide to New York City Restaurants, Markets, Bars*, founded the national office, the association had only a thousand members and twenty Convivia. Now it has fourteen thousand members. In 2004, Martins was succeeded by Erika Lesser, who discovered Slow Food while finishing an M.A. in the food studies program at New York University and joined the national office as a volunteer when it opened in 2000. In 2003, she went to Italy to work as a tutor at the University of Gastronomic Sciences at Pollenzo. Lesser says: "By the time I went back to New York as a director, the organization had become much stronger. The Slow Food philosophy had become popular because it was perceived as a counterpoint to mainstream American food culture. Many people are looking for an alternative. Petrini's ideas have touched a very sensitive nerve in the U.S." The challenge the Slow Food movement now faces is to trace back local food traditions, quality products, nongenetically modified and organic produce and to support American creativity. You can see it in the thousands of micobreweries, in small local cheese factories that produce raw-milk cheese using old-world techniques, and in bakeries whose bread is often tastier than that made in Europe.

Nevertheless, there are many other locally produced items that are disappearing or becoming difficult to find, as U.S. consumers continue to be inundated with standardized food. To address this problem, Slow Food USA brings together food communities and promotes eco-gastronomy through its various programs. Renewing America's Food Traditions (RAFT), The Ark of Taste, and Presidia programs bring visibility to endangered U.S. foods and reintroduce them to the world of consumers and distributors. Slow Food USA works to counter the notion that the United States lacks a diverse or unique food culture. Terra Madre brings together producers, cooks, and others involved in agriculture and food activities from around the globe. The U.S. Terra Madre delegation will represent the country's unique flavors and domestic issues to a larger international discussion about ways of understanding quality food: one that is aware of environmental resources, global balances, the sensory characteristics of food, the dignity of workers, and the health of consumers. Educational projects like Slow Food in School promote the efforts of school gardens, cooking classes, and other taste education projects organized by the local Convivia across the country to provide future generations with a meaningful connection to food.

SLOW FOOD IN GERMANY AND FRANCE

Outside Italy, the Slow Food movement made its first inroads abroad in Germany and Switzerland, two nations where the taste for Italian food and wine was already strong. Rapid sales of the translations of the guidebooks *Osterie d'Italia* and *Vini d'Italia* were in large part responsible for this success. In Switzerland, National Association President Rafael Perez, an importer of Spanish wines who owns a wine store in Zurich, has helped the Slow Food movement attract more than four thousand members. In Germany, where the fiftieth Convivium was founded in 2005, there are more than eight thousand members. If at the beginning there were some problems, due mainly to conflicts among wine importers, today Slow Food Deutschland is well established.

The turning point came in 1996 at a particularly exciting meeting that took place in Ulm, a city in the Baden-Württemberg region between Stuttgart and Munich. The meeting, which Petrini attended, had been organized by a group of new leaders who were not involved in the food industry, among them Friederike Klatt, who runs the cultural center of a pharmaceutical company. With her husband, Lothar, Friederike had become acquainted with Italian food and wines during a holiday in Italy spent at Grattamacco winery, located near the Tuscan coast not far from the town of Castagneto Carducci. In 1986, the couple participated in a dinner of the Arcigola Slow Food at the Frantoio di Montescudaio, a restaurant named for an old olive press. Klatt tells us: "We sat at the table next to people we did not know but soon became friends. We particularly appreciated eating seasonal dishes and talking with the local wine producers. It was really fun to learn about the dishes we were being served and to find out where the products came from and how they were cooked. But there was more to it than food, and shortly afterwards we applied to become members of Arcigola."

The Klatts joined the Slow Food movement and, in September 1992, met with 150 more Germans in Königstein in the Taunus region, to found Slow Food Germany. Klatt, a member of the International

President's Committee since 1997, continues: "For me, food not only has to taste good, it has to look appealing. Studying art history in college, I was not only interested in a visual interpretation of works of art but also their social meaning. I am captivated by the holistic approach of Slow Food. Taste is important, but the source, the means of production, the preservation of plant and animal varieties, the attention for the basic product, and the people involved in the process are equally important. As the curator of a large corporate art collection, I constantly deal with a variety of tastes."

Most recently, Slow Food Germany has become a supporting member of the federal association of consumers and various additional organizations, while also organizing several transregional events, including: the Käsemarkt am Kiekeberg, a cheese market that has taken place annually since 1998 at the Kiekeberg Farming Museum, not far from Hamburg in northern Germany; the Deutscher Käsemarkt, which takes place every other year at Nieheim, in East Westfalia; the Rhöner Wurstmarkt (sausage market); and the biennial Genuss im Nordwesten event in Cloppenburg. In 2005, the Convivium of Upper Franconia sponsored a Slow Beer program in two Bavarian cities, Münchberg and Helmbrechts.

If in Germany there are no Presidia yet, it is because the events organized by Slow Food Germany are in many ways similar to the ones promoted by Arcigola in Italy during its initial phase. By contrast, in France, the home of gastronomy and a Mecca for the founders of Slow Food, there are already five "Sentinelles du Goût," as the Presidia are called in France. They were established by a new group of leaders based in Perpignan, a few kilometers from the Spanish border. These Sentinelles are in turn the vanguard of initiatives devoted to the protection of such specialized local products as the golden lentils of Planèze de Saint-Flour (in Auvergne); the ham made from the black pigs of Gascony; the chicken breed known as the Coucou de Rennes (in Bretagne); the dry rancio wine of Roussillon; and the black turnip of Pardailhan (in Languedoc-Roussillon).

After some tentative beginnings that followed the creation of the movement at the Opéra Comique in 1989, there have recently been two national initiatives designed to give new momentum to Slow Food France. The first, Aux Origines du Goût, was launched in Montpellier in October 2003, with the collaboration of the association of winegrowers from the Coteaux du Languedoc, Saint-Chinian, and Faugères. Inspired by the Salone del Gusto in Turin, the biennial event focuses on the wines, cheeses, and oils of Languedoc. The second initiative was the celebration of the 250th anniversary of the birth of Anthelme Brillat-Savarin, which took place in 2005 in Belley, a town in the Rhône-Alps between Chambéry and Lyon.

Jean Lhéritier, a member of the international president's committee and president of Slow Food France, is a teacher of economic history at the University of Perpignan, where the new official headquarters of the French movement is soon to be established. Lhéritier says: "After all, Slow Food owes a great deal to France, since this is where the pleasures of fine cuisine were first discovered. One pioneer was Jean Lenoir, the inventor of 'Le nez du vin'—little cases of bottled wine aromas designed as a teaching tool that were brought to Bra by the oenologist Jacques Puisais. A few years later, here come some Italians to tell us that the palate is related to the land and the mother.... We already knew that! In the beginning, establishing Slow Food in France wasn't easy, the concept was too Italian. Another problem was the name: many people, public officials among them, objected to the fact that our brand name is in English. Perhaps they have forgotten that fast food does exist. But then, gradually, journalists and intellectuals, together with a group of wine producers of the Languedoc, began to see its importance."

The reaction to Slow Food in France has been strongly "Gallo-centric," as Lhéritier explains: "French people love Italy but do not like to be given a lesson in taste by Italians. Things have changed now that the movement has acquired an international dimension. Inseparable from agriculture and popular culture, the new concept of gastronomy has become very popular, not least because it brings the Frenchman Brillat-Savarin to mind: he was the first to develop a complex, social theory of gastronomy."

TO THE LAND OF THE RISING SUN

Masayoshi Ishida, a thirty-five-year-old from Fukushima, Japan, is relaxing at the worktable in Pollenzo. With a degree in Italian art history, and a passion for food, cars, and Florence, he now works in Bra at the international office of Slow Food, where he maintains contacts with the association in Japan. Ishida points out: "At the end of the nineties, the magazine *Aera*, from the Asahi Shimbun media group in Japan, began talking about Slow Food. There was some interest, but not to the extent of founding the movement. Only later Yutaka Baba, a famous gastronomist who imported food from Italy, got things started: he is currently responsible for the Tokyo Convivium."

The year 2001 was a critical moment in the dissemination of Italian art and culture in Asia. With the leadership of Umberto Agnelli, the Foundation Italy-Japan organized "Italy in Japan 2001–2002," an exhibition that involved all the most important cities and about forty events, including art shows, symposia, and debates. Several delegations of Italian government officials made appearances, including one led in May 2002 by Gianni Alemanno, who was at that time the Italian Minister of Agriculture. During one meeting in which the discussion had turned to the question of Japanese tuna fishing in the Mediterranean, one of Alemanno's Japanese counterparts, an official named Tsutomu Takebe, caused a stir by asking: "Could you tell me how I might go about establishing the Slow Food movement here in Japan? Is there somebody we should talk to?" Alemanno promised to help and put Takebe in touch with Bra.

Some initial difficulties having been overcome, Japan now has more than two thousand members and some forty Convivia scattered across the islands. Publication of a Japanese version of the magazine *Slow* commenced in 2004. Natsu Shimamura, a journalist and critic who is the author of a best seller on Slow Food, is now responsible for the Japanese Ark of Taste, which is focusing on several Presidium projects. One of these is to develop a standardized method of producing a special fish sauce made from liquid reserved during the salting of fish. In Italy, this "anchovy liqueur" is made on the Amalfi coast and is used in a number of pasta sauce recipes. In Japan, it is made not from anchovies but from the haka haka, an unusual fish that lives in the Akita area. Another project involves the Tankaku, a breed of cow that is native to the Inwate area and is occasionally eaten with Italian red wines.

Among the leaders of Slow Food, Giacomo Mojoli has been particularly involved in developing the relationship with Japan, following up on Alemanno's initial contact and meeting the political leadership of the country. He is now honorary president of Slow Food Japan, while the official president is Hirotoshi Wako. In Tokyo, the magazine *Slow* has its headquarters close to the fish market, which is the biggest in the world. The city authorities are now seeking to move this famous fish market, and the association is fighting the plan. Mojoli's Japanese career began with an invitation from the newspaper *Asahi Shimbun* to give a talk on Slow Food. His discussion of such topics as biodiversity, food and the education of the palate, and slow life as a lifestyle in itself and an approach to the world captivated the Japanese audience.

Mojoli recalls: "In those days, there was a great deal of respect for this thoroughly fascinating culture, the incredible richness from an anthropological and social point of view, starting from the tradition of tea, which has much in common with the Slow Food philosophy. The ritual of tea places great value on hospitality, careful attention toward one's guests, dialogue and curiosity as forms of knowledge, and art and taste as a path to harmony. If you think about it, we are really talking of the spirit of conviviality, the need for a way of living that is more harmonious, more tolerable, more slow-paced. The main elements of the Slow Food approach form a kind of secular ritual of observing and experiencing life more deeply."

To the Japanese, food has to be good when one eats it, but good also when one thinks of it. Mojoli adds: "One ends up internalizing the spirit of nature, maintaining a sense of freshness, of the natural, of the real balance between quantity and quality. In this country today, the main challenge is to harmoniously reconcile the relationship between tradition and modernity. In expanding the cultural boundaries of Slow Food, the Japanese are introducing something new in their own country, which has always been capable of borrowing from others by reworking experiences."

In the winter of 2005, Mojoli took Petrini on a tour of Japan. The tour ended on March 6 in Obihiro, on the cold, northern island of Hokkaido, with a meeting with Prime Minister Junichiro Koizumi: it was the conclusion of the national congress of Slow Food Japan.

In addition to the seven national associations, including Italy's, there are various official alliances between the movement and a variety of foreign countries today. For example, an alliance has formed with Brazil through its Left-leaning president, Luiz Inácio Lula da Silva, elected in 2002.

Petrini, as the leader of what has become a global movement, is a highly sought after celebrity the world over and travels constantly. One day he is giving a university lecture in the United States, the next day he's meeting with the Sami people in Sweden, before heading off to the opening of a Slow Food café in New Delhi, India. Curiously, this is the only public establishment in the world which bears the logo of the snail directly on its sign.

chapter 7

∿⊙)

THE UNIVERSITY OF
GASTRONOMIC SCIENCES

A PRAGMATIST'S DREAM: POLLENZO

Once—not so long ago—the manicured lawn was just a field of weeds. The Luserna stone and bricks were marked by decades of pheasant droppings and streaks of lime. A neglected, muddy iron gate led to a church that gave little sign of its ancient splendor. But today, visitors to the Agenzia di Pollenzo, a large estate on the banks of the Tanaro River in the plain between Bra and Alba, begin their visit with a stroll down a pleasant pathway paved with river stones and lined with trees. The building's entrance portal leads one through to a large, square courtyard. On the far side of the courtyard is an elegant hall, decorated with leather armchairs and a tapestry, its windows opening on to a quiet lawn that stretches out toward the Alps. On April 30, 2004, this hall was filled with musicians and acrobats, as the ancient estate of King Charles Albert of Sardinia, of the House of Savoy, officially opened to the public for the first time. The members of the House of Savoy were important leaders in Italian history, tracing their lineage back to the eleventh century and the first counts of Savoy. The family later ruled the Kingdom of Sardinia (a territory that included Savoy and Nice, now part of France, as well as Piedmont, Genoa, and Sardinia), before finally acceding to the throne of a united Italy from 1861 until 1946.

In 2004, Italy was going through a crisis, and the future did not look bright for the car industry, which had been responsible for Piedmont's economic development. The Pollenzo estate, a complex valued at €22 million, the restoration of which took seven years, was inaugurated in front of TV cameras and microphones, before an audience of politicians, local authorities, and the upper classes of oeno-gastronomy. It was all made possible by a pragmatist who had firmly believed in a dream since he had first set his eyes on the estate.

On that day, as everyone smiled with satisfaction at having been able to create a crossroads of all the flavors in the world, Carlo Petrini opened the world's first University of Gastronomic Sciences, an institution he viewed as the fulfillment of "the dream of a lifetime," as the newspapers reported. Petrini was in the mood for jokes: "Please, do not tell me that all I see today is nothing but the product of a dream, otherwise I might think I've spent my whole life sleeping."

On the day that preceded the formal ribbon-cutting ceremony, Petrini had invited all the older townspeople of Pollenzo to a lunch in the estate's restaurant. He wanted them to participate in the event before the streets of their small town were flooded with thousands of guests. People in their seventies, who could still recall the visits of the Savoy royal family before World War II, were first given a tour of the renovations of the royal residence; then they tasted Lidia Alciati's ravioli; and finally they listened to a concert by the State Police band that had gathered in Pollenzo for the occasion. The celebration, conducted with all the conviviality typical of a Slow Food event, went on for eleven days, in conference rooms and in the courtyards of the 13,000-square-meter complex. Many prestigious guests were in attendance: from the art critic and council representative Vittorio Sgarbi, who had delivered a lecture on the "Tastes of Beauty," to Umberto Eco, the author and semiotician, to Enzo Bianchi, the prior of the monastic community in Bose. There were also many artists: Moni Ovadia; the singers Roberto Vecchioni, Francesco Guccini, Gianmaria Testa, and Giorgio Conte; and well-known chefs and wine producers such as Paul Bocuse, Gualtiero Marchesi, Angelo Gaja, Bruno Giacosa, and the Earl Alexandre de Lur-Saluces from Château d'Yquem.

It had all begun on July 27, 1998. Sponsored by Arcigola Slow Food, the "Agenzia di Pollenzo" organization was established with capital of approximately €800,000 from a combination of private and public investors. The organization had 121 private investors. A few weeks after signing the agreement, Petrini met Claudio Altarocca, a journalist for *La Stampa*, and told him about his plan: "Petrini stopped the car. He was now facing a castle of sorts, a church, and a vast stretch of green. Silence was all around, broken only by the crickets and the sound of water. 'Down there once was the Tanaro River. We are just below Bra, and this is the former farm of the royal estate of Pollenzo, conceived by King Charles Albert. Long ago, it was a showpiece, the managerial center of the land properties of the House of Savoy.' But now, it was abandoned and in poor condition. As he entered the dilapidated halls and walked through the incredibly long, grandiose cellars, Petrini, ever the prophet-entrepreneur, envisioned his most audacious gamble yet: in these enormous halls with their neo-gothic details, in the immense courtyard, garden, and park, he saw a hotel, a wine bank filled with precious wines stored for the future, and a European 'academy of taste' similar in purpose and practice to an academic institution, all operating as a public company with €24 million in capital. 'An absolute novelty,' Petrini declared, for food company executives, tour operators, hoteliers, restaurateurs, and the like. 'In four years' time, this will become the Temple of Taste.' Best wishes, Petrini."

Petrini's prediction was close: it took six years, not four. It also took plenty of determination. First of all, he had to find the money to buy the €2.2 million estate from the company that had previously owned it. The property, a hunting lodge known as the "Lake of Pollenzo," belonged to a family of entrepreneurs who had bought it in 1971 from the Savoy royal family. The last king of Italy, Umberto II, was exiled after the 1946 referendum establishing the Italian Republic. After the end of the monarchy, the "Lake of Pollenzo" had four owners, all belonging to the Savoy family, and descending from King Charles Albert. They were Calvi di Bergolo, the Countess Iolanda; Moritz von Hesse, the son of Princess Mafalda, who had died in Buchenwald in 1944; Maria, married to Louis Bourbon-Parma; and Giovanna, the widow of Boris III of Bulgaria, whose son Simeon is now the president of Bulgaria. The property, 360 hectares in size, was the source of a long legal battle between the heirs of the Savoy family and the Italian state: the former royals insisted that the castle of Pollenzo should be considered part of their personal heritage, which meant that it could not be appropriated by Italy's new government. In the end, the members of the Savoy family won, and as soon as the property was officially awarded to them by the courts, they immediately began to sell it off. They sold the first 160 hectares in the mid-sixties, dividing it into several lots. The family of entrepreneurs still owns a sixteenth-century mansion and 200 hectares of land around the Tanaro River.

The founder of Slow Food was at the head of a large consortium of bureaucrats, producers, bankers, and entrepreneurs who were all taking a calculated risk with their capital, in the name of a new eco-gastronomic culture of food. Their goal was the improvement of the region between Bra and the Langhe hills. Unlike the regions of Burgundy or Champagne, this area had no *châteaux-relais* where tourists could be accommodated, nor was there any organization that could serve as a cultural flagship within the wine world. Petrini succeeded in raising approximately €20 million to realize his dream, much of it in donations of €150,000. He knocked on many doors, and all the great wine-producing families of Italy joined in the effort. Numerous local entrepreneurs participated as well, as did the provincial government of Piedmont, working through its public finance company, FinPiemonte. Piedmont's participation was made possible by a regional law that had passed on December 1999 allowing it to invest €6 million in the project. Finally, banks and credit institutes, and the local and regional governments of Alba, Bra, Verduno, La Morra, Cervere, Pamparato, and the province of Cuneo all contributed.

Arcigola Slow Food promoted the public funding, and by December 31, 2004, the Agenzia di Pollenzo company had collected capital amounting to €19 million, subdivided among 322 shareholders, including 314 private investors, who control 68 percent of the public company, while the public funding covers the remaining 32 percent.

Throughout this process, Petrini was assisted by his old friend Giovanni Ravinale, who in 1998 had quit his job as a salesman in the construction industry to devote himself completely to the "dream of Pollenzo." He was soon named director. Ravinale had accompanied Petrini on his first outing inside the semi-abandoned compound. At the end of 1999, bids were accepted from contractors, and work started in January 2000. In three and a half years, 13,000 square meters of indoor space and 37,000 square meters of outdoor space were restored.

With a total investment of approximately €22.5 million, the company that controls the Agenzia di Pollenzo now owns the entire compound and leases it to the tenants, including the restaurant Guido (which belongs to the Alciati and Mongelli families), the Wine Bank, the

Albergo dell'Agenzia hotel, and the University of Gastronomic Sciences. On June 2004, Pirelli Re Agency estimated the value of the estate at €22–25 million.

On the day of the inauguration, Petrini's thoughts were with his friend Ravinale, who sadly could not share the joy of seeing their dream come true: only forty-eight years old, he had died in October 1999 from a sudden embolism. Petrini recalls:

> By the end of the nineties, after the success of the first Salone del Gusto, I started looking for a place, a base on which to build the future of our association, which otherwise I feared was built on sand. We had several employees at the time, and the organization was ready for the next step forward. I was convinced we had to find a symbolic building to protect and maintain Italian wine, a building that could become a sort of grand library of the world's oenologic knowledge. Furthermore, I had in mind to found an "academy of taste," with classrooms where we could continue in a permanent way the workshops we had effectively set up, first at Vinitaly and later at the Lingotto. Thus, I had begun wandering around castles and palazzi in the Langhe and in Roero, when I heard that the owners had possibly decided to sell the Agenzia that King Charles Albert had founded in Pollenzo, keeping for themselves the ancient sixteenth-century castle where they lived, and part of the estate. I went with Giovanni to see the compound in 1997. We got there in the afternoon, and when I saw the courtyard, I was impressed by the beauty of the structure. We knew that someone wanted to turn it into an assisted living complex for wealthy Swiss retirees. The family who owned it was no longer using it as a hunting lodge, and the farms of quails and pheasants located in the old stables had been empty for years—ever since the dramatic flood of the Tanaro River that had swept everything away. But even though the place had been abandoned, the cellars where the king had started experimenting in the production of Barolo wine in the mid-nineteenth century were very beautiful and were a good location for the Wine Bank, a project I had been thinking of for a long time. In addition, I was already envisioning a hotel there, a hotel similar to the ones I had seen for years on estates in France. Ravinale and I intended to raise at least $7 million so that we could start working on the restoration of the Agenzia. Private investors and the

FinPiemonte finance company, which today has a 25 percent share, provided us with that amount. Slow Food bought a €160,000 share and so did the Cooperativa I Tarocchi [see chapter 2]. To invest in this enterprise, we sold our share of a restaurant in Cuneo, La Chiocciola [the snail]. It was not easy to stay on top of all the many aspects of our initiative: the formal constitution of a corporation, the purchase of the compound, the announcement of the competition to restore it, and the selection of the construction firm to carry out the work. Everything was done publicly, because, even though our corporation was private, we wanted to accomplish our objectives with the maximum honesty. Although local authorities were involved, we have never been asked as a favor to give a job to one person or another. I do not exactly know what the standard procedure is, yet undoubtedly this is something they have to be commended for. A committee consisting in part of academics was in charge of every decision, and we have always respected their choices.

KING CHARLES ALBERT AND
HIS OENOLOGIST, GENERAL STAGLIENO

History plays a fascinating role when you walk through the streets of Pollenzo into the silent square beyond the big gates of the Agenzia. During the renovations, some patrician Roman tombs, medieval walls, and the remains of battles that once bloodied the Tanaro River were discovered. All this bore witness to an ancient grandeur which, because of the general state of neglect, seemed impossible to revive.

Pollenzo today belongs to Bra's administrative district and has a population of about one thousand. The Italian Ministry of Cultural Affairs gave the town of Bra €2.6 million for the restoration of the village of Pollenzo. In ancient times, Pollenzo had been called Pollentia and was one of the most important Roman cities in Piedmont, along with two centers founded by Emperor Augustus, Augusta Taurinorum (Turin) and Augusta Bagiennorum (Bene Vagienna, in the Cuneo plain). Pollentia, mentioned by Cicero, Martial, and Pliny the Elder, was conquered by the Romans during the second century AD and became a military bastion. It is also known as the site of an important battle in 402 AD, when general Stilicone, the commander in chief of Emperor

Theodosius, saved the western empire from the first invasion of Alaric, king of the Visigoths. Relics of the Roman age can still be found in the cellars of houses around the Agenzia, while some houses in the historical center of the town are built on the oval foundations of an ancient Roman arena some 200 meters long, much like the houses surrounding Piazza Anfiteatro in Lucca.

Because of its strategic location, the town became a military stronghold in the Middle Ages. During the rise of the Italian city-states in the eleventh century, a time known as the Communal period, the cities of Alba and Asti competed to have control over the town—and succeeded in destroying it. Later, Pollenzo was annexed by the powerful Visconti family, the rulers of Milan. In 1346, it was the scene of another battle, one that marked the end of French rule under the Angevin dynasty. In the fourteenth century, the town served briefly as the seat of the Viscount Antonio Porro, who built a fortified stronghold in 1386. Only in 1762, with Charles Emmanuel III, did the castle of Pollenzo become the property of the dukes of Savoy.

In 1831, Charles Albert Savoy-Carignano was crowned king of Sardinia. A complex personality, Charles Albert had been raised in a francophile environment and was sympathetic to Napoleon Bonaparte (who brought Italy under French rule from 1796 to 1815). After a flirt with liberal and reformist ideas, he later became more conservative, suppressing the democratic efforts of those seeking to establish a united Italian republic. Nevertheless, during his last year of rule, Charles Albert agreed to a constitutional regime that provided the foundation of the later kingdom of Italy.

As a refuge from his court duties in Turin, which was then one of Italy's leading cities, Charles Albert committed himself to the care of the Savoy family's castle and farmhouse in Pollenzo. In 1832, he began a radical transformation of the castle, the village, and its surroundings. He put the Agenzia at the center of the estate, and with economic and financial considerations in mind, he built two square adjacent buildings in order to experiment with modern techniques for growing cereals and vines and raising livestock. In tune with the spirit of the times, the king favored neo-medieval details for his Agenzia: pointed arches in the external façades of the buildings, a tower at one corner, and two turrets with battlements on the main façade.

When the king began producing wine in Pollenzo (as Giusi Mainardi reports in his study of the town edited with Giuseppe Carità, *Pollenzo*), he named the army general Paolo Francesco Staglieno head of winemaking operations. General Staglieno remained in this role for approximately ten years. A Genoese, Staglieno belonged to a distinguished aristocratic family and for years had been in charge of the refinement of the wines of the Grinzane estate (just a few kilometers from Alba), which was owned by the great Italian statesman Count Camillo Benso di Cavour.

In 1835, General Staglieno published an innovative essay on Italian oenology, *Istruzione intorno al miglior modo di fare e conservare vini in Piemonte* (Instructions about the best way to make and maintain wines in Piedmont), which illustrated the new wine production techniques imported from France. The book was a great success because of its suggestions for making a wine that was "completely dry, clear, transparent . . . , generous, alcoholic, and pleasant to the palate." In 1841, in order to test the ability of his wines to be exported without suffering a loss in quality, Staglieno shipped a batch of 141 casks of red wine, white wine, and vermouth to Rio de Janeiro and Bahia. When the ship returned to Genoa two years later with some remaining bottles on board, he deemed the results of his experiment quite satisfactory. The general wrote that, like the great wines of Bordeaux and Burgundy, the "Pollenzo wines came back from America not only unhurt, but also rather improved."

Paolo Francesco Staglieno invented modern, high-quality wine in Piedmont and used the best techniques to make it age well over long stretches of time: dry rather than smooth, clear rather than cloudy, his wines soon became famous. They were sold to many hotels in Genoa, and at court they were so appreciated that on April 10, 1842, they were served at the luncheon held at the palace in Stupinigi on the occasion of the wedding of the heir to the throne, Prince Victor Emmanuel II to Maria Adelaide von Habsburg.

In October of the following year, the Agrarian Association, an organization founded by King Charles Albert for the purpose of standardizing updated farming techniques, held its first general assembly at the royal estate of Pollenzo. This turned out to be a significant meeting, attended by many technical and scientific experts from different branches of agriculture and devoted to themes that are still being explored, 160 years later, in the classrooms of the Pollenzo university.

YOUNG PEOPLE WITH GOOD TASTE

And yet, many of the ideas that were debated at that assembly have in fact vanished. The industrial revolution first, and consumerism later, have relegated gastronomy to the realm of folklore. The story of Slow Food demonstrates that food experts should not be knowledgeable simply in isolated aspects of food culture, such as food safety, diet, or the farming and history of local products. Rather, the movement illustrated the principle that gastronomy should be taught as an interdisciplinary and complex science in which economics and technology, cultural analysis and anthropology, communications and social sciences are all intertwined. Today, the University of Gastronomic Sciences in Pollenzo is the first university in the world where food is the main protagonist. It enrolls sixty students per year, half of them Italians and half from other countries all over the world. After three years of study a student obtains a degree in gastronomy and then may choose to pursue a specialization. The teachers, coordinated by Alberto Capatti, are all oeno-gastronomists who have participated in the development of the Slow Food movement or come to the university from top teaching positions in institutions in Paris, Bonn, Buenos Aires, Mexico City, New Delhi, and Adelaide.

The university admissions office receives applications from all over the world, and especially from the United States, Japan, Canada, Switzerland, and Germany. Students are captivated by the university's innovative curriculum, which requires approximately three months of study abroad each year that alternate with courses on theory. The study abroad subjects are organized with regard to thirty-six regions of the world and the following twelve themes: coffee, sausages, cheeses, and pasta (covered in the first year); the food industry, pastry, animal farming, and rice (covered in the second year); and beer, bread, fish, and bio-agriculture (covered in the third year).

Over their three years of study in the vaulted, brick-walled classrooms and the splendid library with its high wooden trusses, the future gastronomists are shaped into cosmopolitan gourmets, often learning directly from food producers connected with Slow Food. Recent students have included the son of the owner of a historic New York gourmet food shop; the scion of a Turinese family of restaurateurs; a Japanese woman who wants to learn how to feed herself "slowly" once she is back to her native country; a Swiss who is deeply into organic agriculture and dreams of founding cooperatives; and several graduate students from hotel-management schools.

The fee is about €19,000 per year, including room (in little apartments in Bra), half-board, equipment fees, and all travel expenses for the study abroad. Although not particularly low as a university fee, it is nevertheless reasonable when compared to many American or Italian private universities. Furthermore, there are twenty-two grants or scholarships offered by banks, producers, and local authorities.

Opening a private university in less than two years, a process which involved obtaining numerous legal permits and authorizations and preparing courses of study, placed Slow Food under a great deal of pressure. Petrini remembers:

> From the very beginning of this wonderful adventure, I thought that this royal mansion should host not only a cooking school, but also, ideally, a place for studying the food culture we had been observing over the last twenty years. My intention was to stimulate the growth of a generation of new farmers, cultivated gastronomists, and gourmets who would think critically about the sources of their ingredients. What I could not have envisioned was the creation of a university: it seemed such an unachievable objective. Between 1998 and 1999, we were in extensive negotiations with the Minister of Public Education, Luigi Berlinguer, to obtain official status for an academy of taste. We wanted the academy to be authorized to award a college-level degree similar to the ones offered by art academies and music conservatories. We started the legal procedure, and the parliament eventually voted in favor of the institution of the academy. Simultaneously, however, the ministry was in the process of instituting reforms in artistic and musical education; these reforms ignited student protests, and everything came to a standstill. In the meantime, Guido Tampieri, who worked in the Department of Environment and Agriculture of the provincial government of Emilia-Romagna, told me about the ducal palace in Colorno, a few kilometers from Parma. He said it was then undergoing renovation and

might possibly be a good place to teach courses on food production. Pollenzo is at the center of one of the most prestigious winegrowing and wine-producing areas in Italy, while the Parma province is at the top in gastronomic culture, with its *culatello* [a smaller, sweeter, and mellower kind of prosciutto] and Parmigiano-Reggiano cheese. So I thought that this could be a good cultural marriage and decided to aim for the top.

Two different groups then started working on this project. The first group, composed of teachers, was directed by Alberto Capatti from the University of Pavia. It included—in addition to Petrini—the historian Massimo Montanari (University of Bologna), the economist Fausto Cantarelli (University of Parma), who is specialized in food production, and the nutritionist Marco Riva (University of Milan). The other group was in charge of development and raising the funds necessary to launch the project: Vittorio Manganelli, who for years had been a passionate taster and a contributor to the guide *Vini d'Italia*, devoted himself to this endeavor. Capatti, now the president of the University of Pollenzo, explains: "During the initial phase, we university professors were not in the least thinking of founding a new discipline; only Carlo Petrini was thinking along these lines. He had a new way of thinking about how to make the most of the cultural energy that was converging within the food world. The decision to found a university represented a Copernican revolution: we decided to transform gastronomy into a science that would be at the service of the producers. The process was not an easy one, because on some occasions we had arguments with the academic establishment, which was not willing to accept the principle of an interactive and far-reaching pedagogy that could also include the traditional knowledge of a producer of oil or prosciutto. But after thirty-five years teaching in a state university, I threw myself into this new adventure with enthusiasm. Thanks to Slow Food, I saw I had a chance to change some of the traditional ways of learning."

The first agreement among the regions of Piedmont and Emilia-Romagna and the Slow Food leadership dates back to November 2001. In 2002, Slow Food was tasked with writing a feasibility study for the university. The commission presented it on July 16, 2002, and in the summer of 2003, the Association of the Friends of the University of

Gastronomic Sciences, coordinated by Manganelli, was born. The two regions decided to join the association and became founding members of the university alongside Slow Food. Finally, on August 5, 2004, the Ministry of Education issued a decree in favor of the establishment of the new university in Pollenzo, to be launched at the start of the 2004–2005 academic year.

Manganelli, a fifty-year-old head officer of the municipality of Turin who had served first in the division of libraries and then in an administrative department, decided to resign on January 1, 2001, to devote all his time to the project. "The idea of constituting a private university began taking shape in the summer 2002, and from that moment on we began meeting with leading institutional authorities, including Gianni Alemanno, at that time the minister of agriculture, and Letizia Moratti, then the Minister for Education, Universities, and Research. We were informed that universities like the one we had in mind could be founded only every three years; that we would have to overcome countless bureaucratic obstacles in order to be legally recognized, and that we had to raise more funds, aside from what we had already found to restore the Agenzia. Both Mr. Alemanno and Mrs. Moratti helped us. We got down to work, and Petrini, who is erroneously considered a dreamer, but is actually a pragmatist, wanted to be sure about our financial status first. During these years, we gathered 120 investors who supported the university. Today it has a budget of approximately $6 million; there are twenty-eight employees, including permanent and visiting professors and six tutors who are in charge of approximately sixty students (the maximum for each course year)."

Soon the university will be adding to its curriculum a second field of study in agro-ecology, which will aim at being the first academic course for people whom Petrini envisions becoming the "cultivated farmers of the third millennium." Pollenzo "may not be Oxford or Cambridge, but it is already a regular campus," the newspaper *La Repubblica* wrote on January 24, 2005, "where future professionals study the earth and travel to know and taste thousands of different foods, through an interdisciplinary focus on science, history, culture, and taste."

THE MASTER'S PROGRAM IN COLORNO

On February 28, 2005, Slow Food's second academic institution opened in Colorno in Emilia-Romagna, in a seventeenth-century ducal palace that had once belonged to the Farnese family and is only 15 kilometers from Parma. The first master's program in gastronomic sciences and quality products was inaugurated in March 2005 as a one-year-long concentrated compendium of the program in Pollenzo. Starting in 2007–2008, students will be able to enroll in a two-year specialization program. There will be two main concentrations to choose from, the first more focused on the humanities, the second on business administration: Food and Gastronomic Communication Sciences, and Management of Production Enterprises and Food Distribution. The humanities course will be designed for students interested in becoming food critics, journalists, and public relations officers for food companies; the business course will attract future managers of catering and hotel enterprises, managers in the winegrowing and wine-producing business, and head buyers for supermarkets and commercial centers.

Colorno is located at the conjunction of the the Lorno channel and the Parma River. It is an agricultural and industrial center of eight thousand inhabitants. In 1612, it became a property of the Ducal Chamber of Parma, and in the middle of the seventeenth century a summer residence of the Farnese family, one of several powerful aristocratic families in Italy. The palace has been called "little Versailles" for its beauty, and to this day it is a favored location for art exhibitions.

This structure, like the villa at Pollenzo, has a distinctive charm. One difference between the two estates may be that Colorno was decorated and embellished mainly to impress visitors, with no interest whatsoever for any agricultural endeavor. After the Farnese family, Colorno came into the hands of the Bourbons, who asked the French neoclassical architect Ennemond-Alexandre Petitot to restore the interiors. Finally in 1816, Marie Louise of Austria, Napoleon's second wife, transformed the Italian garden into the English park that can now be seen from the classroom windows. Today, the grand staircase, the tower clock, and some sitting rooms still bear testimony to the building's ancient splendor. In 1860, the Savoy family, who owned the palace before the state took possession of it, had all the furniture moved to their residences in Florence, Turin, and Rome. Today, most of this furniture is on display in

Rome at the Quirinale Palace, the residence of the president of the Republic of Italy.

The students enrolled in the master's program at Colorno include Italian and international students from a variety of different backgrounds. For example, there are two young Finnish women who are convinced that quality food products would be a commercial hit in their home country; a young man from Mexico City who has worked for important hotels and wineries in Denver and in Nice; a Japanese freelancer who, fascinated by the Salone del Gusto, moved to Italy several years ago; and a woman who came to Colorno from Canada with the help of state financial aid and is focused on making movies and television shows devoted to good food.

To stress the international character of its curriculum, Colorno has offered an English-language master's degree since November 2005. Titled Food Culture: Communicating Quality Products, this course is taught in English by an international team of highly specialized teachers and professionals. The program is for international students who want to develop an innovative approach to food. Its main aim is to provide students with specific knowledge about high-quality products, which can then be used for communication and promotional purposes. A fundamental goal of the program is to provide students with a deep competence in the anthropological and historical contexts of food consumption, in Italy and other European countries.

The disciplines taught in Colorno include food and wine history and culture; the anthropology, sociology, and psychology of consumerism; food journalism for the web; photography techniques; and communication. While studying these topics, students devote special attention to sensorial analysis, cooking techniques, and food technology.

THE RAVIOLI MIRACLE AND A BANK FOR WINE

Think about how miraculous ravioli are: eggs, cheese, cabbage or borragine, rabbit, veal and pork; then the wine to cook the meat, the aromatic herbs, and the flour; and finally to top everything, the hands that make them. Here in Pollenzo, at the in-house restaurant, Guido, I have seen a beautiful photograph of Lidia's hands. Her hands know how to create ravioli, how to spread out the dough in one second and then, immediately, close and cut them with the *raviolé*, the ravioli maker: her hands and everything are part of the process of making ravioli. Many elements come together to make that delicacy. And just as many people collaborated in making it, so many people enjoy it. I have taken the title for my lecture from a famous saying of the German philosopher L. A. Feuerbach: 'Man is what he eats.' I say that because food is social, man is meant for communion, and he has to consume what the earth provides. Dear Carlin, I am saying this to you, because you know how to make a feast out of food. From China to the United States, all humankind knows how to get together in a convivial way to have a meal.

These are the words of Enzo Bianchi, prior of the Bose Community, an interreligious monastery founded thirty years ago near Turin. It was May 4, 2004, and in the conference room of the Agenzia di Pollenzo, Bianchi was discussing passages from the Bible that refer to food. The beautiful black-and-white photograph mentioned by the prior was taken by the Italo-Belgian photographer Dario Puglia and hangs in the dining room of the Agenzia's Ristorante Guido.

Having left the restaurant in Castigliole d'Asti that Lidia Alciati had continued to run after the death of her husband, Guido, the Alciati family launched into multiple ventures. Lidia and her son Andrea have opened a restaurant in Santo Stefano Belbo, while the other two sons, Piero and Ugo, run the restaurant in Pollenzo, with the collaboration of Savino and Marcella Mongelli, who used to own the seafood restaurant La Noce in Volpiano. This is how Mamma Lidia's *agnolotti* with roasted meat sauce and her *vitello tonnato*, a traditional Piedmontese dish of veal with tuna sauce, came to appear on the same menu with *pescatrice al lardo Arnad* (monkfish with Colonnata lard) and charbroiled jumbo shrimps and scallops with bay leaves. For chefs like Ugo Alciati and Savino Mongelli, a new adventure had begun, and this time it was characterized by a successful harmony around the stove, in a kitchen with modern equipment.

The southwest wing of the Agenzia houses the Albergo dell'Agenzia, a four-star hotel with forty-seven double rooms, three suites, and eighteen smaller rooms tucked under the eaves. With views over the estate's park and the rocky outcrop of Cherasco, the large rooms are tastefully furnished with antiques, yet also fully equipped with modern comforts. Guests are welcomed with old-fashioned hospitality in an elegant and warm atmosphere. The hotel is managed by Firmino Buttignol with the Cooperativa I Tarocchi and other private investors.

The recently restored cellars of the Agenzia di Pollenzo, where more than a century ago General Staglieno organized the production of the royal vineyards, have reopened today as the Wine Bank. A succession of bays and beautiful terracotta vaults offer excellent atmospheric conditions in which to house the many wooden cases of stored wine. The Wine Bank contains approximately sixty thousand bottles that come from more than two hundred companies and were produced between 1997 and 2001.

These oenological treasures have been selected by the director of the Wine Bank, Federico Piemonte, a young oenologist from Friuli. The bottles offer a virtual tour through the best tastes of Italy. The bank is a sort of living museum: wine lovers may reserve the wines they want and then leave the bottles in the bank to age for a predetermined period of time. Piemonte explains: "This is the reason why the Wine Bank is so different in concept from other commercial and promotional structures: its basic philosophy is to create a historical memory of Italian wine that doesn't exist today, except in some collectors' or producers' cellars." The Wine Bank organizes oenological weekends, tastings, and courses for members and journalists.

When Petrini walks through the low-ceilinged naves of this cathedral of noble wines, he is moved when he reaches the end of the cellar, where some medieval walls and a Roman tomb have been found: "All of this will produce its best results in 2030, when the relationship between the Agenzia and the surrounding territory will reach its highest development. In this place, one will find evidence of the most remarkable vintages: from Piedmont's glorious reds to Tuscany's Sangiovese and Super-Tuscans; all the best wines of Italy, from Veneto to Sicily, from Campania to Friuli-Venezia Giulia. I had been thinking about it for ten years: after I saw Italian wine conquering world-class heights, I thought we had to find a dignified place for this national treasure of ours. As we know, with no history there are no great wines. And there are no great wines when we do not educate our taste to capture the pleasure of something that changes and for years to come will offer ever greater and more diverse pleasures."

chapter 8

TERRA MADRE

A MEETING OF THE WORLD
IN THE PALAZZO DEL LAVORO

Through the fog of their jet lag, the first thing they saw was the Palazzo del Lavoro, an imposing gray structure as long as a running track and eight stories high that was designed in 1960 by the Italian architect Pier Luigi Nervi. They had been traveling for two days; the crystal clear light of the fields around their home in New South Wales was now only a memory. The sky was hazy, it was a chilly autumn day in the big city. They were in a suburban area, not too far from the Po River. Barbara Stanich, a gastronomy teacher at the University of Adelaide and the president of Slow Food Australia, had invited them to Turin. Both Geoffrey Brown and Terry Lloyd had accepted the invitation on an impulse. On their farm near Parkes, a city of ten thousand located 400 kilometers north of Sidney, they grow farro, a grain whose flour is full of protein and whose gluten is very digestible. As soon as they got off the bus and saw a big sign with a brown inscription saying: "Terra Madre-World Meeting of Food Communities," Geoffrey and Terry knew they had reached their destination.

Only minutes afterwards, a couple wearing big fishing jackets walked under the same sign. Charles and Marcy Graham had come from the Great Lakes region in Wisconsin, the opposite side of the world. Since 1856, their family has run a trout farm. At the entrance to their estate, Star Prairie Trout Farm, a colored sign explains to visitors that they are welcome to picnic under the pine trees and taste the farm specialties. Erika Lesser, the executive director of Slow Food USA, had reached Charles and Marcy by email.

From a window, a black man with a contagious smile, Clement Kariuki, was watching them enter the Palazzo del Lavoro. Clement had come to Turin from the Rift Valley in Kenya. He lives in an area near the Mau forest, between Nakuru and Molo, a two-hour drive from Nairobi. He came on behalf of a community of nettle growers, which is supported by the NECOFA (Network for Ecofarming in Africa). He had learned about the meeting from two Italians from Bra, Cinzia Scaffidi and Ugo Vallauri, who had traveled all the way to his village in Kenya in order to issue an invitation to him.

Clement, Geoffrey, Terri, Charles, and Marcy were among the first of an army of "earth-intellectuals" who had been called to Turin by Petrini's project of bringing together individuals from food communities around the world. After completing their registrations at the welcome desk, they found themselves in a vast room with an exceptionally high ceiling, three huge projection screens, and five thousand red chairs. The chairs were still empty.

WRINKLED FACES, CALLUSED HANDS, STRONG ARMS

As I welcome you to this extraordinary gathering, I can't hide my joy, my emotion, and my gratitude at seeing you all here in this hall. When we came up with the idea of Terra Madre a year ago, none of us imagined that as many as 1,202 food communities from 129 countries in every part of the planet would be converging here today.

Farmers, fishers, breeders, nomads from the Peruvian Andes to the Argentine pampas, from the Amazon jungle to the Chiapas mountains, from Californian vineyards to the First Nations reservations, from the shores of the Mediterranean to the seas of Northern Europe, from the Balkans to Mongolia, from Africa to Australasia, all organized into what we have decided to call "food communities." We are firmly convinced that food communities, founded on sentiment, fraternity, and the rejection of egotism, will have a strategic importance in the emergence of a new society, a society based on fair trade. Through their labor, they bind together the destinies of women and men pledged to defend their own traditions, cultures, and crops. The communities you represent are repositories of ancient and modern wisdom. They are an important and strategic factor in human nutrition, in the delicate balance between nature and culture that underpins our very existence. It is thus with esteem and affection that I welcome all of you, intellectuals of land and sea, from the remotest corners of the globe.

It is necessary to spread and share the wisdom of which you are the repositories and which represents a great cultural heritage. Nature and culture must progress arm in arm, assisting each other reciprocally.

Over the next few days Terra Madre will be under the world spotlight, but on this opening day I, personally, would like to remind you that the event was front-page news last Sunday in a minor daily newspaper in the Ivory Coast. Significantly, the headline included the word "*fraternité.*"

Yesterday was long and exhausting, and I could see in your faces that you were tired from your long journeys. But you have to realize that our organization hasn't the efficiency of a large company. We aren't a capitalist corporation! Slow Food is a small association that has managed to find the support of important institutions such as the City of Turin, the Piedmont Regional Authority, and the Ministry of Agricultural Policies. But it is also bolstered by the passion and heart of the hundreds of volunteers who are working here today and who have opened up their homes to accommodate you. This is what I mean by the spirit of fraternity! Maybe it isn't utopian to hope that here at this meeting of ours we can create the basis for a food community whose members, albeit distant from each other geographically, can keep in touch and enrich each other through intelligent discussion. That way, many of us will feel less alone, and we will feel prouder of our work and ready to develop the self-esteem that generates well-being and happiness. I hereby wish you all a warm and rewarding stay here in Turin. Over the next few days you will make strong, lasting friendships, exchange experiences of life and labor, and consolidate relations of collaboration and exchange. Memorize these faces, sensations, and sentiments. One day in the not too distant future, you will be able to describe them to your loved ones.

On Wednesday, October 20, 2004, Carlo Petrini was feeling emotional. The five thousand red chairs were all taken by an incredibly varied group of human beings, their languages constituting a veritable Tower of Babel. The audience presented a rainbow of colors to the onlooker; the clothes told so many different stories. There were Canadians and North Americans wearing big casual jackets and boots. People from Peru were wearing ponchos. Scots were wrapped in kilts and tartan scarves. The Afghani had on their traditional *pakul* hats, the Indians their turbans, Native Americans were adorned with eagle feathers. Pointed headgear from Tibet; woolen hoods from the Andes; richly colored silks elegantly worn by Asian women; and headscarves covering the heads of stately African matrons. Everyone had a cheerful and pleasantly surprised expression. The women held in their hands little branches of mimosa. They were all looking forward to beginning an unconventional assembly. There were guardian angels all around: solicitous, multilingual volunteers wearing navy blue vests, and young people representing the Coldiretti, the Italian farmers' association, wearing little yellow hats. The fact that the most important union of Italian farmers was participating in the event and providing lodgings to the delegates of Terra Madre was a small miracle.

None were more astonished than the many journalists in the room, who were feeling somewhat intimidated by the colorful diversity of the crowd. Paolo di Croce, a young Slow Food executive who as the president of the organizing committee of Terra Madre was director of the event, announced in his opening speech that the total number of delegates in attendance was 4,888. Following some applause, the official presentations began.

The mayor of Turin, Sergio Chiamparino, was ecstatic: "This event, the first in history that is at once global and local at the same time, is taking place thanks to the passion, the determination, and the 'sane insanity' of Carlo Petrini." Enzo Ghigo, president of the Piedmont region, said: "Terra Madre represents the other side of globalization." The Minister of Agricultural Policies, Gianni Alemanno, spoke passionately: "The shameful patenting of living creatures, and by that I mean human beings, animals, and seeds, has to be eradicated: big commercial agreements are coming at the expense of local farmers."

Wrinkled skin burnt by the sun, callused hands hardened by shovels, brittle hair, sharp noses, strong arms, and bare legs: the audience was an impressively diverse one. They had all dutifully turned off their cellular phones and now applauded. Those faces reflected the ancient dignity of the farmer. For the first time, these men and women were true protagonists, and, most importantly, they were playing this role without the mediation of unions, political parties, or cultural organizations. Walking through the Palazzo del Lavoro on that day was like leafing through the pages of *National Geographic*. One was aware of a new, virtuous dimension of globalization. As the delegate from Morocco, Amajjar Taarabt, put it: "For the first time, I see the people of the world coming together under one roof."

After the plenary session, which was translated simultaneously into seven languages, including Russian and Japanese, there were two days of seminars on various topics, including seals of origin, meats, spices, coffee, the role of women in agriculture, and indigenous systems of cultivation. Among the Slow Food experts were the agro-ecologist from Chile Miguel Altieri, the Brazilian Frei Betto, at the time undersecretary in the administration of Luiz Inácio Lula da Silva and director of the Zero Hunger project, the researcher Vandana Shiva, and the chef and vice president of Slow Food International, Alice Waters.

PEOPLE UNITED BY A COMMON DESTINY

The sequence of events and ideas that led Slow Food to plan this conference had been rather complex. Petrini and his associates started talking about these issues in Florence at the Commission for the Future of Food, as well as after the award ceremony of the first Slow Food Awards for the Defense of Biodiversity in 2000. What emerged clearly at the time was the fundamental role of the rural communities of which the men and women who received the awards were a part. Slow Food viewed these communities as "destiny communities," that is to say, communities that were sharing food-manufacturing processes and were inspired by some common feelings: even if they were separated from each other by great distances or were in different stages of development, they were nevertheless sharing values and purposes.

For the biodiversity awards, an international jury of journalists, university professors, and cultural figures had been assembled and given the task of identifying heroes to hold up to the world for praise. Making the award was a way of helping strong individuals who had endured adversity and fought to defend a product, a traditional technique, or an ecosystem. Recipients had often shared the cash prize that came with the award with the members of the community that had supported their work. During the award ceremonies, farmers from all over the world had begun to compare notes, to exchange experiences, and to communicate with one another. Seeing this led Petrini to come up with an idea in the spring of 2003: instead of inviting the five hundred journalists who composed the jury and the ten farmers receiving awards, why not reverse the numeric proportions?

Inspired by Petrini's idea, Slow Food established a special task force of about thirty young, multilingual people who were travelers and felt curious about the world. The team worked relentlessly in Bra for fourteen months getting in touch with producers, farmers, and fishermen. Cinzia Scaffidi and Paolo di Croce, who were the organizers, tell us:

> It was a tiring endeavor even by our standards; we are actually used to working long and irregular hours, but that was extraordinary. Many young people worked with only a temporary contract, and yet, they all threw themselves passionately into the process. The image of that audience in the Palazzo del Lavoro has been our greatest satisfaction. Terra Madre is an entity that will continue to function. Since the assembly, there have been very interesting developments in the communities that stayed in touch with one another, like the beekeepers and honey producers. Many communities have already started to launch commercial and technical exchanges with each other. There had never been meetings of this kind before, and one significant aspect of our meeting has been to establish a new model. We talked about agriculture and economics, but this time we related them to ecology, ethics, development, peace, democracy, women, and so forth. In the beginnings, the Convivia in the developed countries did not understand what we meant by "food community." But in poorer countries, it was a familiar concept. It often happened that people we met when we were traveling told us: "This assembly is a great occasion, we'll finally hear somebody else saying what we have been saying for years." The exchange of experiences between the Northern and Southern Hemispheres made it possible for us to begin to understand how the kids who suffer from obesity and the ones that are hit by malnutrition are, after all, two aspects of the same problem. At Terra Madre all the worlds imaginable

met, and each and every one of them had something to learn and to teach. One thing we also realized is that individual behaviors are fundamental. Because there is always somebody in the social scale who pays for somebody else's bad choices.

This statement summarizes a basic tenet of the Slow Food philosophy and how the organization decides what fees it should charge. Approximately €4 million were spent on the Terra Madre event, of which €1.6 million went to pay for the airline tickets of the participants from the Southern Hemisphere: cheese producers from the United States paid for their own trips. In Piedmont, the Coldiretti farmers' association hosted about nine hundred people, while the Ministry of Agricultural Policies, the Piedmont region, and the city of Turin provided the financial backing. Approximately five hundred volunteers helped to ensure that the event went as planned. Now, two years later, the "food communities" are meeting again in Turin for the second edition of Terra Madre from October 26 to October 30, 2006.

ALICE WATERS AND THE VEGETABLE GARDEN OF THE WHITE HOUSE

At Terra Madre 2004, Alice Waters, blue-eyed and blonde, always cheerful but quite determined, gave one of the opening speeches. In it, she recalled the time when she wrote to President Bill Clinton asking him to create an organic vegetable garden at the White House so that he could offer locally grown products to guests who came from other countries: celery or artichoke, she suggested, rather than Coca-Cola. It was a way of demonstrating her commitment to environmentalism and her faith in the Jeffersonian ideal of a government run according to the values of citizen farmers. The White House vegetable garden would have been a highly educational example, but the project never reached fruition.

Sweet but indomitable, Waters wages war against the "fast food nation" in a variety of ways. First, with her own restaurant, Chez Panisse, which she opened in 1971 in Berkeley, California. Then, with the Chez Panisse Foundation and her project to create vegetable gardens in American schools to give children an education in authentic flavors. Third, through books, TV shows, and lectures all over the world. Finally, as an executive of Slow Food. She has already succeeded in involving a thousand students at the Martin Luther King Jr. Middle School in Berkeley in her "Delicious Revolution," and she is now trying to convince the governor of California, Arnold Schwarzenegger, to expand the revolution throughout the state.

At Chez Panisse, her restaurant in Berkeley, a few miles from San Francisco, she has served a different fixed-price daily menu for the past thirty-five years, always using seasonal products provided by local farmers, livestock farmers, and fishermen. Hers is a truly original cooking style, and her ideas about education are equally groundbreaking. Born in New Jersey, Waters majored in French literature at Berkeley before studying the Montessori educational method in London, which she now wants to apply to food education.

This is how she explains her choices: "I realize that Europeans may find it odd that in our country we have embarked upon such activities, but I believe that people in the U.S. *have* to think in terms of 'Slow Food.' We are the ones who took fast food to every corner of the world, and now we have to help everyone understand that fast food is a dead end: besides being damaging to our health and environment, it has changed our culture. Fast food communicates values such as 'fast, cheap, and easy,' which make us think that everything in our life should be fast, cheap, and easy. Fast food has taught us that 'fast is economical,' and that we have endless resources. 'Fast food nations' insist on just one message: hot-dogs and hamburgers taste good and therefore are good. Yet things are changing. In recent years in the United States, we have become more careful with food, especially because of obesity, which is becoming an increasingly serious problem. This is why we have to start with the schools."

Thus Waters is not particularly surprised about the extraordinary growth of Slow Food in the United States. It is becoming increasingly popular in the United States to pay special attention to "good, healthy products," as she calls them, although they are not easy to find, even in the countryside, unlike in most parts of Europe. In a society that considers food as little more than a means of survival, the new food culture has taken hold mainly in the big cities, among the middle class and intellectuals.

Waters, who is vice president of Slow Food International, maintains that we have to put pressure on the schools: "I have been a cook for thirty-three years. I saw how the culture in Berkeley has changed by educating people in food. My idea is to reach every kid, and the only way to do it is to include food education in the public school system. I want to give kids academic credit for school lunch: that way it would be possible to transform the school lunch period into an activity that would be an integral part of every child's education. It is important that young people take an interest in every aspect of food: farming, cooking, tasting, art, history, geography, and literature."

To get people to think more about taste, one could start with two products that are very popular in the United States: wine—especially Californian—and bread. Waters affirms: "Good bread has a taste that everybody can recognize: all of us can distinguish a good loaf of bread from a bad one. It's almost by instinct: bread and wine are two essentials, you don't need to be an expert to enjoy them.

Waters also supports a new generation of local markets that are dedicated exclusively to farmers selling their own products, directly to consumers. This is a model that the United States offers to the Old Continent and to the world, in order to change methods of food distribution. "In these markets, people have to get used to spending a little more money. We want farmers to be paid well so that they can take good care of our fields. Theirs is a gift to our future. It is for this reason that I strongly believe in the idea of Terra Madre. Right before the assembly started, I had a nightmare: I dreamt that only fifteen people participated in it. Then I found out that in the United States, many groups were planning to attend the meeting, and that in Turin I was going to meet some of the most significant people in the field. At that point I felt like it was bound to succeed, as in fact it did. Since I knew that Prince Charles is 'one of us,' I really wanted him to be present. I think it is a good thing to have a prince on our side."

CHARLES, THE PRINCE AND THE SNAIL

On the closing day of Terra Madre 2004, His Royal Highness, The Prince of Wales, the heir to the throne of the United Kingdom, accompanied by a large entourage, appeared on the stage of the Palazzo del Lavoro just before the conclusion of the assembly. He embraced a radiant Alice Waters and shook Carlo Petrini's hand. In the two days that preceded Terra Madre, he had been staying at the Albergo dell'Agenzia in Pollenzo. He and his staff occupied twenty-seven of the hotel's forty-seven rooms. He had walked through a Nebbiolo vineyard and had dined in a simple inn in Verduno. In Turin, Prince Charles gave a nonglobal speech in tune with the philosophy of the snail:

> Ladies and Gentlemen, I can't tell you how pleased I am to be with you today and to share in this vitally important discussion about the future of small-scale agriculture and of artisan food producers throughout the world. The fact that no fewer than five thousand food producers have gathered here today under the "Slow Food" banner is a small but significant challenge to the massed forces of globalization, the industrialization of agriculture and the homogenization of food—which seem somehow to have invaded almost all areas of our life today. I have always believed that agriculture is not only the oldest, but also the most important of humanity's productive activities. It is the engine of rural employment and the foundation stone of culture, even of civilization itself. And this is not just some romantic vision of the past: today some 60 percent of the four billion people living in developing countries are still working on the land. . . .
>
> I have a feeling that by now it may be quite well known that I am inclined to doubt whether genetically modified food, for instance, will be—on balance—a contribution to the greater good of humanity. In doing so, I am not simply being dogmatic. I believe it is both legitimate and important to ask whether the faith some people place in the potential of this and that new technology is a product of wishful thinking, or of the hype generated by vested interests. In the long-term, are these methods really going to solve mankind's problems or just create new ones? And how will we regulate them effectively? There are a great many examples of earlier, well-meaning attempts to control pests or improve the environment which have gone drastically wrong. And I'm simply not convinced that we have absorbed the lesson, which is that manipulating Nature is, at best, an uncertain business.
>
> Even if we discount the potential for disaster, there is still the question of whether this is the right direction to take. If all the money invested in agricultural biotechnology over the last fifteen years had been invested in developing and disseminating genuinely sustainable techniques—those that work with, rather than against, the grain of Nature—I believe that we would have seen extraordinary, and gen-

uinely sustainable, progress. The problem, perhaps, is that techniques such as inter-cropping, agro-forestry, green manuring, composting, and biological pest-control offer less prospect of commercial gain to those who have money to invest. The hundreds of millions of people who would gain are the much-derided practitioners of so-called "peasant agriculture," who have very little money, but who are the long-term guardians of biodiversity....

As Eric Schlosser has pointed out in his brilliant book *Fast Food Nation*, fast food is a recent phenomenon. The extraordinary centralization and industrialization of our food system has occurred over as little as twenty years. Fast food may appear to be cheap food, and in the literal sense it often is. But that is because huge social and environmental costs are being excluded from the calculations. Any analysis of the real costs would have to look at such things as the rise in food-borne illnesses, the advent of new pathogens such as E. coli 0157, antibiotic resistance from the overuse of drugs in animal feed, extensive water pollution from intensive agricultural systems, and many other factors. These costs are not reflected in the price of fast food, but that doesn't mean that our society isn't paying them.

So perhaps, having said all this, you can begin to see why I am such an admirer of the Slow Food movement and of all the hardworking, indomitably independent people like yourselves, all over the world, who are part of it.

Only a few years ago it would have been impossible to imagine that so many people across the world who are either directly involved in small-scale artisan food production, or are interested in consuming the fruits of such labors, should gather together in this way. This, of course, is a great tribute to the unceasing energy of Dr. Carlo Petrini.

Slow food is traditional food. It is also local—and local cuisine is one of the most important ways we identify with the place and region where we live. It is the same with the buildings in our towns, cities, and villages. Well-designed places and buildings that relate to locality and landscape and that put people before cars enhance a sense of community and rootedness. All these things are connected. We no more want to live in anonymous concrete blocks that are just like anywhere else in the world than we want to eat anonymous junk food which can be bought anywhere. At the end of the day, values such as sustainability, community, health, and taste are more important than pure convenience. We need to have distinctive and varied places and distinctive and varied food in order to retain our sanity, if nothing else.

The Slow Food movement is about celebrating the culture of food, and about sharing the extraordinary knowledge—developed over millennia—of the traditions involved with quality food production. So it is important to ask how this gathering can promote those ideals more widely, particularly when we are faced with remorseless pressure to operate on a larger and ever more impersonal scale.

I believe you are in a better position to answer that question than me, but for what it's worth, I do believe that simply by coming together and sharing ideas, and above all by joining the International Slow Food Movement to create, by the extraordinary process of cross-fertilization and invigoration which takes place at gatherings like these, an ever more influential and powerful association that cannot be so easily ignored, the answers will emerge organically. As the old saying goes, there is safety in numbers, and people tend to listen to organizations with a very large membership. They do!

On this theme it does seem to me that the other great food movement with which I am associated, the organic movement, has so much in common with the Slow Food movement and this communality of purpose and direction ought to be a source of cooperation and, also of course, celebration! So I do hope that we may see ever-closer links between these two important movements.

The importance of your movement cannot be overstated. That is, after all, why I am here—to try and help draw attention to the fact that in certain circumstances "small will always be beautiful," and to remind people, as John Ruskin in the nineteenth century did, back in England, that "industry without art is brutality." After all, the food you produce is far more than just food, for it represents an entire culture—the culture of the family farm. It represents the ancient tapestry of rural life; the dedicated animal husbandry, the struggle with the natural elements, the love of landscape, the childhood memories, the knowledge and wisdom learnt from parents and grandparents, the intimate understanding of local climate and conditions, the hopes and fears of succeeding generations. Ladies and gentlemen, all of you represent genuinely sustainable agriculture and I salute you.

chapter 9

THE FUTURE OF FOOD

Papers in English, emails from every corner of the world, the galleys of a magazine, brief notes sketched with a pencil: Carlo Petrini's desk is piled high with work. On the walls, there are plaques, awards, and some posters advertising the Canté i'euv festival. On a small table is a leather bag engraved with the words "Carlo Petrini, *Le Président*" and an image of a little snail that was sent from the West African nation of Burkina Faso. In the foreground, there is the black and red plaque of *Time* magazine with the inscription "European Hero 2004," the least-expected and most prestigious award of all, which he received in London in October 2004. On that occasion, the chef Alain Ducasse described Petrini as the man who "had changed the way we think about food," a "slow revolutionary" with "a broad smile and beaming eyes" whom nobody could resist, a "seducer, a Don Juan of the food world."

Carlin and I have an appointment in his study to write the conclusion of a book which covers twenty years of his life, twenty years of political, cultural, anthropological, and social battles he has waged with irony, determination, and with the style of someone who is eager to enjoy life.

Around him, his staff of assistants is filling Petrini's calendar with the month's engagements. Waiting in the parlor is a journalist who wants to interview Petrini on *Supersize Me*, the movie by Morgan Spurlock that satirizes and denounces hamburgers and French fries. There is a call to make to Buckingham Palace to confirm Petrini's attendance at a dinner with Prince Charles and a trip to plan to Washington, where he will give a university lecture.

Petrini's assistant Laura Bonino, who is as protective as she is unbending, is trying to bring some order to his appointments and incoming calls. Valter Musso, who is responsible for the press office, is setting the date for an interview with an American journalist. A lecture for graduate students at the School of Colorno is to take place the following day. After that, Petrini will travel to Udine in the Italian northeast to present a plan for children's taste education in the Friuli-Venezia Giulia school system. And then on to Naples, where he'll conduct a seminar at the University Suor Orsola Benincasa. Finally, back to Bra just in time to pack for a trip to the United States. In Via Mendicità, there are days that seem to unfold at a flowing pace, marked by the occasional pleasant detour, but more often than not they seem to charge relentlessly forward with all the energy of a locomotive. Carlo and I close the doors of the studio and silently look at each other for a second. We turn the tape recorder on.

Were you expecting success on this scale?
It is obvious that no one can possibly imagine the developments that can take place over twenty years of his or her own life. But one thing is certain: I have made this journey one step at a time. I cannot deny that there were some moments of vision, but generally we have been pragmatic, and what I have accomplished is the result of the participation of the many people who have accompanied me on this adventure. We claimed that people have a right to material and convivial pleasure, and Arcigola was conceived in order to distinguish ourselves from the Left, which looked at this issue with some haughtiness. Then, as one convention followed another, we gradually assumed a different identity in a way that can't be ascribed to the traditional logic of politics.

Don't you think that today you have gone back to your origins as a political "alternative," thanks to Terra Madre? First you broke with the traditional Left, whose members were used to eating burnt ribs at the Feste dell'Unità festival and did not generally care about what they ate. Then you succeeded in convincing many of the members of your group to look for quality in food. Finally, when you reached a unanimous consensus, thanks to the Salone del Gusto and the Presidia, your ideas risked becoming a snobbish trend of fashionable leftists. At that point, you pushed Slow Food toward another turning point, toward the more fertile grounds of nonglobal areas.

No, let me say that I do not agree with this analysis. Even when we developed themes with a strong playful component, my primary source of inspiration has always been to work with other people to form associations. When we started organizing activities around the sensorial experience of wine and dinners dedicated to typical products, exploring lost or unknown flavors, we were always guided by the most wholesome associative spirit. I do not know if I ever told you the story of the great Chinese wise man who, following his own death, asks for permission to go and visit the possible places of his next residence. This is a rare privilege, but he is granted it. The wise man first goes and visits hell, and there he finds a big round table, with all sorts of delicacies. Around the table, there is a railing behind which the damned try to grab the food using long and sharp pointed poles. Although they do succeed in spearing the food, they cannot eat it because the poles are much too long, and so they become desperate with hunger. Undoubtedly, the wise man thinks, it is a horrible fate to have so many delicacies spread before you without being able to enjoy them. Then he goes to heaven. Same scenario: same table, same railing, same long poles. Yet, this time the people around the table are all happy and sated. Why? They are feeding each other. They are cooperating. This metaphor is a way to demonstrate how important it is to show solidarity and to associate. The pleasure of a shared conviviality is what makes Slow Food a reality, not a dream. The identity of a family, a country, and a nation all gravitate around food: at the table rituals and moments of complex cultural exchange take place. Eating in a harmonious way amongst ourselves and with others becomes a way to share a common well-being.

But you can't deny that your attitudes have evolved over time.
Yes, that's true. With time, we have carried the association toward a more complex vision. But I have not changed my philosophy, I want to stress that. It might seem that after leaving politics, I took up a less serious activity, only to return to politics in later life. But that's not so. It's just that those political interests were pursued by a particular movement, the Arci. Generally, however, the politics of our organization were simply filtered through its cultural expressions. I do not for a minute think that there was less nobility in devoting energies to the legitimate recreation of people. Likewise, I think that our current

emphasis on ethics is a sign of the times. We came to it through a coherent itinerary, though.

If you had not been into politics when you were young, the direction [of this itinerary] could have been different, couldn't it?
If you analyze our story from that point of view, then you would be right. We disagreed because of our starting point. I agree with you then: the social dimension we maintained even through our playful phase came from our political and cultural foundation. But if you want to say that we have changed direction, and that from a playful stage in the past we have come to a more committed one today, no, I would not agree.

Recently, after the crises of ideologies, a new political mode has become apparent in Italy. Slow Food was able to anticipate that. The government agenda is in touch today with people's actual problems, like the environment, civil rights, taxes, and eating habits. The novelty of the assembly of Terra Madre can be ascribed to the debate on sustainable development. Some call this type of stance food policy: do you see yourself in it?
The food policy issue is not a new one. I would say that it has been one of the great issues of humankind. My generation gave priority to the ideological aspect of it, rather than to the pragmatic one, which is related to the daily life of countries and populations. The biggest surprise I had in approaching gastronomy as a complex and interdisciplinary science was in reading the definition given by Anthelme Brillat-Savarin in 1825, in his book *The Physiology of Taste:* "Gastronomy is the rational knowledge of anything that is related to man as a being who feeds himself. The goal of gastronomy is to provide survival for humankind through the best possible nutrition.... Therefore, if you think about it, it's gastronomy that makes the farmers, the winegrowers, the fishermen, the hunters, and the large family of cooks move, whatever be the title or quality with which they contribute to the preparation of food. Gastronomy is related to natural history, in its classification of food material; to physics and chemistry, in its testing of their ingredients; to *cuisine*, in its art of preparing foods and making them taste good; to commerce, in its attempt to buy at the lowest possible price what one consumes and sell at the best possible value what one trades; finally, to political economics,

in its impact on the tax revenues and in the means of trade it provides to different countries."

This is indeed a prophetic statement. It almost sounds like a list of the courses offered by the University of Gastronomic Sciences, or a World Trade Organization treaty, or a manifesto written by the Seattle antiglobalization protesters...
Brillat-Savarin talks about political economics and the life of humankind, and he considers food a primary need of the species. He foresaw many of the issues that are of topical interest today. In the history of mankind, food has always been central to trade, power, social life, public health, and landscape designs.

And what about hunger in the world?
Unfortunately, that is a plague that has affected all humankind. It is a planetary shame, which has been enhanced by the squandering of resources for arms and by the growing disparities in wealth. President Lula's administration in Brazil has done well by setting as its first objective the "Zero Hunger" program. Slow Food, too, albeit on a smaller scale, wants to contribute to the program, with a project of sustainable agriculture. As long as human beings populate the earth, food policy will be one of their primary interests.

You spent your life in search of lost and endangered tastes, and you have made many discoveries. In your daily life though, what does food represent?
Food is most important to me as a way of relating to others. Even when I happen to eat by myself in a restaurant, which is rare, I feel I am sharing my meal with the environment that surrounds me. I look around, I observe people's attitudes and listen to the discussions at other tables with curiosity. That way I feel I am an integral part of social life. Sharing food is one of the highest elements of civilization.

I have to ask you a question, knowing that your movement has been born partially in reaction to fast-food restaurants: have you ever been in one?
I think I have. But I cannot tell you where or how, which means that I gave no importance whatsoever to that episode. It would be ridiculous to say that I have never been there, and that I have never tried that type

of food. That, too, is a tasting experience, and especially because I have been there and tried it, I can criticize fast food.

Do you have a favorite dish? Do you generally look for the perfect taste?
I have simple tastes. For example, I like pasta with tomato sauce. Still, there are some dishes that in our experience represent our mothers, and our grandmothers: dishes that transmitted their love for their children and grandchildren. The food I consumed at the house of my grandmother Caterina was the authentic cuisine of the Piedmont lowlands; I was brought up with it. I cannot recall eating a packaged snack, but I do remember *some d'aj*, which was a slice of bread brushed with fresh garlic, with a little olive oil and salt. When I was a kid, I had that as a snack. *Rolatine di vitello* [veal rolls] in green sauce, a typical dish of lower-class Piedmontese cuisine, also comes to mind, or *agnolotti* [a type of ravioli]: at the time, they were filled with meat and also with rice. All these flavors are firmly imprinted in my memory, and yet some of them I have never found again. The taste of those *raviolé* has left an indelible mark inside me. If we wander back in our minds, each of us can dig up memories of interesting tastes and sensations. I recommend that everybody try it at least once.

In the fight against genetically modified organisms, the alignments have been heterogeneous: some administrations of the Center-Right have ruled against the cultivation of transgenic corn, and even the Berlusconi government issued a measure significantly restricting scientific GMO experiments in Italy. The debate ignited by this measure triggered a reaction from some scientists, who made a statement in support of GMO research. Now, aside from scientific issues which are difficult to discuss, why has there been such confusion?
I want to make clear that with the pro-biodiversity campaign launched in November 2004, Slow Food simply wanted to affirm that it was important to have strong and defined norms for growing genetically modified organisms outdoors: it is one thing to do it in the immense North American plains, but quite another to do it in the Po Valley. The risk is that GMO fields may contaminate the adjoining ones. We fought to obtain cautionary norms that would protect traditional agricultural practices against the industrial ones. We refuse to be accused of being trivial or obscurantist. We are convinced that the

real solution to this question can take place only over time, through a dialogue between the traditional knowledge of rural communities and accepted science.

At a certain point in your life, you had to impose on yourself a much slower rhythm because of a long and worrisome illness. Would you like to talk about it?
My doctors found out that my liver was as fat as that of a goose from Périgord: I had a debilitating disease of the liver. I was fortunate enough to be treated in a small hospital in Bra and cared for by my best friends. During that period, I learned that there are three categories of people to listen to: the ill, the elderly, and your enemies. It made me smile that when people met me, after I had lost 20 kilograms, they were alarmed. This was also the time that I began to advocate for better hospital food: my point was that someone who is misfortunate enough to require hospitalization should not also be expected to tolerate tasteless food. That was the beginning of some good collaboration between Slow Food and hospitals.

That illness has deeply affected your life?
I developed a great friendship at that time with the prior of the Bose Community, Enzo Bianchi. I also learned to notice positive aspects in negative episodes of human experience. This illness, for me, has been a great teacher. It made me reexamine my priorities, and it made me appreciate the extraordinary people I had around me. I could concretely perceive the real friendship of many people. That was what really cured me.

Terra Madre has been a great initiative, with unprecedented success and media glamour. Aside from the first meetings of Terra Madre itself, are there going to be other events like this? How will this experience continue?
To the more than one thousand communities who participated in it, the Terra Madre initiative has given a deep sense of self-confidence and a universal vision of the issues that the "intellectuals of the fields" had been unable to share with men and women of other continents. Among them—I'd like to say among us—a fond relationship based on common destinies as well as a network of contacts has developed, and with this network we'll be able to discuss all our concerns on a regular basis.

Our approach would involve displaying the foods of the world in the same way as we have done at the Salone del Gusto. Although this will be incredibly complex to organize, we think it will be a winning solution. In fact, I think that without adding a new international dimension to it, the Salone del Gusto risks becoming repetitive and stale. The participants in the Terra Madre 2004 have repeatedly asked that, instead of following up on that meeting with the smaller-scale "Training Exchanges" we have organized around the world, we launch a project that would enable them to relive the feeling of companionship they experienced at Terra Madre and to discuss their future without the mediation of political parties, associations, and unions. This is why Terra Madre, which now has an internet chat room, is a great novelty: we have committed ourselves to creating a portal and a forum for keeping these contacts alive. There are also advanced—and not too expensive—technologies that enable us to put people in touch with one another via satellite and computer, even if they live in remote villages in Africa. We need a source of energy to maintain a connection, via audio and video. These are the paths we want to take. Yet, I have to say that without the heart, the web alone won't do.

Slow Food is trying to build a permanent network for Terra Madre to connect different communities. This would be an important step forward so that all participants can feel represented.
The primary goal for the future of Terra Madre is to get all the food communities online. The web in this sense is not only a technological tool. After all, I would not like to think that I have relied too much on a tool that makes life go faster. Today, we consider it valuable to be able to communicate with everybody and to do that with increasingly accessible instruments: to me instead, it is the consequences of this communication that are important. Exchanges of experiences, common objectives, and shared knowledge will become a reality, this is our commitment. For this reason, Slow Food has scheduled to celebrate the second Terra Madre conference in 2006 with the participation of many international universities and great chefs of the world.

The farmers will be close to the people who cook their products?
At the second Terra Madre conference in Turin, we expect at least a thousand cooks from all over the world to come and express their thanks

to the communities that produce the raw material we use daily in the kitchen. The most famous chefs will be there, along with women who, whether in their kitchens at home or working professionally in restaurants, are the obstinate keepers of traditions. Since poetry is not enough, we want all these men and women cooks to begin promoting endangered products—products we have to protect. We will create a protocol, a list of participating members. Until now, gourmets have devoted all their attention to cooks and all their praise to the exceptional dishes they may savor. We will shift the focus on to the producers.

What are your plans with the University of Gastronomic Sciences: are you working on a degree in agrology, or do you have other projects?
Well, we want our institutions in Pollenzo and Colorno to become the center of another network, the network of the academy. One hundred international universities have already joined us for a project on the reality of farming: in our project, professors will have to put themselves at the same level as farmers. I think that professors, in particular, need this kind of contact. A new "diplomacy" of knowledge on an international scale may come out of this, while on the other hand everyone should contribute to the debate on GMOs, biodiversity, and sustainable agriculture. The cooks could also initiate another project, a new academic discipline in cooking techniques. It would be advisable for ordinary cooks, who may have a reputation but no background whatsoever in the humanities, to know who Brillat-Savarin was and to have read something about Platina [the noted Renaissance thinker]. In order to cook, one should have a feel for marketing and an attitude toward cultural exchange that is not yet common among chefs because they generally are very jealous of what they know. To the critics who accuse us of being too much involved in the third world and of forgetting about tasting wines and dishes, we answer that we have already gone beyond that: gastronomy is so complex that it requires an interdisciplinary approach.

You are just back from a great number of trips and contacts: Sweden, Canada, Japan, United States, France, Spain, United Kingdom, Israel, Mexico...
In the countries I just visited, I could see for myself that the communities that had participated in Terra Madre have already started exchanging information and contacts. They welcomed me with the kind of

warmth and passion that is typical of people who have been through a significant experience. Thus today I feel I have to strengthen these meetings. I wouldn't be surprised if this long trip could become one of the important steps in the consolidation of Terra Madre.

At the end of the most recent Salone del Gusto, you promised to launch an agreement between farmers and producers to go around the big distributors and to make the pricing process more equal: we pay too much for vegetables at traditional supermarkets, while the farmers receive a seventh or tenth of that price. Who is to establish an equal price? Who is to certify that these goods are genuine? Slow Food, maybe?
I think it is feasible. For the time being, we have decided to create a special membership status within Slow Food for the food communities of Terra Madre. This way, our movement will include not just those who want to buy food or develop their knowledge of food.

So Slow Food is about to change its stripes yet again: from an association of gourmet consumers and knowledgeable people to an association of producers?
Exactly. We keep organizing Convivia in order to support the traditional activities of our members. But I want to point out that I do not like a term like "consumers." It implies "consumption" of the land, of the environment, of anything that is around us. Consumption has become too invasive a term. I prefer to define the members of the Convivia as co-producers. They have to be responsible for complex mechanisms: it is up to them to learn about food and to understand the environment that it comes from and how that ecosystem can be sustained. All these issues play a role in a new relationship between producers and co-producers.

What does this mean in terms of Slow Food's role in the economics of food?
Our new historic phase will consist in achieving just and profitable sales opportunities for the farmer. We are deeply committed to achieving these benefits for the producers and fostering trade that offers a dignified life to the people who work in the food sector. We shall work for producers and co-producers to find the same voice and dignity in our association. In doing this, we won't forget about pleasure, which was the reason why we were born: it will just be a more responsible kind of pleasure.

appendix

TWENTY STORIES OF PRESIDIA
AND FOOD COMMUNITIES

BIODIVERSITY AND ITS TASTES

Eating is an agricultural act.
—Wendell Berry, from "The Pleasures of Eating"

The crust of the mountain bread is soft, its dough chewy and brown. You can taste the rye and the fennel seeds. If you spread a veil of butter on it and eat it with some Irish wild smoked salmon, you feel like you've already got one foot in gourmet heaven.

A drop of golden oil from Morocco's Argan nut, with its sharp taste of slightly toasted hazelnut, enhances a simple dish of boiled and drained Punjabi Basmati rice from Dehradun. The resulting delicacy is a mixture of light and pleasant sensations. Then, just to add a dash of color, you might throw in some Manoomin wild rice, a green indigenous North American grain with a crunchy herbaceous firmness.

Undoubtedly sharper in your mouth is the salty, smoky aftertaste of the cured reindeer meat known as *suovas*, an ancient product of the nomadic Sami people in Sweden. Yet it goes perfectly with the flavor of zolfino beans from Pratomagno in Tuscany—particularly when baked in the oven with traditional Tuscan herbs and generously sprinkled with olive oil and a few twists of freshly ground black pepper.

In Italy, you have to reach the heart of Sardinia to taste two uncommon kinds of pasta: the incredibly thin handmade *filindeu* (angel hair pasta) from Nuoro and the *tagliolini* (a thinner kind of tagliatelle) cooked in sheep broth and dressed with saffron and *casizolu* cheese, handmade by the women of Busachi. The dish is called *su succu*, and it is a dream for the palate.

A robust sprinkle of *bottarga* (cured roe of tuna or mullet) from Orbetello in Tuscany honors Italy's national pasta by giving spaghetti an unexpected kick.

And, unless you're willing to miss one of life's great joys, you must taste the tender and succulent meat of England's Old Gloucester cow, and let your palate be tickled by the rich sea flavors popping out of every bite of a dish of fried *moleche* (soft-shell crab) from Chioggia.

Even the most knowledgeable gourmets are surprised by the bitter flavor of black turnips from Pardailhan in France, not to mention the unusual flavors of ancient, indigenous root vegetables from Argentina.

To taste raw milk cheese is to experience a whole new taste sensation: in the United States, bold and pioneering cheesemakers are defying the government's rigid hygienic norms with handcrafted cheeses made from unpasteurized cow's and sheep's milk. Another flavorful surprise lies in store with your first bite of smoky *oscypek*, a traditional sheep's milk cheese from Poland's Tatra Mountains.

Sweetness comes from Bosnia's sublime plum preserve, *slatko*. You could accompany it with a few slivers of chocolate from São Tomé and a handful of succulent raisins from Herat in Afghanistan, before concluding the meal with some coffee from Huehuetenango in Guatemala: try sweetening its intense floral bouquet with a dash of manna, an almost Biblical natural sweetener from Sicily's Madonie Mountains.

This menu was not dreamed up by some multiethnic or politically correct chef. Rather, it comes from twenty stories of biodiversity. The stories are all narrated by their authors—members of Presidia and food communities who were present at Terra Madre. They remind us that eating is an "agri-cultural" act.

UR-PAARL BREAD

Above the town of Malles in the Venosta Valley of Alto Adige (a region in northern Italy that borders Austria), there is a Benedictine monastery where the monks preserved the ancient recipe of *Ur-Paarl nach Klosterart*, which in German means "the original double rye bread made in the style of the monastery." It is a food that might easily have disappeared with the death of the last monk. Today, a group of bakers supported by a Presidium funded by the Bolzano province and the local chamber of commerce has begun to produce it again.

Ottilie Bobitzer
(baker at the Bäckerei-Konditorei Schuster in Malles)
Paarl is one of the typical breads of Alto Adige, made for long preservation. It is 80 percent rye and 20 percent farro and is seasoned with spices that grow in the Venosta Valley, such as fenugreek, cumin, and fennel seeds. Fenugreek is fundamental, because it gives the bread a peculiar taste, rather strong and pungent. Today we eat it every day with butter and *speck* (smoked prosciutto). Originally, though, it was baked two or three times a year and was put on special racks so that it could dry without being attacked by mold. It was used in soup, in milk, and in coffee.

Ur-*Paarl* actually has its origin in a beautiful tradition: shaped into a figure eight, it was considered the bread of newlyweds since it would break into two equal halves. The keeper of the "mother" recipe was Friar Alois Zöschg, the last baker of the monastery of Monte Maria, above Burgusio. It was he who revealed the precise ingredients to a group of bakers, including my husband. So, between 1990 and 1994, about a dozen bakers learned how to make *Ur-Paarl* as in times past. The idea was to boost the cultivation of rye in Venosta Valley; the production of this type of bread has helped many farmers. We now are able to keep forty rye fields active, and for us this is a great result.

At the beginning, there was more enthusiasm for this bread, and in the valley many people started to eat it regularly. Since then consumption has diminished a bit, but it is still worthwhile to produce it. These days it also sells well to tourists. The price is profitable for everybody: we sell it for around $6 to $7 a kilogram, more than regular bread. There are also some variations, with candied fruit, or bits of apple or pear. Many connoisseurs now buy it here, especially after our participation in the Salone del Gusto.

ARGAN OIL

The Argan tree grows in a hot and dry area of Morocco's south coast. Similar to the olive tree, the Argan tree produces a fruit with a hard-shelled nut. Since time immemorial, Moroccan women have extracted the oil of the Argan nut, which tastes somewhat like hazelnut oil. Argan oil is an important ingredient in the local cuisine, and is often added to almonds and honey to make a traditional custard. In Tamanar, a university professor has succeeded in creating several women's cooperatives centered on the production of Argan oil, which has now become a Slow Food Presidium. In France, Argan oil has been adopted by many chefs.

Zoubida Charrouf
(chemistry professor, president of the Ibn al-Baytar Association, and a 2001 winner of the Slow Food Award for the Defense of Biodiversity)
Since 1984, I have studied the Argan tree in-depth, because it has a most important function in our country: it is a barrier against desertification. The mission of the Ibn al-Baytar Association is to transform an ecological problem into an economic resource for the communities who live in the areas where these trees grow, which extends over some 800,000 hectares. The fruit is harvested from mid-June to mid-August and can be stored for a long time without being processed. Once the hard shell of the nut is broken—usually with a stone—the oil is extracted from the little kernel inside it.

Originally, Argan oil was used exclusively within Morocco and was practically unknown outside our country. Only after 1998 did it start gaining some popularity in Europe. Before the cooperative and the Presidium started, the oil had a value of $3 to $4 per liter: the women relied on men to sell it on the streets in homemade packages. Today, there are five cooperatives which employ more than five hundred women, and we can get up to $30 per liter. It is generally used to season vegetables, fish, meat, and couscous, but can also be good for cosmetic purposes. We have created one main co-op for the export market, and nowadays almost all our oil production is headed to Europe: the small quantity that remains in Morocco is sold to tourists.

Khdija Ibnou El Kadi
(manager of an Argan oil women's cooperative)
The most significant aspect of our project is not the economic one, although we are obviously pleased with the fact that at this point many women can make between $70 and $140 per month: in extremely

deprived villages this represents a substantial income. Our interest, however, lies in the social aspect: with this enterprise our communities can now actively protect the forest, and women have gained more autonomy. Men at the beginning looked at us with some suspicion, but now they have let us work because they understand that the earnings can be used to send their kids to school and to buy them books and school supplies.

Some villages have no electricity, so we divide our tasks; where possible, more modern machinery has been installed. There are three types of cooperatives: the first picks the Argan fruit and shells the nuts, the second extracts the oil, and finally the third supervises the marketing of the oil. The ground where the Argan trees grow does not belong to us. The state owns these wild and uncultivated stretches of land, and our cooperatives retain the use of them.

SUOVAS: SMOKED REINDEER MEAT

The nomadic Sami people live in northern Scandinavia, close to the Arctic Circle. In Sweden, the Sami, with a population of approximately twenty thousand, are spread over a vast territory, and their culture is safeguarded by the government. The main activities of the Sami are hunting and breeding reindeer in the wild: out of the reindeer they make lean meat filets that are subsequently salted and smoked over the fire for eight hours. *Suovas*, now protected by a Slow Food Presidium, can be savored in two different ways: fresh and charbroiled; or seasoned, thinly sliced, and served with red berries. *Suovas* has a delicate, aromatic taste.

Olov Sikku
(researcher with the Samiid Riikasearvi Association and a breeder)
The Sami are keepers of an Arctic culture that we are trying to protect with the help of financial support from the Swedish government. We are not yet totally satisfied with our accomplishments. At the moment a political confrontation is going on: we are asking for territorial autonomy, and we are considering becoming the Sami Nation.

Our food culture is deeply linked to nature and to the reindeer. Thanks to Terra Madre, we were given the opportunity to compare ourselves with other communities similar to ours. We may now start exporting more *suovas* meat; for now, we are exporting only about 5 percent of what we produce. I think the most important goal is to protect the *suovas* market in Sweden, where the Sami community lives, before we start exporting the meat to large foreign cities. Apart from any other considerations, this is a product that cannot be produced in great quantities.

Edvin Rensberg
(breeder in the Ruvhten Sijite village)
I am fifty-eight years old, and I have a daughter who works with me. I own about six hundred reindeer, and the slaughtering takes place mainly between November and December. From that moment on, the production of *suovas* begins. The filet of the reindeer has to be coated with salt for three months, and then I smoke it with a fire made of fresh birch wood. I finally hang it and leave it to dry for at least three weeks—the period may vary according to the weather conditions. For our own domestic consumption, we need approximately five or six reindeer per year. I am personally a breeder, but there are also craftsmen who devote themselves especially to the smoking process, like my neighbor who buys the meat and then cures it.

Currently in Sweden we are unable to fetch a good price. The live animal is usually sold for approximately $3.60 per kilogram, while the smoked *suovas* can reach $30 fresh and goes to $48 when it is dried.

I have participated in the Terra Madre, and I have met people from different countries who maintain a similar lifestyle. I spoke with nomads who wander around with their herds of cows or camels. I was surprised by the tales of some of them: in Spain for example, they cover as much as 80 kilometers per year, while here we do not go more than 10 kilometers per year.

WILD ATLANTIC SALMON

In the waters of County Cork in southern Ireland, the fishing of wild Atlantic salmon was once very profitable, providing a living for the many families who smoked and preserved it. Today, however, the number of wild fish has considerably declined, while the number of farm-raised salmon has increased on the international market. Four craftsmen are seeking to protect this tradition, with the help of a Presidium supported by the Irish wine company Febvre & Co. Each craftsman has his own recipe for preserving the fish, but they all use wild Atlantic salmon fished on the open sea, when the fish is at its fattest and most flavorful. The Atlantic salmon found in rivers is swimming to its spawning grounds, a journey that makes it considerably leaner.

Sally Barnes
(smoked salmon producer in Castletown, County Cork, Ireland)
Having married a fisherman, I arrived in Castletown twenty-five years ago from Scotland. They were hard times then; Ireland was poor, and there were few buildings in the area. I was mainly giving a little help on my husband's boat. Fishing was a daily endeavor: fishing boats went to sea in the morning and came back in the evening, staying within 6 miles of the coast. At that time, there were no limitations. But today, fishing at sea is allowed only two months a year, in June and July, so that the salmon can swim upstream in the rivers to reproduce.

Our fishing life has changed according to the rules set by the government: there was a time when you could go fishing from March to September. We were supposed to sell the fish immediately after fishing, because the boats were not as equipped as today: we did not even have ice on board. In the evening, we unloaded our cases on the ground, and we had to be content with the first buyer. As a result, we could make money only during the period the boats went out to sea. One year, we managed to sell our product to only one buyer. But he did not pay us. Instead, to pay off his debt, he gave us the equipment to smoke the fish: since then, I quit fishing and opened a little company for smoked salmon.

The quality of the salmon is of the utmost importance. Today it is mass produced, and many people cannot distinguish between wild salmon and farm-raised. The latter grow in salt water but inside nets and are fed with fish food. The fish that we catch is already four years old and has spent one winter far from the coast, in Iceland and in Greenland. It then tries to go into fresh water to complete its reproductive cycle. The salmon is a predatory fish, and in open sea it feeds on other fish, which makes it fatter and tastier.

Our smoked salmon is sold at $84 per kilogram (while fresh salmon generally costs $17 to $19 per kilogram), but we don't rely entirely on this for our livelihoods. We work also with tuna, herring, mackerel, and haddock. I have to update my equipment soon, and I may get some financial aid from the government to do it. But I do not want to expand, otherwise I'll be obliged to smoke farm-raised fish, as well as the wild.

The assembly of Terra Madre thrilled me. I felt I was participating in a sort of United Nations of Food and Tradition: I attended every plenary session and then every seminar.

THE BASMATI RICE OF NAVDANYA

The Navdanya Foundation, created by the scientist Vandana Shiva, has lent its protection to the famous Basmati rice of Dehradun, which is cultivated at the feet of the Himalaya Mountains without the use of pesticides or industrial farming. The name Navdanya means "nine seeds," and the foundation brings together more than sixty thousand farmers from all over India, promoting seeds banks and forms of sustainable agriculture. Every year, the Subcontinent produces 650,000 tons of Basmati rice, which is the most costly among the rices imported by the European Union (at $850 per ton). Today, there are twenty-seven different varieties of Basmati rice, and Navdanya collects and distributes fourteen of them. The Slow Food Presidium, supported by the Sicilian wine company Planeta, is active in Dehradun and has selected three varieties. The headquarters of Navdanya are in New Delhi, where there is also a store and a Slow Food café.

Maya Jani
(co-director of the Navdanya Seed Conservation Movement in
New Delhi, India)
Everything started in 1997, when the Texas-based company RiceTec patented what to them was a "new" variety of rice and decided to call it "Basmati": it was in fact a mix with American varieties of Indica rice. A movement of Indian farmers opposed this form of bio-piracy, and in 2001, we won our legal battle against a monopoly that wanted to take possession of our rice and endanger the livelihoods of thousands of farmers. From that moment on, we have worked with Slow Food to constitute a Presidium capable of safeguarding the characteristics of our rice varieties; today five hundred people work for it. The Navdanya Foundation takes care of collecting, moving, and packaging the rice. The farmers are provided with free packing and seeds so that they can reduce

their costs and support their choice of using nonchemical products, as this implies a smaller yield. Every family owns small stretches of land, never bigger than 1 hectare: for their own survival, rice alone would not be sufficient, hence they also grow legumes, turmeric, a root that, along with cardamom and ginger, is the base for curry, and other spices.

NATIVE AMERICAN WILD RICE

In five American states—Montana, North Dakota, Minnesota, Wisconsin, and Michigan—and in three Canadian provinces live the descendants of one of the largest nations of Native Americans, the Ojibwa, also known as the Anishinaabeg. Members of Minnesota's White Earth reservation (whose capital, Ponsford, has seven hundred inhabitants) harvest the "wild rice" that grows in the lakes of the area. The rice is called Manoomin, which in the language of that community means "the good grain." Manoomin grows naturally only in Minnesota and Wisconsin: it does not need to be either planted or taken care of while it grows. The plant produces long grains of a dark green color, which are crunchy and have a strong flavor. From the scientific point of view, this cereal in fact has nothing in common with the rice of the Oryza type: rather, it belongs to the Zizania family of grasses. Manoomin is under threat from a "fake wild rice," whose characteristics are radically different, which is cultivated in California and sold at a low price. The Slow Food Presidium aims to defend the natural product and is run by the writer and activist Winona Le Duke. The Presidium is supported by the Tutela Vini Oltrepò Pavese Consortium.

Sarah Alexander
(coordinator of the Wild Rice Project, which supports the White Earth Land Recovery Project in Ponsford, Minnesota)
In Minnesota, the Ojibwa natives number approximately twenty-five thousand today, although many of them do not live on the reservation anymore. In the lakes of the White Earth reservation, Manoomin is picked in September by hand from a canoe. The man who mows sits at the bow and drives the canoe, while astern a beater, who is often his wife, beats the ears to make the grains fall to the bottom of the canoe. Two people in a canoe can pick between 200 and 300 pounds a day, but the

weight will be cut by half during the drying process. In the winter, Manoomin used to be a precious food resource for the Ojibwa natives, who ate it in soup, with buffalo meat, or mixing it with other kinds of rice. Today, the White Earth Land Recovery Project buys it from the pickers and then sells it at about $8 per pound.

Problems started in the 1950s, when the University of Minnesota, conducting research on the wild rice of these lakes, succeeded in creating a variety that could grow in rice fields. In California it grows well, but does not have the same flavor: the rice is black rather than green, has much less flavor, is not as crunchy, and is difficult to cook. It is sold at $2 per pound, and people buy it because it is a low price, and because they do not know the difference between the two. And this is not all: the University of Minnesota is now at work to find a way to create a genetically modified wild rice. The project is financed by a private company from California, Norcal, which has already patented some other varieties of rice.

THE PASTA FROM SARDINIA: *SU SUCCU* AND *SU FILINDEU*

In Sardinia, a popular tourist destination famous for its coasts, bread and wheat by-products are significant elements in the life of the island's rural communities. Symbolic hard-dough "breads" of various shapes—dolls, roses, or flowers with inscriptions—play a ritual role in social and religious functions like weddings and the festivals of patron saints. In Busachi, a small town of 1,600 nestled in the hills between Oristano and Nuoro in the heart of Sardinia, three ladies decided to open a bakery in January 2004. They named the business after one of their specialties: "Su Succu." *Su succu* is an ancient baked pasta dish made with cheese and saffron and cooked in a terracotta pot. In Nuoro, another lady makes *filindeu*, an angel hair pasta that is added to the special soup for the feast of St. Francis of Lula. She is the only woman in town still possessing the extraordinary manual dexterity required to make this pasta.

Giovanna Fadda, Angela Fois, Isabella Fadda
(bakers in Busachi, Oristano)
Until the 1970s, our town followed an ancient tradition for wedding celebrations: rather than sending presents, relatives and friends competed for the lunch menu. One brought the bread, another the homemade

tagliatelle, somebody else the hens ... The delicacies were brought to the bridegroom's house in a small procession with traditional costumes. In Busachi, many people are still making bread and pasta at home. We are a little isolated from the rest of the world, and nowadays the young leave Busachi because of unemployment. Our children are now adults, and we decided to join forces to launch a business, taking advantage of the funds offered by the region to develop local enterprises. In January 2004, we opened this bakery with the idea of preserving the ancient recipes. We have invested our money in it as well. We make the traditional bride-groom's bread, to be hung in the living room as a memento of the wedding: it has the five Hail Marys engraved on it and depictions of wheat, grapes, and all the gifts of the earth. The bread is made exclusively of durum wheat: we call it *su zicchi* and sell it at $5.50 per kilogram. We also produce a semolina focaccia, the *farrigongiada*, a soft potato bread, and a raisin bread.

However, our specialty is *su succu*, a Busachi dish that used to be made only for weddings. It is made in terracotta pots and consists of handmade *tagliatelle*, with a few eggs, cooked in a broth made from three different meats—chicken, sheep, and beef. To the broth you need to add a generous amount of saffron from San Gavino Monreale: it gives the pasta a beautiful yellow color and a lot of flavor. You sprinkle the dish with a good handful of grated *casizolu* [an excellent cow's milk cheese from the nearby plateau of Montiferru, made mostly by women and now with a Presidium of its own] and slices of fresh *casu* cheese, and finally you bake it in the oven. Every September, the fair of *su succu* takes place and everybody enjoys the dish together.

Paola Abraini
(housewife and producer of su filindeu *in Nuoro)*
This pasta of durum wheat bran is called *su filindeu*, which means "threads of God." It's a very thin angel hair pasta that is made by hand. I learned to make it from my mother-in-law, who had learned it from her mother. I have made it for thirty years for the feast at the sanctuary of St. Francis of Lula, an old church in the countryside near the town of Lula, but it basically is a feast for the people of Nuoro. It takes place every year at the beginning of May, beginning with a *novena* [nine consecutive days of prayers]. During these days, the pilgrims stay by the

church day and night in special *cumbessias*, shelters built by the priors of the feast. All the people from Nuoro are offered a bowl of sheep broth with *filindeu* pasta, and some pieces of slightly acidic cheese.

To prepare this pasta, I have built myself a disk of wood with a diameter of about 80 centimeters: it is useful for kneading the pasta and letting it dry. I knead the flour and water together by hand. I start with small quantities as big as a fist, and then I divide it many times among my fingers until I have very thin threads. It's like a mathematical process: every time I do it, the yarns double in my hand. I do it eight times, to obtain a total of 250 *filindeu*, each the length of my arm, and then I lay it down on the disk. I repeat this process until I completely cover the disk, with three layers one on top of the other crosswise. Finally, I let the pasta dry, until I have a net which has the consistency of a thin pastry layer.

It takes less than an hour to make a kilogram of *filindeu*. I can produce three or four kilograms of this pasta a day. I begin in January and end in April, and I make about a quintal. I work all by myself: my daughter, who is twenty-four, does not want to learn how to make it. At times, some ladies come to help me, but they don't have sufficient manual skill: they stay with me for a few days and then give up.

THE OLD GLOUCESTER COW

This native English breed of cow takes its name from Gloucestershire county, about 200 kilometers west of London, in rural England. Its milk has been used since the thirteenth century to make cheese. It is also renowned for its high-quality meat, which begins to reach its peak quality when the animal is two years old. The breed came close to extinction in the 1970s, when the Gloucester Cattle Society, which kept its registers, had to close down. The breeder Charles Martell from Dymock is now relaunching the association. For his tenacity, he received the Biodiversity Award in 2003. Today, the Old Gloucester cow has an active Presidium with ninety-nine breeders; the Gloucester Cattle Society supports it.

Paul Gurney
(butcher in Newent, a town of four thousand inhabitants, 6 kilometers from Dymock, in Gloucestershire county, United Kingdom)
Following the outbreak of mad cow disease, the British Parliament

passed a law that protects production techniques. Animals older than thirty months cannot be slaughtered, and this creates a problem with the Old Gloucester race, because the meat gets better with age, especially for the males. The cows weigh approximately 280 kilograms, and the males get to be 370 to 380 kilograms. Calves are suckled by the mothers and then spend their first winter eating corn and oats. In the summer they go to pasture, and in their second winter they eat exclusively hay. This gives their meat an exquisite taste and not much fat.

After the inevitable drop in demand for meat due to mad cow disease, people are willing to pay more to get high-quality cuts of meat. In the small city where I have my store, I have never raised the prices: people know me, they are used to eating this product and would not understand. A whole cow is worth about £600 ($1,060), but its price varies according to the cut: a filet may cost as much as £20 ($35) per kilogram.

Charles Martell
(breeder in Dymock, a village of five hundred inhabitants; director of
the Presidium)
On my mother's side of the family, we have always been breeders, while my father and grandfather were sailors. When I was a little kid, my grandmother gave me as a present a beautiful book with the image of an Old Gloucester cow and the inscription: "This race has been saved from extinction in 1919 thanks to registered breeders." What we are doing today was already going on in the 1920s, and then in the 1970s: we have a bond with these animals.

In my company, there are 30 acres of pasture and some twenty heads of cattle, with only six cows for the production of cheese with Gloucester milk. There are five of us: myself, my young wife, a nineteen-year-old student who milks the cows, and two other employees of the dairy. To make the cheese, we sometimes buy milk from other companies. I do not own a tractor and have no debts. Our main source of income is the dairy: I make about £4,000 a month (roughly $7,000), and we make a living from the business.

CHIOGGIA *MOLECHE*

The green shore crab lives everywhere in the Mediterranean Sea, but in the lagoon of Venice it is fished as *moleche* (soft-shell crabs). In Chioggia, about 60 kilometers south of Venice, the *molecanti* (crab catchers) have been operating for at least three centuries. Moleche can be caught twice a year, in autumn and spring, when this species molts its shell. The fishing cooperatives select them according to maturity, consistency, and size. The crabs are caught just before they are expected to molt; then they are put in big baskets and kept in shallow seawater until they have shed their shells. They are taken alive to market: at that point, the crab's body is soft and pale green. To cook *moleche*, you dust them with flour and fry them, turning them into bite-size, crunchy delicacies. There are four cooperatives of *molecanti* scattered among the cities of Chioggia, Venice, and Burano, and a Presidium supported by the Veneto region and Veneto Agriculture helps them.

Gigi Boscolo
(director of the Presidium in Chioggia and Venice)
Crab catching dates back to at least 1680, when the species *Carcinus aestuarii* was identified by a Venetian naturalist. *Moleche* live in brackish water in lagoons and are caught at certain times of the year: the *moleche* that are expected to molt in a few weeks are considered the most commercially desirable. There are no scientific studies of *moleche*, but an ancient tradition distinguishes the *boni* crabs—the "good" ones that will abandon their shells in a few weeks—from the *spiantani*, which are expected to shed in a couple of days, and the *matti*, which will not shed at all. From a catch of 1,000 kilograms, you can keep 10 to 15 kilograms. The selection process is quick, but it requires attention and skill. The crabs are put in the baskets, and the molting process is carefully monitored: when they lose their shells, they become *moleche* and are ready to be sold and eaten. *Moleche* are an old and very popular dish that is not hard to cook but must be made with fresh crabs.

When in season we can sell *moleche* at about $60 per kilogram; still, there is no one who is capable of picking more than 3 kilograms a day. They are costly because they are rare, but in the end, the income of a *molecante* is similar to a worker's. In other periods of the year, there are other shellfish: the famous *schie*, for example, are miniscule crayfish that are good in risotto or fried. My cooperative has approximately three hundred members, but only fifty members or so devote themselves to the *moleche*, two or three months a year. The residents of Venice and Burano have learned how to catch crabs from the inhabitants of Chioggia, although there have long been rivalries among these people.

ROBINSON CRUSOE ISLAND AND THE *BOTTARGA* FROM ORBETELLO

In Italy, in Tuscany's Orbetello lagoon, Massimo and Vincenzo make a good living from fish because they have succeeded in transforming it into a high-quality product that they serve in their own restaurant, which is invariably filled to capacity on weekends. But Teodoro, who lives on Robinson Crusoe Island, 674 kilometers west of Santiago de Chile in the Juan Fernández Archipelago, can hardly make ends meet, although he catches the best lobster in the Pacific Ocean. Though separated by thousands of miles, these fishermen share the same struggles. Slow Food and Terra Madre brought them together.

After Massimo and Teodoro met, they began to collaborate: the Chileans have visited the Tuscans to learn their techniques of smoking fish, and they now hope to form a consortium and buy the necessary equipment. At the end of the eighteenth century, the island took its name from the protagonist of the novel by Daniel Defoe. The island is part of a UNESCO-designated natural park, famous for the unique species of plants and animals that live there. Fishermen catch the *Jasus frontalis*, a lobster that lives only in those waters, using small wooden boats that are similar to old whalers' longboats. There are many other excellent fish, but they are not considered equally valuable. This Slow Food Presidium was created to safeguard a unique ecosystem.

Life for the Presidium in Orbetello, which is dedicated to *bottarga* (gray mullet roe), is not as adventurous. The sixty-six members of the cooperative take care of the lagoon of Orbetello, concern themselves with environmental issues, and catch sea bass, sea bream, eel, and gray mullet. The fish enter the lagoon attracted by the plankton and are then caught in traps and nets. The most lucrative business consists in extracting the roe of the female grey mullet, which can be done for only a couple of weeks in September.

The exchange between the little island in the Pacific and the lagoon of Orbetello is an example of cooperation among Presidia. The Tuscans, after having hosted the Chileans, are raising funds to help their colleagues.

Teodoro Rivadeneira Recabarran
(fisherman from the Juan Fernández Archipelago, Chile)
I have been a fisherman for the past twenty-five years, since I was seventeen. My father was a fisherman, too; he took me and my brother to sea when I was eight months old. On our island there is nothing else to do. I am one of the eighty-four members of the Union of Independent Workers and Traditional Fishermen of the Juan Fernández Archipelago; I have a small, 9-meter motorboat called Cumberland, named after one of the island's most beautiful bays. Until the eighteenth century, our island was called Más a Tierra. When Defoe wrote his novel based on the adventure of a real sailor, Alexander Selkirk, who was marooned here, the island's name was changed to Robinson Crusoe. I make my living fishing lobsters, but recently we have started freezing fish filets to sell on the continent. Between October and November, I receive an average of $12 per lobster, then the price goes to $17 around Christmas. During the low season, a lobster is worth only $10, and in May the fishing period ends. In refined stores in Santiago, lobsters are sold for $36 each; during the holiday season, they go for $60. Ours is a problem of logistics: we depend on the people who bring the fish to Santiago with a small airplane; for the frozen fish, there is a ship that goes back and forth to and from the island once a week. We were really pleased to get to know Orbetello and to see how fish can be smoked, through the project supported by the region of Tuscany. We hope to get the equipment and do this work ourselves: that way we could count on a steadier income.

Vincenzo Lupo
(cook and member of the Orbetello Lagoon Fishing Cooperative,
Orbetello, Grosseto, Italy)
I have always been a fisherman: I learned this profession from my father. For ten years, I have worked in our fish farms. In these fish farms, you can catch the female gray mullet: when the tides ebb, the females try to

swim from the lagoon to the open sea to lay their eggs. In the process, they are trapped in *lavorieri*, and from there, we channel them into the area where we actually catch them: we call it the "chamber of doom." At this point, we cast the nets and choose the females and then we take them to a lab to extract the *bottarga*. For several years, I have also been a *martavellaio*: the *martavello* is a creel net that we cast in the lagoon from flat-bottomed boats to catch eels. We then treat them so that they may become *sfumate*, really spicy, the way we like them here in Orbetello.

I am now the cook in a little restaurant of the cooperative that we opened in 1999: initially it was a store for members only, almost a toy. However—and unexpectedly—it was a success, and now it is always full.

Massimo Bernacchini
(president, Orbetello Lagoon Fishing Cooperative,
Orbetello, Grosseto, Italy)

The lagoon of Orbetello is our life. It has a surface of 27 square kilometers: the Monte Argentario delimits its southwest border, along with two thin strips of sand, the Giannella to the north and the Feniglia to the south. Three channels connect the lagoon with the sea. We are personally involved in the protection and conservation of the environment. This is an extremely delicate ecosystem, which can generate an income only through sustainability. We practice farming and fishing, we sell fish, and, as of recently, we also help in our restaurant: by doing so, the entire production cycle comes full circle. The headquarters with the store and the restaurant are in a building near the old city gate owned by the town of Orbetello; it dates back to 1612 and has been restored in 2000. Today the co-op has sixty-six members, but with our enterprise we give work to approximately one hundred people, which is remarkable since we are in a relatively depressed commercial area. The only other resource here is tourism of the Argentario.

Our revenue is about $4.8 million, of which 35 percent is from fishing and 25 to 30 percent from farming. The rest comes from the retail of our delicacies. The product we are most proud of is possibly the *sfumata* eel. It requires a long preparation: the fish is eviscerated, rinsed, marinated, dried in the oven, tossed with a special homemade sauce, and put back in the oven. It has a strong flavor, is sold almost exclusively to people in the area, and costs about $34 a kilogram.

The highest surplus value is from *bottarga*: its preparation is condensed in a few days, when the female gray mullets lay their eggs. The final revenue from the fishing phase is barely 17 percent. The retail price is approximately $300 a kilo. We also produce smoked gray mullet filet. In addition to that, we sell about 4,000 quintals of fresh fish, all year long: sea bream, sea bass, and eel. Our farming is an extensive one, for we let the fish live in its natural habitat. We do not yet have a registered trademark for our fish, but we are working on it. We are proud that many of our members are young. We have demonstrated that aquaculture can be practiced through respect for the environment, so that while the lagoon is kept alive, it also provides a living. We have participated in the Slow Fish trade fair in Genoa, and we have hosted tastings, workshops, and dinners almost everywhere in Italy. For us, Terra Madre has been a pivotal passage; there we became aware of the results we have obtained.

TUSCAN ZOLFINO BEAN

In a small area in Tuscany, an excellent, small, pale yellow bean has been cultivated for centuries. It has been called "zolfino" (sulphurous) for its color; it is prized among Italian beans for its sweetness and creamy consistency when cooked. The production area of the zolfino bean is a narrow one, between the Arno River and the Pratomagno massif, on hills whose altitude ranges from 300 to 600 meters. The production of the zolfino is most significant in towns like Loro Ciuffenna, which is located 50 kilometers south of Florence. This town is headquarters of the Guardian Farmers Association, which protects typical local products; not far away, the town of Terranuova Bracciolini is home to the Zolfino Bean Association of Pratomagno. This is one of the first Slow Food Presidia, and it is supported by the provinces of Arezzo and Florence, the Arezzo chamber of commerce, and the Pratomagno Mountain Community.

Viviano Venturi
(farmer and agronomist of the Pratomagno Mountain Community,
and director of the Presidium, Loro Ciuffenna, Arezzo, Italy)
This type of bean is cultivated only in seven towns around the Pratomagno, a mountain 1,700 meters high, which has been the destination of Maremma herds since time immemorial. To cultivate the zolfino, or the

coco nano bean, is a bit of a gamble, because it is grown on small plots of steeply graded land, where no mechanization is possible. Furthermore, there are boars and other artiodactyls who feed on beans, so it is important to fence the fields. The plant itself is quite delicate: excessive heat can kill the flower before it transforms itself into a pod. In addition, the plant needs the right amount of humidity: as a consequence of these many factors, the crop may vary from year to year. In 1999, before the Presidium was born, the zolfino was sold at about $6.60 per kilogram. Now we have gone to $21 for the farmer and $33, if the beans are packed, for the consumer. However, a problem arose: the reputation of the zolfino has introduced a lot of imitations into the market. In the future, we have to improve the experimentation we are working on with the University of Florence to select particularly resistant varieties. To create new hybrids is pointless, one just has to plant and re-sow until the best comes out. It is such a long process. Getting a good result takes eight or nine years. Thanks also to the law passed by the provincial government of Tuscany to safeguard seeds, we should be able to boost production. We are beginning to work to get the protected designation of origin, the DOP, which should stop the production of fake zolfino beans.

Luigi Giovannozzi
(farmer and president of the Guardian Farmers Association,
Terranuova Bracciolini, Arezzo, Italy)
We founded the association before the Presidium, because we really feel strongly about protecting our territory, as so many people from the mountains have moved to the city and the factories of Arezzo province. I joined my father's company when I was fifty: before that I was in computer science, but then I fell for the countryside. Aside from beans, we produce wine, which is our main activity, and olive oil in small quantities. The one thing we are not short of is customers, although I believe we should do more to promote the territory: it would be a good idea for instance to make a permanent tasting center. My beans can be at their best if cooked in a flask, sprinkled with some olive oil, and even with a bit of onion. I advise against eating them with something else. They are good by themselves. Furthermore, they represent a complete meal, with all the nutritional components they have. With 15 liters of water, you can grow enough beans to obtain the same amount of protein as a

hamburger, which—if you consider the full process—has been made with 5,000 liters of water.

We hope to get the DOP and obtain some support from all the necessary bureaucracies. Many people now grow plants organically, even without certification from the AIAB (Italian Association for Biological Agriculture). It is too pricey to pursue certification for 10 quintals of beans a year: the producer has to pay for the visit of the association technicians who conduct the quality inspection. So much public funding is granted to agriculture, but none of it goes to support the expenses one has to sustain for the quality control of a bean. I think this is absurd. The assembly of Terra Madre gave me some confidence. It was memorable. I felt like I was a member of the family, apart from the pride of representing this historical Presidium. I am expecting some continuity to result from that meeting: we need support to solve our problems.

THE BLACK TURNIP FROM THE PLATEAU OF PARDAILHAN

The black turnip has long been cultivated on the clayey limestone plateau of Pardailhan, a village of less than two hundred people, some 45 kilometers north of Narbonne in the Languedoc. A quite well-known product, the black turnip has recently been revived by some local chefs. Now, one can find it in the farmers' markets of the cities around the plateau— Bézier, Saint-Pons, Narbonne—from November until January. It has a rather aggressive taste, at times hot and at times slightly bitter, and can be served in various ways: cold with a vinaigrette, warm if caramelized, or in some soups and stews. Generally considered to be the "black gold" of a poor village, it has become one of the five French Sentinelles du Goût (the French term for the Presidia). It is championed by the province of Hérault and the Parc Naturel Régional du Haut-Languedoc.

Eric Lorton
(farmer from Pardailhan, Haut-Languedoc, France)
I became a farmer because I am a gourmet; I used to be a bricklayer and did various little jobs. In 1999, at thirty-four, I took over a farm on this plateau 500 meters high, some 50 kilometers from the sea, where the climate is particularly favorable to cultivating tubers. I come from the Burgundy region and had no connections here in the Languedoc. I

bought 2 hectares of land and began raising chickens and pigs. I have two children and the government gives me some social aid, but none to protect high-quality products. I have always invested in searching for new varieties, selecting plants and tubers to grow, and now I can offer turnips, carrots, and other quality vegetables that are sought after by some local chefs. This does not exactly make a big businessman out of me; still, it is my major gratification, for a job that is slightly crazy and has to be done with much passion. The price of the black turnip is today rather good: at the beginning of the season in the markets, it goes for around $3.6 per kilogram, and tends to go down to $2.4 later.

Terra Madre has been a moment of pure joy. I received an injection of confidence from it; the pleasure I feel in tasting my products, and in seeing that they are appreciated by the gourmets, pays me back for the labor.

THE ARGENTINIAN YACÓN AND COCINA DE LA TIERRA

In Argentina, the wild and beautiful area called Quebrada de Humahuaca consists of a long and steep gorge leading northwest into Bolivia. It is here that the descendants of pre-Columbian communities cultivate an ancient root from the Andes, the Yacón. It tastes as sweet as a cantaloupe and can be used to make fruit preserves or fruit juices. With its dry leaves, it makes an especially aromatic tea. An agronomist's work has revived this ancient cultivation, and the Piedmont region finances a Presidium to protect it.

An Argentinean chef has turned her passion for farming and organic cooking into an association called Cocina de la Tierra, which today represents two hundred family-owned businesses. She travels the world to attend workshops and tastings, presenting her organic dishes, many of them made with the ancient and traditional vegetables of Argentina's past.

Magda Alejandra Choque Vilca
(agronomist engineer, researcher for the environmental development
foundation Fundandes, and officer of the Presidium, San Salvador
De Jujuy, Argentina)
As an agronomist, I am convinced that food and cooking represent my country's history. In Argentina, one senses this history from our corn dishes, from traditional Andean cultivation like potatoes, and from the

Yacón and other products threatened by extinction. We value biodiversity highly, and I often hear people talking about it in a theoretical way, but we link it strictly to nutrition. Now, thanks to what we have accomplished with twenty families, an entire village that was bound either to die or live on welfare assistance now subsists on this traditional food. The entire community has been involved in the production: as a result everybody begins to appreciate farmers again. It is important to persuade people that biodiversity is critical to our future: actually, it makes it possible to avoid crises by offering us different options to defend ourselves against poverty and hunger.

In our country, the laws and norms are either too generic to effectively protect these products, or too focused on particular and specialized issues. The paradox is that, while government does not understand it, the farmers are deeply aware of the importance of their labor, as was evident at Terra Madre. Farmers have a holistic perspective on reality and consider their own lives and nature in an organic and global manner. To them, the concept of biodiversity is inherent to nutrition. In Argentina, on the one hand development is pushed toward GMO farming, but on the other, people are proud that UNESCO has designated certain areas for protection.

Maria Calzada (organic chef and director, Cocina de la Tierra Foundation, Buenos Aires, Argentina)
As a chef, I have specialized in the products of organic agriculture for twenty-two years. I work in Buenos Aires and am in touch with companies all over the nation. In addition to me, there are eight other cooks in my organization: together we travel through Latin America to explain the importance of this kind of food, with an eye to enhancing local specialties. With the help of our foundation, various cooperatives can present their own products, as well as the identity they represent. We want to demonstrate that this type of cuisine is modern, good, easy to execute at home, and not just a relic of the past.

I am also interested in helping the two hundred families that contribute to the project of marketing the products of their land. I want to favor the domestic market over the export market. Once they realize that their fruit, vegetables, corn, and organic wines are better and reflect their traditions, the Argentineans could become the leading supporters of biodiversity.

It's true, our country has been through a serious economic crisis, and obviously it is not easy to convince people to spend some more money to eat better. Nowadays, it is mainly an elite who consumes organic products. We are committed to reversing this situation, enabling the farmers to understand that it will do them good to opt for organic rather than industrial farming.

AMERICAN RAW MILK CHEESES

To talk about biodiversity and food traditions in the United States is a complex matter: for instance, it would not be at all possible to create a Presidium in a traditional sense, as Robert LaValva, director of the Slow Food Presidium dedicated to American raw milk cheeses, explains. Through tastings and meetings across the country, LaValva works to coordinate and strengthen the activity of the thirty or so cheesemakers who have defied government regulations on cheese production and who are using various European models of cheesemaking. This new school was born in the 1970s and is active in California, Connecticut, Indiana, New Jersey, North Carolina, Oregon, Vermont, Virginia, and Wisconsin. They are small businesses that sell to local markets or to restaurants. Selling through the Internet is also gaining momentum. Two couples from Vermont and one from Virginia tell their story.

Ann and Bob Work
(cheese producers, Peaked Mountain Farm, Vermont)
We used to live in Connecticut and work in New York, I as a landscape gardener, my husband as a real estate agent. But we got tired of city life and in 1998 decided to move elsewhere. My parents-in-law had an abandoned farmhouse in Wisconsin, but we figured out that it was too cold for us. So we opted for Vermont and bought an estate in Townshend, a small village with nine hundred inhabitants. We have always had a passion for food, and we saw the farm as an opportunity to experiment with what we had read in books. There are many New Yorkers who venture here looking for genuine products. Now we have 125 sheep: of these, eighty provide us with the milk for the cheese, and we also sell the meat. We buy cow's milk from another farmer, and we use this to produce raw milk cheeses, too.

Gari and Mark Fischer
(farmers and cheese producers, Woodcock Farms, Vermont)
Our story is very similar to Ann and Bob's. I am fifty and used to work as
a TV producer in New York. I moved to Vermont before them, fifteen
years ago. We were looking for a simpler lifestyle that would be in touch
with nature. At the beginning, it was not easy to find a job: I ended up
working as a tiler. We then decided to devote ourselves to something
more attuned to our passions, like food. We started to sample all the best
sheep's milk cheeses in order to refine them following the French model,
which here in the States is rather unfamiliar. After a year of activity, we
realized that we would make a better profit producing our own cheese.
And that was that. It has been five years since we produced our own
sheep *toma*: we have about one hundred animals and 45 acres of land, 30 of
which are for pasture; we are pleased with the results we have achieved.

Rick and Helen Feet
(farmers and cheese producers, Meadow Creek Dairy, Galax, Virginia)
We lived in Washington, D.C., an area less rural than the one we later
moved to, and I was a carpenter. We then came to Galax, a city of ten
thousand inhabitants at the foot of the Blue Ridge Mountains. The
parkway passes nearby, bringing a lot of people here for gastronomic
tourism, which is still a novelty in the United States. They look for
dairies like ours, for wine producers, or small breweries. To get here, it
takes twelve hours by car from New York and six from Washington.
Today, our farm has 170 acres, half pasture and half woods, and we own
approximately one hundred Jersey cows. We produce milk of excellent
quality and four kinds of cheese, which my wife learned to make attending several courses in England and in New Zealand: the Galax, inspired
by the Dutch; the Mountaineek, similar to Alpine cheeses; the Grayson,
with a washed rind; and the Appalachian, which is a *toma*. We made these
cheeses thinking about European cheeses and reinterpreting them with
our type of milk. I know that other producers have had problems with
the American "hygienist" law that prohibits the sale of raw milk cheese
seasoned for less than sixty days. We age our cheese for more than two
months. In recent times, we have been able to compare notes with other
producers, organize tastings, and match our cheese with American beers
and wines. Six or seven years ago, the federal government wanted to ban

raw milk cheese, even the seasoned one, but we got organized to fight it, and the bill did not pass. Fortunately, our two children, who are about twenty, help us: they travel all over the world to learn how to make cheese, and then come back to Galax to work in our business.

OSCYPEK SHEEP'S MILK CHEESE

Oscypek is a smoked sheep's milk cheese made in the Tatra Mountains of Poland, between Krakow and the Czech Republic. Looking something like a spindle made of two cones attached at the base, the cheese has a rather intense flavor. *Oscypek* is a specialty produced by the *batza* community, shepherds who take their sheep to pasture in the high mountains, between 800 and 1,500 meters, from May until October. The cheese gets its shape from the molds used in its production. After processing, *oscypek* has to be brined and later slowly smoked: this gives it its yellowish bronze color, shiny and homogeneous. Five shepherds and cheesemakers belong to the Presidium, which is supported by twenty-three wine producers of the Roero area.

Wladek Klimoski
(shepherd and farmer of the Tatra Mountains)
I am a shepherd and a farmer: I own six and a half hectares that I cultivate organically. I am fifty-six years old and have three sons. My main activity is to stay in my hut in the summer and take care of my six hundred sheep in the pastures. One has to milk them three times a day; it's hard work that requires at least three assistants. We make a living by selling *oscypek* and *bunc*, a fresh cheese. For the first, we are paid $5 per kilogram; for the second, half that. Unfortunately, now that our molds have gained a reputation, imitations made with cow's milk have multiplied. This causes more difficulties for us, and we cannot always succeed in selling our products at lucrative prices. One has to remember that to produce just one 700-gram cheese, we have to use the milk of twenty-five sheep, milked three times a day: each milking results in only one glass of milk. The sheep are mountain sheep—their milk is of excellent quality, but scarce. If things keep going this way, notwithstanding the publicity made around *oscypek*, I believe that it will be difficult to continue doing our job, and, as has happened in the past, many more shepherds will leave the mountains.

Jacek Szklarek
(trustee of the Slow Food Presidium)
Working for Slow Food is exciting for me: I studied radio and TV journalism in Italy and then took a doctorate at the Pontifical Salesian University. I was a teacher at Krakow University, which is 80 kilometers away from the Presidium, but changed my mind and decided to deal with food and tourism. With the Presidium, we are trying to rescue this ancient traditional recipe, which everyone in Poland is now familiar with. Pope John Paul II, when he was still the bishop of Krakow, loved to come to the Tatra Mountains to have *oscypek* cheese and meet with *batza* like Wladek.

Until five or six years ago, there were 250,000 sheep grazing on the Tatra. Now there are only forty thousand of them. There is no slaughterhouse, and after the years of Communism, shepherds are afraid of forming a cooperative: being very individualistic, and knowing that the activities controlled by the state have all been failures, they are skeptical. We do not know what will happen after Poland joins the European Union: one thing is for sure, today the income of these cheesemakers is below that of a factory worker. If they had the assistance that farmers of the EU countries can count on, they could definitely survive better.

THE MONKÓ COCOA OF SÃO TOMÉ

The Swiss are leaders among consumers of chocolate with an annual consumption of 11 kilograms per capita, the Germans come second with 10 kilograms, and the Italians ring in with almost 4 kilograms. The world production of the cocoa plant is concentrated mainly around the Ivory Coast, Ghana, Indonesia, Cameroon, Brazil, and the Caribbean area. In recent years, the chocolate world has significantly changed. World trade in chocolate now focuses more on the production area and "cru," rather than on the percentage of cocoa butter contained in chocolate bars. As a process, it is analogous to the one that has made the success of certain vineyards and areas of wine production. This is why the most valuable plantations have sought to enhance their production of aromatic cocoa. If it represents a fashionable trend, it is also a way to better remunerate the farmers.

The Monkó cocoa produced in São Tomé, an island off the coast of Gabon, has played a preeminent role at Terra Madre, thanks to the work of an Italian who went to live there and produces a unique form of rustic chocolate.

Claudio Corallo
(agronomist and cocoa plantation owner, São Tomé)
In 1822, Brazilians introduced the *Forastero* type of cocoa to the nearby island of Príncipe: it was the Monkó, but various hybrids later supplanted it. In the 1980s, after my agronomy studies, I came to Africa to follow some international cooperation projects. I had to leave Zaire because of the war. When I arrived in São Tomé, I started working in the old cocoa plantations after I had cleared the brush that was overwhelming them; I did a lot of drainage work. I also tried to master all the special techniques of growing cocoa: a major factor is to pay attention to the fermentation of the beans. The next step, the drying process, is where the activity of cocoa producers normally stops, because they send sacks of beans to Europe still needing to be toasted. On the contrary, I wanted to try to produce it locally, so I started making a cocoa *"non concato,"* which is to say not mixed for seventy-two hours in a container at the temperature of 45°C. This type of processing was invented in Switzerland by the Lindt company, and today practically all the chocolate makers do the same thing. However, you lose the aromas and perfumes of the cocoa that way; in my chocolate bars, which contain various percentages of cocoa butter, from 70 to 100 percent, they remain intact. Italian chocolate makers liked my product, and for this I am grateful to Terra Madre and the Salone del Gusto, where I was able to exhibit my Monkó cocoa.

I have taught the farmers to execute the fermentation correctly and to make a better income out of cocoa. Unfortunately, international cooperation has mutated here into a sort of neo-colonialism: the Westerners who work here create a fake economy that destroys ancient work practices. Here, when a project is over everything collapses.

I am particularly pleased, though, that many kids on the island for the first time could taste chocolate. They had no idea.

André Aureliano Aragão
(lawyer and cacao plantation owner, São Tomé)
I am a lawyer, and my family is of Brazilian origins: we have lived on the island for at least two hundred years. I own a plantation, and along with

Claudio Corallo, I was involved in the Monkó cocoa revival project. I have links to international associations of attorneys and could easily leave this island and go to live in Europe, however I have decided to stay to work on cocoa, sticking to the high-quality philosophy. I think this is the only way to improve the country's economy, even though there is a lot of talk these days about oil and tourism. Sadly, on the island there has been a significant decrease in farming, with people rushing to the city. The situation is changing now, and many have decided to come back to the plantations.

PLUM *SLATKO*

The production of *slatko*, which means "sweet" in the Bosnian language, is traditional in the Drina High Valley, close to the city of Gorzade, in Bosnia-Herzegovina.

Slatko is a plum marmalade that takes a long time to prepare. Before Communism, this area was renowned for its fruit. Today, the inhabitants of Gorzade are trying to revive this kind of cultivation. A Presidium supported by the region of Tuscany, with the Agropodrinje Cooperative and the Bologna-based European Committee for Development and Agriculture (ECDA), and with the collaboration of Aida Živojevič, director of the Presidium, is trying to revive a small local economy centered around *slatko*.

Jasmina Sahovic
(farmer from Filipovic, Drina High Valley, Bosnia-Herzegovina)
I am a housewife, and the ECDA volunteer workers convinced me to attend the Salone del Gusto to present, with four friends of mine from the village, this specialty that we have always made at home for our own consumption. In our region, female unemployment is very serious, hence we would like to figure out if is possible for *slatko* to become a viable activity for us. These plums come from my orchard. My husband takes care of a bell pepper greenhouse and we work together in the fields, but we can hardly make ends meet. We have decided to use our plums for another traditional product, *slivovitz*, the grappa of our area. We shall keep producing preserves as well. We came back to Bosnia three years ago, after the war ended, and the recovery is very slow and hard. I never gave up though: we

got married when the fighting was still raging. If I make something like $6 for a jar of *slatko*, we may have a chance to face a less rigorous winter.

THE RAISINS OF HERAT

During the second day of the Terra Madre assembly, an improvised little market of handicrafts, seeds, and tea was organized under the vaults of the Palazzo del Lavoro in Turin. Everyone was attracted by the extraordinary raisins that a group of Afghani people had neatly displayed on a little counter, in many little bags: these were the famous raisins of Herat, a city in the northern section of Afghanistan, which has many excellent varieties of raisins and is famous all over the Middle East. Herat raisins used to be exported everywhere in the world, but then with the war against the Soviet Union and later the rise of the Taliban, business came to a stop. Today the economy is recovering, and one possible source of income could come from this extremely sweet and unique delicacy. Helped by the agronomist Faiz Abdullah, and by a Japanese NGO, farmers are going back to their traditional growing techniques, like the use of dry walls to trap water for the vines and to protect them from the wind.

Azim Abdul Walli
(raisin farmer in Herat, Afghanistan)
The city of Herat spreads along the margins of the desert where, for four months of the year, incredibly strong winds blow. We grow the raisins in little gardens on walls slanted 45 degrees: every vine is planted in a trench a meter deep. The vine branches get out of their hole, follow the stones of the wall, and reach the subsequent trench, forming angled shapes that resemble factory roofs. This growing method allows the raisin to withstand the wind and the winter cold. Until some time ago, we had seventy-two varieties of raisins here, all in small bunches and quite sweet. Before the war, we exported them in several countries: India, Russia, and the United States. Now we are exporting only to India. Everything revolves around the clan here. We have 1 hectare of land, and to cultivate it we need three men at least. There is often the problem of water, because here the drought never gives any respite, and if someone does not have a well, he has to pay for water. The price of raisins varies according to quality, but usually is $1.20 per kilogram.

THE COFFEE FROM HUEHUETENANGO

One of the highest-quality coffees in the world grows in Guatemala. Thanks to the currents of warm air coming from the isthmus of Tehuatepecone, you can grow coffee at altitudes of up to 2,000 meters on the Huehuetenango plateau. This Presidium is at work on many projects. In 2002, a coffee-roasting company from Padua, in Italy, Caffè del Doge, bought the first batch of the Presidium's coffee directly from its producers. In 2004, a Tuscan coffee company owned by Andrea Trinci joined forces with Caffè del Doge, to be followed in 2005 by the Piedmontese company Mokafé. In May 2005, there was a proposal to create a coffee-roasting company in the Vallette prison in Turin. Managed by the Pausa Caffè cooperative, a group of detainees works daily to learn slow coffee-roasting techniques from several great Italian coffee masters. Fifty percent of the revenue goes to the producers in Guatemala. Aided by the Italian Foreign Ministry and the Cooperation for Development, the Presidium is also committed to the creation of a roasting company in Guatemala.

Marco Ferrero
(officer of the Presidium and president, Pausa Caffè cooperative)
We have created a Presidium in the mountains between Guatemala and Mexico, in Huehuetenango. Coffee production is a global business that will be decisive for the future of small producers. In 1999, the price of coffee collapsed, and it has remained at the lowest level in the last thirty years. The production costs to the farmers are at times greater than the prices they can get when they sell the coffee itself. People in Guatemala thus emigrate to the United States, sometime illegally, putting their lives at great risk: some of them die even before crossing the border, while others are sent back, often to join the four million poor people who live on the outskirts of Guatemala City. At Huehuetenango, they produce one of the best coffees of Central America—highly aromatic and with a good body, balanced and low in acidity. It is normally used to improve other blends of coffees. But we want it to be appreciated in its pure form. We are now working to sustain the traditional growing method, with the coffee growing in the shade of trees. Farmers have little *fincas* (farms), and they produce about 100 or 200 quintals a year.

Julio Herrera
(manager of a cooperative of coffee farmers, Huehuetenango, Guatemala)
Rivas Gilardo
(coffee farmer in Huehuetenango, Guatemala)
In this area we have been growing coffee for generations. It is our only
activity, the alternative being to cross the borders and emigrate to the
United States. The harvesting phase is thus very important to us and is
celebrated with a big village feast, where one eats and dances for days.
Till now we have always sold the coffee in the form of raw beans. For our
daily use, we roasted our own in a big frying pan, but we cannot roast
large enough quantities to sell it packaged. That would be a way to get a
much better income, but to do that we would need costly equipment.
Luckily the price of coffee has recently increased a little, and because we
are good at maintaining a high level of quality we get up to $125 a quintal,
while before it was sold locally for $75. We have joined forces with a
cooperative of two hundred members, and through our Presidium we
are able to directly export our product. Before, we depended on *coyotes*,
the big buyers who gave us $70 for a sack of beans, to later sell it to the
international market for $125. The co-op we founded in 1965 has been
our most powerful tool to defy the people who only want to depreciate
our labor. We are now trying to improve our coffee production techniques, but often people are so poor that they cannot even get started.
They ought to get loans from the banks, but the banks are too busy giving money to somebody who already has it.

MANNA FROM THE MADONIE MOUNTAINS

There once was a time when ash trees grew all over the northwestern
section of the island of Sicily. In the summer, each tree was tapped and
with rising temperatures would yield a whitish resin. As the resin hardened, it formed *"cannolicchi"* (little cannoli), as the farmers call them, of
manna. This sweetener, which is mentioned in the Bible, was until the
1960s used largely by drug makers for its laxative and detoxifying properties. The production of manna has almost disappeared today except in
the towns of Pollina and Castelbuono in the province of Palermo in
Sicily. Since the establishment of a Presidium supported by the region of
Sicily, several traditional small factories have been producing local

desserts using the purest kind of *manna eletta* (a superior-quality manna), which is made according to a very exacting process.

Giulio Gelardi
(farmer and director of the Presidium, Pollina, Palermo, Italy)
In my family, we have always lived with manna: my grandfather was already producing it, and I continued that tradition. With a different spirit, though, because I wanted to come back to Sicily after having been away for twenty years. I remember that, years ago, manna was collected only in order to sell it to industries: it had many impurities, and we had no control over the price. I then found a method to obtain the purest manna by hanging yarn on the tree at the moment when we tap it. This year, which has been a very good year for the harvest, I was able to produce 350 kilograms of manna, of which 150 are excellent, and as many are of medium-high quality. My family owns some land—we have six hectares—but only three of them are cultivated with the ash trees for manna. We have approximately five hundred plants, while the rest of the land is cultivated with olive trees. I make a living with my activity as a farmer, and I have devoted my life to manna: not just through farming, but also through research, articles, and books. Manna has an almost mystical quality; it is not like any other product that is for sale. During the winter, I looked for information on manna in libraries and in ancient treatises; I found out that manna used to be produced not only in Sicily but also in Calabria, on the Gargano promontory, in the Caserta province, around the Castelli Romani, and in the Tuscan Maremma. At the end of the eighteenth century, these production areas began to disappear, and now we in the Palermo region are the only ones who are still at it. I learned there have been some painters, including Tintoretto, who were fascinated by the mystical qualities of manna.

I sell the manna I produce as "*manna eletta* from the Madonie Mountains." This is the best available, and we sell it for $120 per kilogram, in packages of 50 grams each. In Castelbuono, there is also a company which produces the *mannetto*, a small panettone cake with an icing made of chocolate and manna.

INDEX OF THE PRESIDIA

To find contact information for the individuals coordinating Slow Food's efforts at preserving these endangered tastes, go to SlowFood.com

ITALIAN PRESIDIA

Valle d'Aosta
GRESSONEY *TOMA*
The Valle d'Aosta is usually associated with fontina cheese. But high up in the area of Gressoney Saint-Jean, many small dairies also produce the Gressoney *toma* in pastures at altitudes of up to 2,200 meters. Made with raw cow's milk only in the summer months, this is a classic Alpine *toma*, slightly smaller but taller than others, and weighing in at around 3 to 5 kilograms. A wonderful, soft cheese, it is excellent when left to mature for a year.

Piedmont
CAPRAUNA TURNIP
Caprauna is a small village in the upper valley of the Tanaro River with a few hundred inhabitants and an excellent local variety of turnip: large, very sweet, and with an unusual white-and-yellow color. Typical of the Piedmont Alps, the turnip was an important part of the local diet in centuries past, but was later replaced by the potato. It is difficult to conserve once harvested and therefore best left underground until ripe in

the autumn and winter months. The Presidium hopes to safeguard its cultivation around Caprauna, an area particularly suited for turnips that is currently at risk of depopulation.

CARMAGNOLA GREY RABBIT

The Carmagnola grey rabbit is the only native Piedmontese rabbit breed. This rabbit has soft fur, grey with a lighter mark on its nape in the shape of a triangle. Of a medium size, the rabbit has a long body and muscular haunches. The meat is fine and tender—flavorful, white, and not at all tough.

CARMAGNOLA OX-HORN PEPPER

This capsicum comes in splendid colors—from intense yellow to bright red—and a curious long, tapered shape (over 20 centimeters long) with three or four lobes. Reminiscent of the *spagnolìn*, the first oblong pepper to arrive from the Americas, the Carmagnola ox-horn pepper has a sweet flavor and thick, fleshy pulp. It's best eaten roasted, grilled, *bagnà 'nt l'euli* (raw immersed in extra-virgin olive oil), or with *bagna cauda*.

CLASSIC *ROBIOLA* OF ROCCAVERANO

This *robiola* is Italy's only historic origin-controlled goat cheese. The Presidium variety is made exclusively with raw goat's milk. Each form has its own unique flavor. Typical perfumes on the nose are yogurt, fresh grass, and hazelnut with piquant, mossy nuances on the palate and a long finish.

COAZZE *CEVRIN*

Some call it *toma*, some call it *robiola*, but the only real name for this cheese (in local dialect) is *cevrin*. Produced from mixed raw cow's and goat's milk, it is rounded, with a thickly ridged and moist crust. The outermost shell of the cheese is colored deep amber-yellow. Though the curd of the cheese near the crust is a pale yellow, the innermost curd is pure white. Aged Coazze *cevrin* has intense and long-lasting flavor. The primary aromas are musky, with notes of dry wood and freshly mown grass. In the mouth, the cheese has a long-lasting flavor of hazelnut, butter, and—at times—spices.

COGGIOLA *PALETTA*

A prosciutto made from pork shoulder has always been produced in this small commune in the Valsesia district. It is called *paletta* (spade) because it utilizes the ham shoulder bone, cut in half lengthwise to make four small, spade-shaped hams from every pig. After the meat is rubbed with salt and spices, it is left to rest for twenty days and is then encased in the pig's bladder. Coggiola Paletta is eaten raw in thin slices or briefly boiled and accompanied by apple mostarda and polenta.

GARBAGNA BELLA CHERRY

The Garbagna Bella cherry has been neglected in recent years because of the fruit's poor resistance to humidity. It is the classic *ciresa* ("cherry" in the Piedmontese dialect) of old, a sweet and crunchy variety that is particularly well suited for preserving whole in alcohol. Conserved in this way, it will not disintegrate and will maintain its consistency and flavor. These cherries are best coated with chocolate or used as the base of liqueurs. With cinnamon or cloves, the cherries offer an interesting and unusual accompaniment for meat.

GAVI *TESTA IN CASSETTA*

Testa in cassetta (headcheese) is a cured meat made in the winter from pig's head, tongue, and muscle, and cow's heart. These cuts are boiled, and the head is chopped down into a semi-liquid paste. In Gavi, the *testa in cassetta* mixture is flavored with salt, spices, red pepper, pine nuts, and rum. It is then stuffed into a cow's intestine and left to rest for a day in a very cool place.

HERITAGE PIEDMONTESE APPLE VARIETIES

At the start of the last century, thousands of varieties of apples were still being cultivated in Piedmont. Since then the development of industrial agriculture has made a cruel selection, with the market preferring foreign apple varieties—bigger, prettier, and more adaptable to modern techniques. This Presidium is working to save varieties such as Grigia di Torriana, Buras, Runsè, Gamba Fina, Magnana, Dominici, Carla, and Calvilla. All are good apples, aromatic and rustic, with a definite future even on the contemporary market.

LANGHE SHEEP *TUMA*

This cheese achieved DOP (designation of protected origin) status under the name "Tuma di Murazzano." However, Tuma di Murazzano may be made with up to 40 percent cow's milk (pasteurized milk included). The Presidium is recovering the historic version, made exclusively with raw Langhe sheep's milk (and no more than 5 percent goat's milk). Hence the choice of a new name. In 1950, there were over forty-five thousand sheep in the Langhe; now there are no more than 2,500. This cheese is normally eaten ten to fifteen days after production, but it can also be vacuum-packed and preserved for a longer time.

MACAGN

Macagn takes its name from a foothill of Monte Rosa. Smaller than similar Piedmontese cheeses, it is a typical mountain cheese made from whole raw cow's milk. The curd of the cheese is compact, slightly stretchy, with thinly spaced holes. It is straw-white in color when young and tends to go gold with aging. Produced twice a day in the summer, *macagn* has a distinctive fragrance with aromas of pasture and flowers.

MONDOVÌ CORNMEAL BISCUITS

The Presidium's biscuits are produced according to tradition from a mixture of wheat and corn flour, butter, fresh eggs, and sugar. The dough is kneaded into round oblong or crescent shapes. Yellow and crunchy, the biscuits melt in your mouth. They are neither greasy nor overly sweet, and the grain of the corn flour bran gives a pleasant consistency. The lingering flavor is slightly toasted.

MONTÉBORE

Montébore is produced in and around a town of the same name near Tortona in Piedmont. This cheese dates back at least until 1400 AD, when it was first mentioned in a written document. The shape of the cheese recalls a tiny wedding cake, with three diminishing tiers, one atop the other. Legend has it that the shape was modelled on an ancient tower in the town of Montébore. Montébore is made from raw milk: 75 percent cow's milk and 25 percent sheep's milk. The flavor of Montébore is initially buttery with strong milky flavors. The closure has notes of chestnut with a light herbiness. Montébore can be eaten fresh, slightly aged, or grated.

MOROZZO CAPON

The Morozzo capon is usually of the Piedmontese yellow breed. It has a long black tail with metallic highlights and glossy brick-red feathers edged with blue or green; it has no crest or wattle. Castration (the term "capon" designates a castrated rooster) is usually carried out by women since the operation requires deft, skilled hands. It has soft, tender, delicate meat that is sometimes used in pies or stuffed. Purists prefer it boiled and dipped in salt.

MOSCATO PASSITO WINE FROM VALLE BAGNARIO

The passito from the Valle Bagnario di Strevi is a sweet dessert wine made with the pick of the grape harvest, the very finest bunches, which are laid on grills to wither. In November, they are pressed and left to ferment with some of the skins, devoid of pips and other waste matter. Thanks to the quality of the Muscat (*Moscato*) grapes of these old, steep vineyards, the wine's aromas blend perfectly with its beautifully balanced, not overrich bouquet.

NIZZA MONFERRATO "HUNCHBACK" CARDOON

Grown in sandy soil, the cardoon plants adopt their unique hunchback shape thanks to a particular cultivation technique. Once they are tall and vigorous, the *cardaroli* (growers) bend the plants over and cover them with soil. As they seek to regain sunlight, the plants swell and curve. The stems lose all their chlorophyl and turn white and tender. The hunchback cardoon of Nizza Monferrato may also be eaten raw and is eaten as an accompaniment to one of Piedmont's greatest dishes, *bagna cauda* (a sauce of olive oil, garlic, and anchovies).

PIEDMONTESE WHITE OX

Like all autochthonous white oxen, this is a very ancient breed indeed. It was only in 1886, however, that a mutation led to the birth of a bull with huge haunches and extremely muscular thighs. This was the progenitor of the so-called Piedmontese *vitello della coscia*, or "thigh calf." At the start of the twentieth century, there were still 680,000 head, but today the number has dropped to fewer than three hundred thousand. Piedmontese beef is unique, with just the right amount of intramuscular fat to make it lean and flavorsome. Traditionally, it is flattened with a knife and eaten raw with extra-virgin olive oil, salt, and a tiny pinch of pepper.

PIEDMONTESE YELLOW HEN AND SALUZZO WHITE HEN

The yellow hen of Piedmont has a golden-tan plumage, a tall, black tail with metallic highlights, a yellow beak, and an erect crest. The white hen of Saluzzo is similar, but is all white, tail included. The Presidium breeders adhere to a strict discipline (natural feed, 5 square meters of open space for each bird, et cetera). Traditionally, in Piedmontese restaurants, both birds are cooked *alla cacciatora*, with onions and chopped tomatoes. The meat is also excellent boiled with its own stock, in gelatin, or with salad.

POIRINO TENCH

A relative of the carp, barbel, chub, and bleak, the tench is humped in shape with a gold skin—hence its name *gobba dorata*. It has always been raised in the ponds of the plateau of Poirino, where man-made lakes have existed since the thirteenth century. Its flesh is soft and tasty, without the taste of soil that is often typical of poor-quality produce. The Presidium tench is a star ingredient in the typical cuisine of the Roero. The classic way to prepare it is *in carpione* (fried, then marinated).

SAMBUCANO LAMB

The Sambucano breed is a medium-large sheep with a long, muscular rump and slender but solid, not overlong limbs. Its smallish head is hornless and bare, with a slightly ramlike muzzle and floppy ears. Most have straw-white fleece, but some rare specimens have black fleece and a small star-shaped patch on the head. The breed is valued for its wool and, above all, for its meat—excellent oven-baked or in a pie with Jerusalem artichokes. Sambucano liver paté with chestnuts is a delicacy not to be missed.

SARAS DEL FEN

Saras in local dialect means ricotta. The habit of wrapping this cheese in hay (*fen*) was born of the need to transport it down from the pastures of the Val Pellice. Saras del Fen has grassy, milky perfumes on the nose that gain intensity with aging; it is rich and smooth on the palate.

TORTONA STRAWBERRY
Similar to the blackberry—large, sweet, and highly scented—the Tortona strawberry is a great rarity. This treat is available just ten days of the year, in the second half of June. This strawberry was developed from a wild species that grew in the hills of Tortona in Piedmont.

TORTONA VALLEY SALAME
Pig farming is an integral part of the history and peasant culture of the Curone, Grue, and Ossona valleys. These valleys are near Tortona and are circumscribed by Lombardy, Emilia-Romagna, and Liguria. The traditional products of this area include all the items in the classic repertoire of Italian pork butchers, but the foremost specialty of the area is raw salami, made by a good number of small-scale, artisan producers and aged naturally in a particularly favorable hilly microclimate that conserves the finished salame so well that less salt than usual is needed to protect the meat from decay.

VAL D'OSSOLA MORTADELLA
In Italian, the term *mortadella* means "meat crushed or minced in a mortar." The Val d'Ossola mortadella is made of raw pork and a small amount of pig's liver. The pig's liver and the addition of *vin brulé,* or mulled wine, give it its distinctive flavor. It is aged for about two months and eaten sliced with the local Coimo black bread.

VALLI VALDESI *MUSTARDELA*
Like all *sanguinacci* (blood sausages), *mustardela* came into being to exploit every single part of the pig (including the head, the throat, the tongue, and the skin). It is made by boiling, boning, and grinding all the various parts and mixing them with lardons, onions, and leeks sweated in pig fat, with pig's blood as the final ingredient. Eggplant-purple and sausage-shaped, the Valli Valdesi *mustardela* is smooth and soft in the mouth with a spicy, vaguely sweet-and-sour flavor. The sausage is eaten simply boiled, with potates or polenta.

Lombardy

BAGOLINO BAGÒSS

Bagossi are the inhabitants of Bagolino, a small village in the Caffaro Valley in the province of Brescia, and Bagòss is also the name of the cheese produced in the valley. An uncooked curd cheese made with partially skimmed raw milk, Bagòss is a traditional *toma di montagna*, or mountain cheese, with unique characteristics. Wheels are larger than those of normal mountain *toma*. Bagolino Bagòss cheeses range from 16 to 22 kilograms in weight. This cheese begins to express all its complexity after at least ten to twelve months of aging.

BITTO OF THE "BITTO VALLEYS"

Bitto is one of the symbols of Lombardy cheese production. This cheese descends from an ancient tradition of high-mountain cheesemaking. Slow Food created this Presidium to help augment and maintain the production of Bitto cheese from Alpine meadows. Presidium members are engaged in maintaining and promoting a list of traditional practices: from the rearing of local goats (the cheese is made with 10 to 20 percent goat's milk) to the rationing of pastures, and from manual milking to the use of *calècc*, ancient stone huts that serve as mountain dairies.

LODI *PANNERONE*

Also known as "white gorgonzola" (due to its large shape), Lodi *pannerone* is one of the very few cheeses in the world that is not salted. The name comes from the word *panera*, which means "cream" in local dialect. This cheese is made exclusively from creamy whole milk. Lodi *pannerone* typically has wide holes and is consumed fresh: initially sweet and soft, the taste quickly develops bitter almond notes.

MANTUAN PEASANT CASALIN SALAME

Bright strawberry-red in color, and firm yet soft, Mantuan salame is rough textured with spots of white and pink fat. Its flavor is balanced and complex, with a subtle garlicky aroma. The Mantuan salame owes its flavor and aroma to the damp air of the Po Valley and the white, dove-grey mold that grows on its surface. When ready for sale, the *norcino* (meat curer) carefully blows off this mold without destroying it completely.

VALCHIAVENNA GOAT *VIOLINO*

This singular cured meat is made with the leg and shoulder meat of goat. It is shaped like a violin (*violino*, in Italian): the hoof represents the neck of the instrument and the muscular mass the body. Native to the Valchiavenna, where the processing and salting of meat are age-old traditions, Valchiavenna goat *violino* weighs from 1.5 to 3 kilograms, depending on the cut of meat used (front shoulder or rear leg). The tastiest, most fragrant *violinos* are aged slowly and naturally.

VALTELLINA BUCKWHEAT

Rustic, hardy, and parasite-proof, buckwheat was a staple of the peasant diet of the Valtellina and the Alps until the start of the last century. Its flour is the basic ingredient for the typical dishes of the Valtellina: *pizzoccheri, sciatt,* and polenta *taragna.* Today only a few cultivations survive, and most of the buckwheat processed in Italy is imported.

Trentino Alto Adige

AURINA VALLEY *GRAUKÄSE*

This is a cheese with a long tradition in Alto Adige, a region heavily influenced by its northern neighbor, Austria. It takes its name from the greyish (*grau*, in German) color of its body. *Graukäse* is obtained by acid coagulation only. Nothing is actually added to the milk. The cream is allowed to rise to the top, and the milk is then part-skimmed before being heated to 25°C and left to coagulate naturally, a process that may take as long as thirty-six hours. The soft curd is then stirred slowly and the mixture is cooked briefly at 40°C. It is removed and pressed for about half an hour. It is then crumbled, seasoned with salt and pepper, and placed in molds, where it stands at a temperature of 20°C for twenty-four hours. Subsequently, the cheese is matured for a week in a cellar with very high humidity. In the mountain dairies of Monte Cavallo near Vipiteno/Sterzing, *graukäse* is sometimes matured by hanging the cheese from the ceiling near the fire so that it undergoes light smoking.

BANALE CIUIGHE

The history of *banale ciuighe* reflects the extreme poverty of the old Giudicarie Esteriori territory. Here, families used to sell the best parts of the pig, using only the least desired parts, with the addition of turnips, to make *ciuighe*. Now 150 years later, the custom has been preserved and the recipe perfected. Today, the noble cuts (shoulder, coppa, pancetta, neck) are also used, along with a lower percentage of turnips.

MOENA PUZZONE

Twice a day, mountain dairies in the heart of the Dolomites send milk to the cheese factory in Predazzo that produces *puzzone*. Only forms bearing the letter "M" belong to the Presidium. The secret of *puzzone* is the aging, during which each form is washed once a week, from a minimum of sixty days to as much as six to seven months. All this gives the cheese an intense, pungent perfume—hence the name *puzzone*, which means "stinky," and its unmistakable red rind.

NON VALLEY MORTANDELA

Families in the Non Valley used to buy a piglet at the All Saints' Fair and raise it for twelve months on potatoes, bran, leftover vegetables, and hay. The pork from the animals was used to make *mortandela*, one of the most typical cured meats of the valley. This traditional delicacy is made by boning the pork (from which the fat and gristle have been removed), mincing it, and mixing it with spices. Then the meat is flattened out, placed on wood boards, and smoked.

SANTO TRENTINO WINE

Santo Trentino is a sweet wine made from the sparse, well-ripened bunches of the native Nosiola grape variety. The grapes are left on mats to dry for five to six months until Easter Week, called *Settimana Santa* in Italian—hence the name. The must is fermented in small oak barrels for at least six to eight years: after bottling, the wine can then be aged for up to fifty years or more.

TRENTINO LUCANICA

Lucanica—made of lean pork, cured lard, salt, ground pepper, and garlic—is the Trentino salame par excellence. There are a number of varieties and the further one travels north toward the Alto Adige, the more the *lucanica* reflects the South Tyrol smoking tradition. Today, each valley has its own variation on this relatively simple theme. Some add beef, goat, or mutton, and the spices used vary according to personal recipes.

UR-PAARL

"Ur-Paarl nach Klosterart," which literally translates to "original double rye bread made in the style of the monastery," is the oldest type of *Vinschger paarl* of the Venosta Valley. Traditionally, the bread is shaped like a flattened figure eight, made by combining two round loaves—hence the bread's name, *paarl*, which means "couple." This bread can be 10 to 30 centimeters in diameter and 2 to 3 centimeters thick. The origins of the recipe for Ur-Paarl can be traced to Benedictine monks from the Monte Maria monastery; bakeries that follow this recipe faithfully bake loaves of this bread from a combination of rye and spelt flours and *pain levain*.

VEZZENA

Vezzena cheese is made like those Alpine cheeses produced from partially skimmed milk, but its unique flavor and characteristics can be attributed to the herbs of the Lavarone plateau and to the extended aging of the cheese. Presidium Vezzena is produced in summer with milk from two mountain dairies. It can be recognized by the "M" inscribed on its wheels. After a year or more of aging, the "eyes" disappear and the bright yellow body develops a light graininess. The aromas grow more complex with pleasant hints of grass and spice.

Veneto

ALPAGO LAMB

A small- to medium-size native breed that is hornless with tiny ears, the Alpago lamb has a ramlike profile with unusual dark spots on its head. Its fleece is dense, with fine, wavy wool. These lambs are raised in a semi-natural state, and their feed is supplemented with local hay and cereal meal. The meat of the Alpago lamb is extremely tender with just the right balance between fat and lean and is flavored with aromatic herbs.

BIANCOPERLA CORN

Until the post-World War II years, it was customary to make white polenta in the Polesine and Treviso districts of the Veneto region. Down on the plain, white polenta was considered finer than the rustic yellow polenta typical of the mountains. The corn used was and is (though increasingly less so) the local Biancoperla variety. The cobs are tapered and have large pearl-white kernels. White polenta is excellent served with humble fish varieties, such as *marson, schie, moleche, masenete,* shrimp, and *baccala*, or salt cod.

GOOSE *IN ONTO*

Veneto farmers once bred varieties of grey geese and geese with grey and white patches, which were eventually replaced by the great Roman white goose. With these geese they made salame, smoked leg, and goose *in onto*, a conserve made from the most perishable part of the bird. Every household prepared its own supply, as it was a good way of preserving the goose meat for several months. After the goose is slaughtered, the meat is cut into small pieces and packed under goose fat in terracotta or glass jars. Whenever needed, a small quantity can be used to make sauces or roasts.

GRAPPA MORLACCO CHEESE AND BURLINA COW

In the pastures of Mount Grappa, cheesemakers once produced a soft cow's milk cheese, low in fat, with an uncooked curd from local (and now near-extinct) Burlina cows that was named after their native region: Morlakia. Today, Grappa Morlacco cheese is once again produced on Mount Grappa with skimmed milk from the evening's milking mixed with whole milk from that of the morning. After fifteen days of aging, the cheese is ready for consumption, but it can be left to age for up to three months.

GRUMOLO DELLE ABBADESSE RICE

This rice is a variety of Vialone Nano rice that was introduced to Grumolo delle Abbadesse, a small village between Vicenza and Padua, by Benedictine nuns, and it has been grown there since the sixteenth century. The rice grown in Grumolo delle Abbadesse has tiny kernels, and its exceptional quality can be attributed to the area's soil and water. This rice swells up considerably when cooked, the kernels remaining intact and distinct, while absorbing cooking liquids—the perfect characteristics for a good risotto.

HIGH MOUNTAIN AGORDO CHEESE

In this particular area of the Veneto region, there are many Alpine meadows still in use for pasturage and for making rustic cheeses. The cheeses produced here are classic examples of Alpine skimmed-milk cheeses, made from cow's milk with a percentage of goat's or sheep's milk. Compared to the cheeses of other areas, the high-pasture cheese made in the Agordo area is slightly smaller. It is intended for long aging in natural caves, where the cheeses rest for six to eight months.

MALGA MOUNT VERONESE

Cheesemaking traditions in the Lessino region reach back to medieval times, when Cimbri shepherds would move there from the high plain of the Asiago. Mount Lessini's traditional semisoft Mount Veronese cheese has been granted origin-controlled status. Until recently, the cheese made from the precious milk of high summer pastures was not properly valued, and for this reason the few remaining *malghe* (shepherds' huts) were at risk of disappearing—a loss that would have had grave consequences for the mountain ecosystem. The Malga Mount Veronese Presidium focuses on cheese made from milk of cows grazed in high mountain pastures.

MOLECHE

Shore crabs that have lost their hard shell while molting and are in the process of growing it anew are known as soft-shell crabs. When caught in this delicate phase during the spring and autumn, shore crabs are tender and soft. *Moleche* are green soft-shell crabs that are not farmed but are gathered during the molting period and harvested at the moment they shed their shells. They are cooked alive in boiling oil after they are lightly dusted with flour.

PADUAN HEN

The Paduan hen, which ranges in color from black to white, gold, tan, or silver, has a whiskered visage, with a long beard and plumage extending from the bird's crown over its eyes. This hen was probably brought to Italy by Marquis Giacomo Dondi Dall'Orologio, a fourteenth-century

Paduan doctor and astronomer, who returned from a trip to Poland with a few specimens with which to adorn his gardens. The Paduan hen is used to prepare the classic dish *gallina a la canavéra*.

SANT'ERASMO PURPLE ARTICHOKE
Tender, meaty, elongated, and thorny with violet leaves, the Sant'Erasmo purple artichoke is cultivated on the islands of the Venice lagoon. Growers transport their crop by boat to the Rialto and Tronchetto markets. Eaten raw, the *castraure*, or first sprouts, are a real delicacy, or they may be dipped in batter and fried, or cooked in butter and served cold with lemon. It is often used to accompany *schie* (tiny prawns native to the lagoon).

SETTE COMUNI ALTOPIANO MALGA STRAVECCHIO
Asiago is one of Italy's most common DOP cheeses. The Presidium, however, is dedicated exclusively to an Asiago cheese known as *stravecchio d'Allevo*, an extremely rare product of outstanding complexity that is made in mountain dairies on the Asiago plateau and aged nineteen months or more. The aromas of this cheese recall freshly mown hay, ripe fruit, and moss. The cheese initially tastes sweet and grows gradually more pungent, offering hints of toasted hazelnuts and grilled bread.

Friuli-Venezia Giulia
PITINA, PETUCCIA, AND PETA
The peasants of Pordenone used to preserve mutton, goat meat, and doe venison for the winter in the form of round cured meats called *pitina*, *peta*, or *petuccia*. Different herbs were used in the three variants, and the *peta* was the largest of the three. The meat was minced and flavored with salt, garlic, black pepper, rosemary or wild fennel, and juniper berries, shaped into balls, dipped in corn flour, and smoked in the *fogher* (the typical valley fireplace). *Pitina* is usually eaten raw after two weeks' aging but is also excellent cooked.

RADÍC DI MONT
During the month of May, when the snow has receded, mountain shepherds venture some thousand meters high up in the Alps to gather the tenderest wild chicory. In scientific nomenclature, this variety is known as

Cicerbita alpina; in Carnia, it is known as *radìc di mont* or *radìc dal glaz*. Even today these foragers, armed with their cloth sacks or baskets, go up the mountains to gather this delicacy in spring. The shoots are preserved in oil.

RESIA GARLIC

Resia garlic, called *strok* in Resian dialect, is a variety native to the Resia Valley. The medium-size bulb is enveloped in a pink-streaked skin; inside, its white cloves are securely attached in a ring formation, peculiar for its lack of internal layers of cloves, but typical of this variety. Resia garlic once flourished on the market, reaching markets even in Ljubljana and Vienna.

Liguria

ALBENGA VIOLET ASPARAGUS

This asparagus with large spears and intense violet color is unique to Liguria. Albenga violet asparagus is cultivated entirely by hand, and the harvest takes place from mid-March until the beginning of June. Soft and buttery, without the fibrousness of some other varieties, this asparagus is excellent boiled al dente and anointed with extra-virgin Taggiasca olive oil or as an accompaniment to more subtly flavored dishes, such as boiled, steamed, or baked fish, white meat, or refined sauces.

BADALUCCO, CONIO, AND PIGNA BEANS

The main differences between these three bean types, cultivated on terraces inland from Imperia, are their shapes and sizes. Pigna beans are kidney-shaped and slightly larger than conio and badalucco, while the other two are oval-shaped and smaller. All are fleshy, soft and delicate, excellent fresh or dried. These beans are best boiled and served with extra-virgin olive oil. The most typical local recipe pairs these bean varieties with stewed goat.

BRIGASCA SHEEP *TOMA*

The Brigasca sheep is a local breed whose name is linked to the border territory between Liguria, Piedmont, and Provence. Descended from the Frabosana breed and likely crossbred with Langhe sheep, the Brigasca is a rustic animal, perfectly adapted to the ancient tradition of transhumance. The sheep winter in lowland pastures and are then led by herders to high Alpine pastures, where they spend a minimum of six months. With the milk of the Brigasca sheep, three different kinds of cheeses are still produced: *sora, toma,* and *brus.*

CINQUE TERRE SCIACCHETRÀ

This noble passito (a dessert wine) is produced from Albarola, Vermentino, and Bosco grapes cultivated on the dry stone-wall terraces of the Cinque Terre National Park and left to dry out of the sun. The walls, built by winemakers centuries ago, are nearly all in ruins. To keep local viticulture alive, it will be necessary to preserve this unique landscape and guarantee a future to the locals who devote their lives to working the land. The Presidium has been created to inspire experimentation with the production and commercialization of quality Sciacchetrà wine.

CLASSIC GENOESE FOCACCIA

Focaccia, or *fugassa* as it is known in local dialect, is a Genoese specialty. Soft inside, classic Genoese focaccia has a crunchy exterior and an intense, delicious aroma of olive oil and yeasty bread. The interior is ivory white and slightly oily with a fine crumb. The ingredients are simple: extra-virgin olive oil, flour, water, and coarse salt. The use of lard or inferior oil is strictly forbidden. It is delicious served alone, with figs—as it was enjoyed traditionally—or with Sant'Olcese cured sausage, a speciality from Alta Val Polcevera.

DRIED CALIZZANO AND MURIALDO CHESTNUTS

The technique of drying chestnuts in *tecci* (small stone huts with pine roofs) was once common throughout the Ligurian Apennines and Piedmontese valleys and still survives in the Bormida Valley. The chestnuts are smoked for about two months over low fires fueled by chestnut husks. They are either eaten dried or used as ingredients for biscuits, preserves, and ice cream. At Christmas, it is traditional to eat *viette* (dried chestnuts) soaked in water for five hours.

MONTEROSSO ANCHOVIES

Until thirty years ago, fishing was the principal activity of Monterosso. Today, there are few fishermen left, but the salted anchovies of this little village in Cinque Terre are still highly prized, and the technique of night fishing with lamps has remained unchanged. Salting used to be the responsibility of local women, who would wait for the boats to come in, clean the anchovies, and salt them in terracotta pots. Salting is a complex operation, since the fish are extremely delicate. The process of aging thus needs to be followed with considerable care.

NOLI ANCHOVIES

Called *cicciarelli* in Italian, these anchovies are known as *lussi* or *lussotti* in Noli dialect. These anchovies have always been fished using sweep nets, called *sciabica*, an exclusively in-shore fishing technique. One boat floats over the fish, while another surrounds them with the net, describing a horseshoe shape. Small, tapered, and silver in color, *cicciarelli* are excellent prepared *in carpione* (fried, then marinated) and in mixed fries.

ROSE SYRUP

The rose most suited for syrup production is the muscose or musk rose. Highly perfumed, with doubled flowers and fringed, violet-dappled silver-pink petals, this heirloom variety was selected between the end of the eighteenth and nineteenth centuries. The syrup, a Genovese tradition, is obtained by immersing petals in boiled water to which a little lemon juice has been added. After twenty-four hours of maceration, the liquid is filtered, the flowers pressed, and sugar is added. The syrup is then boiled for ten minutes before bottling.

SAVONA CHINOTTO SOUR ORANGE

This small citrus tree of Chinese origin has grown on the Savona coast since the sixteenth century. Its limbs yield an incredible quantity of flowers and fruit for their diminutive size. With time, clusters of the sour oranges turn from brilliant green to orange, releasing their own singular, intense perfume. The small, somewhat bitter, thick-skinned sour orange, or chinotto, keeps for a remarkably long time and is eaten either candied or with Maraschino liqueur.

VESSALICO GARLIC

Vessalico, a tiny village in Alta Valle Arroscia, is home to a very ancient variety of garlic. Cultivation is entirely manual and harvested bulbs are woven into long, intricately-laced networks, called *reste*. Intensely flavored, with a slight spiciness and a delicate aroma, Vessalico garlic can be easily conserved. This garlic variety is the essential ingredient in one of the area's most typical dishes, a mayonnaise made with extra-virgin olive oil and crushed garlic.

Emilia-Romagna
CERVIA ARTISAN SEA SALT
The origins of the Cervia saltworks are lost to history. Some have attributed their construction to Etruscans, others to Greek colonies (Cervia's former name, Ficocle, supports the Greek hypothesis). One thing is certain: salt production was already thriving in this area in Roman times. In fact, it began with a single small basin, the Camillone saltworks, which continues to produce superior salt with ancient methods to this day.

CLASSIC BOLOGNA MORTADELLA
The Presidum's Classic Bologna Mortadella is made from pork from heavy Italian pigs and a minimum of preservatives. It is flavored with salt, whole black pepper, ground white pepper, mace, coriander, and crushed garlic. It is then cooked in stone ovens at a central temperature of 75 to 77°C. The casing is made strictly of pigs' bladders. When sliced, the meat is not red and pinkish like the industrial variety, but pale brown with much more complex aromas.

COCOMERINA PEAR
The flesh of the rare Cocomerina, or "little watermelon," pear becomes an intense red when harvested late in the season. Fragrant, fragile, and difficult to conserve, the Cocomerina pear is ideal for jam, but few trees remain, and the pear is at risk of extinction. An association has been created to save this ancient variety, and the group gathers pears every year and produces excellent jams from this fruit.

CORNO ALLE SCALE CHAR
A relative of the fario trout and the Alpine char, the Corno alle Scale char is named for the Corno alle Scale Regional Park, a small nature reserve that bridges the Tuscan and Emilian Appenines. This char has

white-edged fins and a brown back with yellow, olive-green, or red stripes fringed with blue. Raised in spring water (without the addition of antibiotics or other chemicals), it has firm white flesh.

MARIOLA

Mariola is one of the most traditional cured sausages of the plains of Parma, Piacenza, and Cremona. It is made with the leftovers of the pig, after the neck, hams, and shoulder have been transformed into cured meats such as *culatello*. *Mariola* comes boiled or raw. Raw *mariola*—which must be aged before consumption—has a complex musky scent, with a pleasant hint of mushrooms. It melts in the mouth and has a lingering flavor. Boiled *mariola* is very reminiscent of *cotechino*, a fresh pork sausage that is also eaten boiled, but is leaner.

MODENESE VACCA BIANCA

The Vacca Bianca of Padana, which has also come to be called Modenese, is derived from the Red Reggiana cow. Today the Vacca Bianca is raised primarily for the production of the milk, but its meat is also good. The breed is known for the intensely white color of its hide; the hooves are black, as are the tips of the horns. The adult males can weigh as much as 1 ton, while the females do not exceed 650 kilograms. The milk has a fat content of 3.36 percent and a protein content of 3.47 percent, making it optimal for the production of Parmigiano-Reggiano. The objective of the Presidium is to boost the production to such a level of excellence that there is a Parmigiano DOP (origin-controlled) cheese made entirely from Modenese Vacca Bianca milk.

MORA ROMAGNOLA PIG

Romagna's native pig breed, the Mora Romagnola, once risked extinction. In 1949, a record 22 million head grazed throughout Italy, but recently the figure has dropped to fewer than fifteen. This pig has dark brown skin, almond-shaped eyes, and long tusks. Like many traditional breeds, Mora Romagnola pigs are sturdy and fatten well and are ideal for outdoor conditions. The pig's flavorful meat is soft and dense, ideal for *culatelli* and *spalle crude* (see Zibello Culatello and Spalla Cruda, below).

RED REGGIANA COW

The red Reggiana cow was supposedly brought to Italy by the Lombards, a theory supported by the resemblance—their similar red mantles—between the highly regarded Emiliana breed and those still found in central Russia and Ukraine. These are the cows that have given the world Parmigiano-Reggiano. In the postwar years, industrialization and the introduction of cows that yielded greater quantities of milk threatened to make this breed extinct. These cows produce a milk that is particularly rich in protein, calcium, and phosphorus, and is of the best quality.

ROMAGNOLA COW

In 1953, there were around half a million Romagnola cows in Italy, grazing from Veneto to the Marche. Today only around fifteen thousand remain. Recognizable by their grey-white coats, they are impressively muscular with strong, robust legs. The females have black, lyre-shaped horns, while the males' horns are half moon-shaped. Romagnola cows are more resistant to the elements than any other white breed and thus usually graze outdoors. Their meat is also excellent—particularly the cutlets, which are fatty and flavorful, comparable to those of the more famous Chianina breed.

SALAMA DA SUGO

The Salama da Sugo, or *salamina*, as the people of Ferrara call it, is a refined cured meat with an exotic flavor. It combines the potent aromas of the spices used with the meaty flavor of the pork and the fruitiness of red wine. When it is ready for cooking, it is boiled on a string and wrapped in linen to prevent it from touching the sides of the pan. To set off its strong, almost pungent taste, it is served on a bed of mashed potatoes or pumpkin.

SPALLA CRUDA

In most Italian regions, pork shoulder is ground in a mixture used to make salame and *cotechini*. In the province of Parma, however, it is regarded as a superb cured meat, both with its bone and without. No preservatives are used, making the aging of this meat a delicate process.

When *spalla cruda* is well cured, it is absolutely extraordinary: sweet and fragrant, with hints of chestnut and a slight note of pepper.

TOSCO-ROMAGNOLO APENNINE *RAVIGGIOLO*

This rare cheese has been made for centuries in the valleys of the Romagna Apennines from the milk of local cows. The curdled milk is drained and its surface is salted, all without breaking the curd. In the Forlì valleys, a part of which extends into the Foreste Casentinesi National Park, some dairymen still make this cheese with raw milk. *Raviggiolo* is produced only from October to March and does not keep for more than four days. This cheese is buttery and white, with a delicate, sweet flavor.

TRADITIONAL MARINATED COMACCHIO VALLEY EEL

The first factories for producing marinated eels were built in the Po Delta in the eighteenth century. Until the 1960s, one company in Comacchio continued to operate. The eels were brought there live in vine baskets—called *bolaghe* in local dialect—and were roasted in the factory's dozen fireplaces. The Presidium has helped recover this ancient product made by spit-roasting the eels and conserving them in wooden jars packed with brine. The secret to the flavor of the marinated Comacchio eel lies in the quality of the eels themselves.

ZIBELLO CULATELLO

One of Italy's most highly regarded and rarest cured meats, Culatello di Zibello is produced from the finest parts of the pig through an extensive and delicate processing procedure. Only about seven thousand of those produced a year bear the Consorzio Produttori di Zibello stamp, whereas thirty thousand boast the DOP mark. Only the *culatello* of the Consorzio is completely hand-processed and aged without refrigeration.

Tuscany

BAZZONE PROSCIUTTO

The name *bazzone* refers to the shape of this prosciutto, which is particularly elongated and resembles an especially pronounced chin—*bazzo* in local dialect. The pigs are obtained in a semi-wild state and are then fed spelt, apples, pears, chestnuts, acorns, and *scotta*, or leftovers from area cheese production. The resulting rosy-colored prosciutto is unctuously delicate, offering up a musky scent of acorns and chestnuts. This ham is best enjoyed with Garfagnana potato bread.

CARMIGNANO DRIED FIG

Dottato figs are the preferred variety for making Carmignano dried figs, known locally as *picce*. The figs are split open and set out on cane mats, called *canniccioni*, for four or five days. They are steamed with sulphur, then dried directly in the sun. After resting for a month in a cool, dry place (during which time a sugary patina or *gruma* forms on the skin), the figs are layered in a figure eight. Anise seeds are placed between each pair of figs. The figs are eaten either as an accompaniment to Prato mortadella or as a dessert with vin santo wine.

CASENTINO PROSCIUTTO

The Presidium has revived the old Casentino tradition of making ham from the meat of pigs raised in semi-wild conditions. Aged at least twelve months, Casentino prosciutto is round, flat, and long and bright red in color, with a fair percentage of white fat. Its scent is heady and pungent, while the flavor is delicate, with a slightly smoky finish.

CASOLA *MAROCCA*

The name *marocca* appears to come from the dialect word *marocat*, which means "unpliable." In the past, in fact, this bread used to have a very hard texture. It is made by mixing chestnut and wheat flour with mashed potatoes. Today, this traditional Lunigiana bread is produced year-round with the year's unperishable stock of chestnut flour. This flour is always available in the mountains, unlike wheat, which grows best on the valley floor.

CERTALDO ONION

Cited in Boccaccio's *Decameron*, the Certaldo onion is a symbol of its town of origin. Two varieties exist. The statina is round in shape and purplish in color with succulent flesh; it is best eaten in the summer months. The bright red and pungent vernina is harvested from the end of August through the winter months. Both varieties are excellent for soups and for *francesina*, a dish of boiled beef and puréed onion.

CINTA SENESE PIG

The only Tuscan native pig breed to avoid extinction, the Cinta Senese has a long snout and a black coat with a white band around the chest—hence the name, as *cinta* means "sash" in Italian. Thanks to breeding in the natural or semi-natural state, the meat is evenly veined with fat, with an outstanding flavor and aroma. A whole range of cured meats are made with the various parts of the animal: *lardo, rigatino, gotino* (or *guanciale*), prosciutto, salame, *capocollo*, and so on.

CLASSIC CHIANINA OX

One of the oldest and most important breeds in Italy, the classic Chianina ox is tall and powerful—the world's largest ox—and has a white coat and a sleek, elegant head. The ox adapts well to pasture. Once kept in stables, it now lives in a wild or semi-wild state in the mountains. Its meat is famous the world over, hence the need to distinguish between the genuine article and imitations.

COLONNATA LARD

The special pork lard made in Colonnata, near Carrara, has qualities that place it above typical lards. A seasonal product (it is made only from September to May), Colonnata lard benefits from the area's microclimate, the local marble used for the aging tanks, and the extensive variety of local aromatic herbs and spices used to season it. Colonnata lard is ready after at least six months but can age for a year or more. Slices of the lard are very white, soft, and subtly scented.

GARFAGNANA *BIROLDO*

The *biroldo* sausage of Garfagnana is an old-fashioned blood sausage made with boiled and boned pig's head, blood, and spices and is seasoned with wild fennel seeds, nutmeg, cloves, cinnamon, star anise, sometimes garlic, and salt and pepper. The mixture is cured and boiled for three hours. Garfagnana *biroldo* is soft and balanced on the palate. The lean head meat, blood, and spices offer delicate, lingering aromas.

GARFAGNANA POTATO BREAD

In Garfagnana and part of Serchio Valley, the tradition of making this potato bread, also called *garfagnino*, lives on. The bread is a combination of 85 percent wheat flour and 15 percent mashed potatoes, which make it softer and give it a fuller flavor. The huge 1- to 2-kilogram loaves are sliced and served with the salty cured meats of Garfagnana, a traditional Tuscan pairing.

GOYIM CUISINE OF THE TUFA CITIES

In the sixteenth century, the towns of Pitigliano and Sorano in Tuscany's desolate and little-known Maremma region became home to a Jewish community fleeing persecution elsewhere. This Presidium honors a variety of food specialities that developed out of the fusion between the Jewish tradition and the local cuisine of the "tufa cities" (so called because they are built on an outcrop of tufa rock). *Sfratto* is a cigar-shaped biscuit consisting of a wafer-thin casing filled with chopped walnuts, honey, orange peel, aniseed, and nutmeg. *Bollo* is a sweet, round or figure-eight-shaped bread flavored with aniseed. These two pastries are influenced by Jewish traditions, although they are not actually kosher, hence the name "goyim" cuisine.

MALLEGATO

The tradition of *sanguinaccio*, or blood sausage, made without pork (save for a little lard) still survives in San Miniato. In the classic version, the fresh blood is encased and enriched with lardons, salt, nutmeg, cinnamon, pine nuts, and raisins. In the Volterra variant, the mixture is enriched with *pappa* (stale bread crushed by hand and soaked in water). *Mallegato* is dark—almost black—in color and is an acquired taste. The flavors of this cured meat meld the aromas of the herbs with the sweetness of its blood base.

MAREMMA OX

This native breed has large lyre-shaped horns and a pale coat with hints of grey. Hardy and outstandingly robust, it is not suited to life in the stable. The Maremma ox roams free on the range and is herded by *buttero* (cowboys). Being raised in this natural state is beneficial to the well-being of the animals and the flavor and wholesomeness of the meat. The classic local recipe is *spezzatino* (stew) made with the most muscular cuts.

ORBETELLO *BOTTARGA*

In Orbetello, the art of preserving fish was probably introduced by the Spanish, who were smoking eels and dressing fish with *escabece*, a vinegar sauce, as early as the sixteenth century. In Orbetello, they still make *anguilla scavecciata* (eel in vinegar) and *anguilla sfumata* (smoked eel). *Bottarga* (from the Arabic *botarikh*, meaning salted fish roe) has always been produced from the roe of the grey mullet. Tender and amber in color, it is excellent sliced thin with a splash of extra-virgin olive oil and a squeeze of lemon.

PISTOIAN MOUNTAIN PECORINO

In the mountains around Pistoia, there are still families of shepherds and dairymen who make pecorino as was done a century ago: the sheep are taken to high-altitude pastures and only natural rennet and raw milk are used. The milk comes from the Massese breed, which has black wool and dark spiralled horns. The cheesemakers produce three types of Pistoian Mountain Pecorino: *fresco* (aged seven to twenty days), *abbucciato* (aged at least thirty-five days), and *da asserbo* (aged from two to three months to a year).

PRATO MORTADELLA

In Tuscany, mortadella was historically simply a means of using up left-over cured meats and poorer cuts of pork. Flavored with spices and liqueur and boiled in water, hunks of mortadella were cured in Prato and parts of the province of Pistoia at the start of the twentieth century. Mortadella di Prato has a distinctive dull pinkish color, the result of the addition of a few drops of alkermes liqueur to the mixture, which exudes exotic, spicy aromas.

REGINA DI LONDA PEACHES

Also called the Regina d'Autunno, the Regina di Londa is a late-ripening variety of peach discovered by accident in the 1950s. It is particularly suited to the Moscia River valley and its tributaries and does not require any chemical treatment. After it matures in the second half of September, the Regina di Londa is the only white peach available in Florence until October. Large and highly perfumed, it has white-green skin and firm, fragrant flesh.

SORANA BEAN

This unusual variety of cannellini bean is small and very thin-skinned with a squashed, almost flat shape. Flavorful and easy to digest, the bean is grown in a small valley in the province of Pistoia, on the shores of the Pescia River. It is cultivated on very little land and is still picked by hand and left out in the sun for three to four days to dry. The beans are conserved in a special container with whole peppercorns, valerian root, or bay leaves until the winter months.

TUSCAN SEA PALAMITA

Wrongly believed to be of lesser quality than tuna, the Tuscan sea palamita is a delicacy best enjoyed conserved in oil with bay leaves, pepper, and chili. Fished throughout the Tuscan Islands, it is a member of the tuna and mackerel family. It is a long fish (sometimes up to 80 centimeters), with a wide mouth and sharp teeth and is electric blue in color with black stripes.

VALDARNO CHICKEN

The Valdarno chicken is tall and loose-limbed, with sturdy thighs and a small breast. It has white feathers with a plumed, sickle-shaped tail, an erect blood-red crest, well-developed wattles, large cream-colored ears with red veins, and yellow beak, feet, and skin. The bird grows slowly and reaches optimal weight after four to six months. Both meat and eggs offer excellent flavor. The eggs have ivory shells and, though smaller than the supermarket variety, have much larger, yellower yolks.

VALDARNO *TARESE*

The most salient feature of this pancetta—known locally as *tarese*—is its enormous size. An entire Valdarno *tarese* measures 50 by 80 centimeters. It is made with both the back and stomach of the pig and is seasoned with red garlic and a mix of pepper, orange peel, and spices. After about ten days packed in salt, it is cleaned and weighted down to dry for a day.

The process of salting and spicing is repeated, and then it is covered in pepper and left to age for two to three months.

ZERI LAMB

This sturdy medium-large size sheep has a well-proportioned head and white fleece. Zeri sheep are pastured year round, save for winter. The milk is high in nutrition (especially protein) but is used only to feed lambs. Because of this diet of mother's milk and pasture grass, the lamb's meat is exceptionally tender and wonderfully scented. The most traditional local preparation is *agnello al testo* (roast leg with potatoes).

ZOLFINO BEAN

Also known as "one hundred beans" (because they are sowed on the hundredth day of the year) or "buttery beans," zolfino beans are small, round, and yellow with a soft skin. These beans are cultivated between the Arno and Pratomagno, usually 230 to 300 meters above sea level and sometimes up to 600 meters. When cooked, they melt in the mouth like butter. They are eaten boiled, dressed with extra-virgin olive oil and piled on toasted bread, or served as a side dish with *bistecca alla fiorentina*.

Umbria

CANNARA ONION

Round, with bright red skin and coppery white flesh, the Cannara onion plays a part in many of the region's most traditional recipes, from soup to *cipollata* (a rustic antipasto of onions, eggs, and tomatoes). Cannara onions are sweet and easy to digest. They are excellent eaten raw in salads with olive oil and salt and are a fine accompaniment to meat and game. Because of their extraordinary sweetness, these onions are particularly good with liver, lamb offal, and foie gras.

LAKE TRASIMENO BEAN

This tiny bean, about the size of a grain of rice, comes in colors ranging from salmon pink to black and brown, though the most common color is white. Soft, buttery, and flavorful, the dried beans are eaten boiled and anointed with a little extra-virgin olive oil. When fresh, called *cornetto*, these beans are stewed with tomatoes and garlic. Cultivated on the terraces around Lake Trasimeno, they were popular until the 1950s, but have nearly disappeared since then.

TREVI BLACK CELERY

The black celery of Trevi has stalks of a dark green color that are free from strings and encase a tender and pulpy heart. The process for cultivating black celery is rigorous and has not changed over the centuries: It is seeded during the waning moon, around Good Friday. It is believed that the plant in this period grows most quickly and the flowering is delayed. By October the celery are ready to be harvested. The black celery has a limited production, being cultivated in one small strip of land between the village and the Clitunno River.

Marche

FABRIANO SALAME

Fabriano salame is a highly regarded cured meat made by chopping the most prized part of the pig—the hams. Lightly covered with a dark brown mold, Fabriano salame is hard and coarse. The meat is firm and flavorful, deep red in color, and dotted with white lardons. When sliced, it exudes a beautiful scent, sometimes smoky, but without any hint of meat. Fabriano salame has a lingering flavor, with nuanced vanilla notes.

FIG CAKE

An old product of the Marche peasant tradition, Lonzino fig cake is made with figs (of the dottato or brogiotto varieties), dried in the sun and then mixed with almonds, pieces of walnuts, and aniseed, sometimes mixed with a little *sapa* (slow cooked grape must) or *mistrà* (a liquor made by macerating aniseed in alcohol), and wrapped in fig leaves. Fig cake is excellent with a medium ripe cheese and a glass of passito wine.

PORTONOVO WILD MUSSELS

The name *mosciolo* from local dialect refers to the wild mussel (*Mytilus galloprovincialis*), a naturally reproducing species that lives attached to the submerged rocks along the Conero coast. Consumption of these wild mussels dwindled due to the popularity of competing farmed mussels. Promoting the fishing and consumption of the wild shellfish helps protect their natural habitat and the strong historical ties between this shellfish and the region.

SERRA DE'CONTI CICERCHIA

A rustic, humble pulse, *cicerchie* were once common throughout the Marche. They are cultivated in spring, between rows of corn with beans and chickpeas. The Serra de'Conti *cicerchie* variety is tiny and irregular in shape. Its color ranges from grey to brown, and it has tender skin and a flavor that is far less bitter than that of other varieties. The pulse was once at risk of extinction, but some farmers in Serra de'Conti have continued to cultivate them, thus saving them for posterity.

SIBILLINI MOUNTAINS PINK APPLE

The Sibillini Mountains pink apple has been cultivated in the Marche since ancient times, particularly at altitudes of 450 to 900 meters above sea level, from the foothills of the Apennine Valleys to the Sibillini Mountains. These apples are small, irregularly shaped, and have a very short stem. Though not particularly striking in appearance, they are delicious nonetheless. The different types of this fruit share the same sweet, slightly acidic flesh and intense aromatic scent.

TENERA ASCOLI OLIVE

As their name suggests, the distinguishing characteristic of these olives is their softness. They also stand out on account of their size, their oval shape, the richness of their flesh, their smooth, pale yellow-green skins, and the sweetness. The most common method of conservation is in brine. The classic way of preparing these olives is to stuff them and fry them, a dish commonly referred to as *olive all'ascolana*.

Lazio

CACIOFIORE OF THE ROMAN COUNTRYSIDE

In Roman times the use of wild cardoons in the cheesemaking process was quite common. Some cheesemakers are trying to revive the tradition in the Roman countryside, where artichokes and cardoons flourish. Eight shepherds, some of whom practice transhumance, have agreed to experiment using thistle flower, specially cultivated for use as rennet in the raw-milk sheep cheese that recaptures the flavor of the ancient *caciofiore*. Until a few years ago, *caciofiore* was still produced in the Abruzzo and Marche regions, but it originated in Lazio.

MARZOLINA

This diminutive cheese was once produced only in the month of March, when the goats had just started to give milk, hence the name, which comes from *marzo* (March). The production of *marzolina* was once at risk of disappearing, but fortunately one of the last remaining cheesemakers passed her recipe on to other producers. *Marzolina* is shaped like a long cylinder. It can be eaten fresh, but tradition calls for a few days of aging, where the cheese rests on a wooden grate. The cheese can also be aged packed in oil in glass jars.

ONANO LENTIL

The lentils of Onano, in the province of Viterbo, have been cultivated in a very limited area for centuries. These legumes are mentioned in documents dating back to 1561. The variety is large, round, and flavorful, and is light brown in color with shades ranging from lead grey and ashen-red to greenish and marbled. This lentil "of the popes" grows well in the ideal, sandy, light volcanic soils of Onano. The skin is almost inexistent and the inside velvety, fine, and creamy with aromas of hay and chamomile.

Abruzzo

CAMPOTOSTO MORTADELLAS

Egg-shaped and joined on a string in pairs, Campotosto mortadellas are related only by name to the commercial product hung on strings in tourist shops throughout central Italy. Two producers still make the delicacy according to tradition, using finely minced prime lean pork, salt, pepper, and a secret mixture of herbs and spices. Slices are bright red in color with a central white cube of lard. The meat is firm and compact, while the lard is sweet and crunchy.

CASTEL DEL MONTE *CANESTRATO*

The pastures of the Gran Sasso National Park have long been used for transhumance: in past centuries, shepherds walked to the high pasture of Campo Imperatore with thousands and thousands of sheep, mostly of the Sopravvissane or Gentili di Puglia breeds. But every year the number of people making the trip up to high pasture with their sheep is smaller, as the difficult circumstances in which the cheese is made in these pastures discourages shepherds. With the high-pasture milk, the shepherds make a rough pecorino that is formed in wicker molds and can age up to a year. The flavor is strong and spicy, and the cheese is good sliced and excellent grated.

FARINDOLA PECORINO

This sheep's milk cheese is perhaps the only cheese in the world made with pig rennet. Use of this unusual rennet dates back to Roman times, and the preparation of the rennet today is the job of local women. The sheep, which are hand-milked, descend from the Pagliarola Appenninica breed and are raised in semi-wild conditions. Because of the rennet and the production technique, Farindola pecorino has a granular, straw yellow, slightly moist interior, even when aged. The moistness creates a mossy perfume and wonderful mellowness.

SANTO STEFANO DI SESSANIO LENTIL

Just a few millimeters in diameter with a spherical, wrinkled shape and thin skin, the dark brown Santo Stefano di Sessanio lentil is grown 1,000 meters above sea level and only on the pristine slopes of the Gran Sasso National Park. The cultivation of lentils in this area was already cited in monastic documents dating from 998 AD. Here, the small legume has found an ideal habitat in the long, severe winters and short, cool springs of this impoverished, stony terrain.

SIGNORA OF CONCA CASALE

The *signora* is a traditional cured meat of the Conca Casale region. The shape recalls a bit that of the *cotechino* sausage. The taste, however, is that of a raw, coarse-grained salame, with a strong citrus flavor. This flavor comes from the washing of the sausage casing during its preparation with a mixture of water and lemon, spiked with wild fennel. The *signora* is always made by hand with great care taken to fill up every fold of the casing.

VASTESE *VENTRICINA*

Vastese *ventricina* is made with the best cuts of pork flavored with salt and ground sweet pepper in equal quantities and occasionally with wild fennel seeds and pepper. Eaten either chopped in sauce with pasta or sliced raw, this cured meat is orange-red in color with a fragrant, spicy aroma—the result of long aging. The lingering taste of Vastese *ventricina* is predominantly spicy but does not overwhelm the flavor of the meat and seasonings.

Puglia

ACQUAVIVA RED ONION

The Acquaviva *cepodde* (the onion's name in local dialect) is cultivated in the area surrounding the city of Acquaviva of Fonti. It is noted for its sweet flavor and is eaten raw. With its platterlike shape, the onion is carmine-red with a stark white interior and boasts a sweet succulent flavor. The onion is featured in local festivals, where it can be sampled in *rustici*: a kind of focaccia stuffed with the onions and strong ricotta.

CARPINO BROAD BEANS

The calcareous, clay-rich soil of Carpino is perfect for the cultivation of broad beans. After the harvest, the plants are well dried and crushed by horses. Then the beans are removed from their pods with a wooden pitchfork and thrown into the air from wooden paddles to eliminate tiny particles of dirt. Small, with a dimple in the base, Carpino broad beans are green when harvested, but take on a sandy white color with aging.

GARGANO CITRUS FRUITS

The citrus fruits of Gargano ripen all year round: the Durette at Christmas, the Bionde oranges from April through May, the lemons in June and so on. The orchards, or *giardini* as they are called here, are clustered around farmhouses and protected from the wind by dry-stone walls or reed or holm-oak and laurel wood fences. The Presidia producers use the oranges and lemons of Gargano to make excellent marmalades, candied peels and fruits, and limoncello liquor.

GARGANO GOAT

The Gargano goat is a particularly rustic breed, perfectly suited to roaming free in the barren and rocky pastures of the area. It has raven-black long hair, a large and stocky head, a forelock on the forehead, and a long beard under the chin. The horns are light and open toward the tips, describing an arc. The Gargano goat is prized for its milk, from which several different types of cheese are made including a delicate fresh ricotta, but also for its meat. Fifteen years ago this breed numbered some thirty thousand heads, but today it is reduced drastically to less than three thousand. The Presidium wants to recover the value of the cheese and the meat of the Gargano goat.

GARGANO PODOLICO *CACIOCAVALLO*

This cheese is made with the milk of the Podolica cow (which yields very little milk and only in certain months). The breed used to be one of the most common in Italy but is now confined to parts of the south where pasture is sparse and water rare. The production of *caciocavallo* (with its typical large round base and small ball top) is an operation that requires great skill and ability. But the results are excellent. Well aged (from three months to even eight to ten years) it is exceptional.

GARGANO PODOLICA COW

The Podolica is a breed raised on the open range that produces a particularly aromatic milk and a robust and flavorful meat rich in mineral salts. While the Podolica breed's versatility and adaptability, its hardiness and resistance to disease initially favored its use throughout the territory, it is precisely these characteristics that are precipitating its decline, for it is also not easily stabled, produces little milk, and has a tougher, more fibrous meat.

MARTINA FRANCA *CAPOCOLLO*

The best cured meats in Puglia have traditionally come from Martina Franca, and the most highly regarded is *capocollo*, the name used in the south of Italy to refer to cured pig neck. To counter the climatic conditions of the area of origin—unsuitable for meat curing—a practice has developed where the meat is slightly smoked, marinated in brine, and soaked in mulled wine. The procedure, which serves to preserve the meat, also gives it its extremely rich flavor.

TORITTO ALMOND

In the province of Bari, the cultivation of almonds was once very common and has profoundly influenced both the shape of the countryside and its popular culture. Today, the only area in which almond production still plays an important role is Toritto, on the border between the Pre-Murgia and the High Murgia. In this area one can find various ancient varieties of almond that have survived the invasion of higher-yielding Californian varieties. They are named for famous citizens of Torrito, such as Antonio De Vito and Filippo Cea.

TRADITIONAL ALTAMURA BREAD

Traditional stone ovens are still common in Altamura. Made in the nineteenth century with typically tall hoods, and requiring extremely long-handled peels, these ovens can hold 300 kilograms of bread or more. The superb bread of Altamura is baked in huge sombrero-shaped loaves, made from the ground durum wheat bran of the Alta Murgia district in the province of Bari, which is mixed with natural yeast, sourdough starter, warm water, and sea salt.

Campania

AMALFI SFUSATO LEMON

Amalfi lemons date back to ancient Roman times, and images of lemon trees very similar to the Sfusato variety appear in the ruins of the Casa del Frutteto in Pompei. The Amalfi Sfusato lemon has an elongated shape and a very pale yellow skin. With juicy, acidic pulp, few seeds, and intense aroma, this lemon is perfect for the preparation of traditional limoncello.

BAGNOLESE PECORINO

Produced from the milk of Bagnolese sheep, this pecorino has a dense brownish-yellow crust and a firm, unctuous, straw-colored paste. A rustic, simple cheese with a very specific and assertive flavor profile, fresh Bagnolese pecorino is always offered on Irpinian tables as an antipasto —

according to southern Italian tradition—or cooked in various preparations. When aged, the cheese retains a decidedly spicy flavor and is good for grating.

CASTELLAMMARE VIOLET ARTICHOKE

Also known as the Schito artichoke, this blossom has green bracts with purple shading. Traditionally, the first cluster (the *mamma* or *mammolella*) is placed under a terracotta cover to protect the plant from the elements, allowing it to grow while remaining tender and delicate. Roasted over the grill and seasoned with salt, pepper, parsley, fresh wild garlic, and olive oil, it is served as a symbolic Easter dish. This artichoke is also prepared as *m'buttunata*: stuffed with cheese, chopped salame, eggs, salt, pepper, parsley, and stale bread.

CILENTO GOAT *CACIORICOTTA*

The Cilento goat is an indigenous breed from the province of Salerno and is especially populous in some areas of the Cilento National Park. Cilento goats are raised according to traditional practices and thrive on the poor pastures of noncoastal areas. The goat's milk is used to produce *cacioricotta*, a unique cheese made with a technique common in both Puglia and Basilicata. The name of this cheese reflects an unusual kind of coagulation of the milk, partly acidified and curdled with rennet (typical of *cacio*) and partly curdled through heat (typical of ricotta).

GIOI SOPPRESSATA

First cited in an agronomic document in 1835, Gioi Soppressata is produced in Gioi Cilento. It is one of the oldest, most unusual Campanian cured meats and is made only from the finest cuts of pork, from which the cartilage and gristle are carefully removed. To produce this sausage, the meat is chopped with a knife, flavored with salt and pepper, and encased in pig's intestine. A piece of lard as long as the intestine itself is then fitted into the center, both to add a decorative touch and to keep the mixture moist after smoking.

ISCHIA CAVE RABBIT

So called because it is raised in 3 to 4 meter caves from which the warrens extend, the Ischia cave rabbit boasts meat that is firmer and tastier than that of caged rabbits. On Ischia, rabbit is a popular holiday dish, a symbol of the inhabitants' love of their island. In the past, the *conigliata* was a feast held to celebrate the completion of a *casa a carusiello*, or domed house.

MENAICA ANCHOVIES

The Menaica anchovy fishing technique dates back to ancient times. Once widespread throughout the Mediterranean, this fish survives only in the Cilento district because of the fishermen who still go out at night with their boats and nets (both called *menaica* or *menaide*). Once delivered to the harbor, the anchovies are immediately washed in brine, then salted and layered in terracotta jars, where they are left to rest for at least three months. Menaica anchovies are distinguished by their pale pink flesh and intense, delicate aroma.

MONACO PROVOLONE

Monaco is a *caciocavallo*-type cheese without the characteristic ball of curd decorating its top. Called provolone, but in no way related to the provolone produced industrially in the Po Valley, Monaco provolone is made exclusively in the Lattari Mountains at the bottom of the Sorrentina peninsula. Smooth when fresh, it releases heady perfumes of green grass and hazelnut. This cheese was used in Neapolitan cuisine as an ingredient for a number of dishes, and it deserves recognition as a great table cheese.

MOZZARELLA IN MYRTLE

The use of myrtle (*mortella*) as natural packaging was born of the necessity to protect this cheese during transport from the pastures where it was made to the valley below. Myrtle also gives the cheese a special fragrance. With time, this mozzarella has become a product in its own right in southern Italy.

NASSA SHRIMP

The *parapandalo* is a pink shrimp with a long beak. Its ideal habitat is a dark underwater grotto. It is caught using the *nassa*, a large reed and myrtle basket handwoven by fishermen. Thanks to the quality of the "food" available to the shrimp in its dark habitat (strong currents keep a steady supply coming), its flesh is especially sweet and firm. Connoisseurs eat it raw or sautéed with a pinch of salt and ground pepper.

PAPACCELLA PEPPER

Papaccella is a sweet pepper with a small round shape. It has a vibrant yellow color, but it is also sometimes red or green. At the market younger shoppers confuse it with the ordinary sweet pepper, but older people will remember it well if they happen to come across it. Optimal for use in flavoring dried sausages, it was typical of the outskirts of Brusciano. The region of Campania has recovered the germ plasm and is experimenting with reproducing the original seeds, which the Presidium hopes to then make more widely available for cultivation.

PIENNOLO SMALL TOMATO

Named for their tendency to grow hanging in bunches like grapes, these tiny tomatoes (around 20 to 25 grams each) can be distinguished from the famous Pachino tomatoes by the two grooves down their sides and the point at one end. The skin of this tomato is thick, the flesh firm, compact, and parched by the strong Vesuvius sun. Both its flavor and aroma become more intense with time.

PIETRAROJA PROSCIUTTO

The first mention of the existence of this prosciutto dates from 1776, when the duke of Laurenzana of Piedmont ordered some for his refectory. Since then, the centuries-old stone walls of his canteen have always welcomed these hams (each weighing 9 to 13 kilograms) for aging. Pietraroja prosciutto is not served in slices, but cut into small pieces, accompanied by a glass of Aglianico rosé.

ROMAN *CONCIATO*

This cheese just might be the most ancient cheese in all Italy. It is made by curdling sheep's, cow's, and goat's milk with goat rennet, then washing the resulting cheese with the cooking water of *pettole*, a type of homemade pasta. The traditional technique for producing Roman *conciato* requires covering the cheese with a mixture of oil, vinegar, thyme, and chopped spicy pepper.

SAN MARZANO TOMATO

Even some of Italy's most famous vegetables are at risk of extinction: the San Marzano tomato is just one example. A very delicate variety that is difficult to grow and tend, this tomato develops an extraordinary fragrance when ripening, reminiscent of freshly cut grass and spices. The San Marzano tomato is inextricably linked to pizza Napoletana, and is also an ingredient in traditional Neapolitan *ragù*, a meat sauce that cooks for at least five to six hours.

TRADITIONAL CETARA ANCHOVY EXTRACT

Anchovy extract, a traditional Cetara product, is an amber-colored liquid produced by aging salted anchovies from the Gulf of Salerno, caught from March through the beginning of July. Immediately after they are caught, the anchovies are cleaned by hand and salted, then layered in oak containers. After four or five months, the liquid that drips out from a small hole in the base of the container is collected and used as a unique condiment, particularly well suited to spaghetti or linguine.

WHITE PERTOSA ARTICHOKE

During the 1920s, this vegetable was a much-sought item in all the markets in the area. Today, it has almost disappeared: a mere thirty farmers cultivate it in small quantities amidst their olive trees. There are many traits that set this artichoke apart: its resistance to low temperatures, its light green—almost white—color, its sweet taste, and the extraordinary tenderness of its inner leaves and choke. It is an excellent artichoke to eat raw, drizzled with extra-virgin olive oil.

Basilicata

BASILICAN PODOLICO *CACIOCAVALLO*

Podolico *caciocavallo* is made using the *pasta filata* technique developed in the south of Italy over the centuries to ensure the preservability and security of cow's milk cheeses. This cheese is especially prized because it is produced with the milk of a rare local breed, the Podolica. Suitable for aging up to four to five years, Basilican Podolico *caciocavallo* is superbly complex when very mature. This cheese has a vast array of aromas because of the excellent milk of the Podolica cow.

FERRANDINA BAKED OLIVES

The first documention of the baked olives produced in Ferrandina dates back to 1700. Production stipulates that these olives first be toasted then dry-salted and finished in the oven at 50°C. This method accentuates the flavor of the naturally delicious Majatica olive and maintains its characteristic sweetness. Best eaten on its own or with Lucan cured meats or aged sheep's milk cheese, Ferrandina baked olives are also added to orange salad, yellow squash soup, and stewed salt cod.

MATERANA MOUNTAIN *PEZZENTE*

The name *pezzente* (beggars) likely documents the peasant origins of this sausage, which is made exclusively from less desirable cuts of meat and mixed with crushed sweet and spicy Senise peppers, wild fennel, fresh minced garlic, and sea salt. The most convivial way to enjoy this salame is in slices accompanied by good homebaked bread. It can also be used as a base for tomato sauce for homemade pasta, or a savory second course with vegetables (chicory, Swiss chard, escarole) cooked in an earthenware crock.

MOLITERNO *CASIEDDU*

Produced in the summer months by the shepherds of Val d'Agri, this cheese is a type of *cacioricotta*, a goat cheese from the Puglian-Lucanian Apennines. Traditionally wrapped in fern leaves, Moliterno *casieddu* is a small white or hay-yellow sphere (depending on its age). The cheese has a strong perfume of milk and a delicate aroma of *nepeta* (an herb added to the milk during the cheesemaking). These same aromatic characteristics are present in the cheese's flavor, providing a pleasing contrast to the natural sweetness of the goat's milk.

ROTONDA RED EGGPLANT

Brought to Rotonda at the end of the nineteenth century, this eggplant variety is probably of African origin. These unusual Rotonda red eggplants are as small and round as apples. Bright orange in color with green and reddish streaks, they resemble tomatoes or persimmons. Their pulp is fleshy and retains its creamy color even hours after being cut. The aroma is intense and fruity (reminiscent of prickly pears), and the flavor is spicy with a pleasantly bitter finish. These eggplants are delicious eaten marinated in oil or vinegar, and even the leaves are good to eat.

Calabria

COSENZA STUFFED FIG

After the harvest, the figs—only the Dottato variety are used—are sun-dried on *cannizze* (cane grilles), baked in the oven, flavored, and stuffed. These figs are relatively small and yellowish in color, with tiny seeds that are almost imperceptible in the mouth. Cosenza stuffed figs are either skewered on small crosses or on sticks, or arranged in crown, plait, or ball shapes and flavored with fig honey.

DECOLLATURA SOPPRESSATA

The true secret of this soppressata is the meat, which comes from free-range pigs that are fed chestnuts, acorns, and household leftovers. The pigs are slaughtered, still lean, at ten to twelve months of age. The meat is chopped and shaped by hand, seasoned with salt and a sauce made from Pizzo Calabro peppers, and then encased in pig intestine. The sausage is smoked for ten days and then aged four to ten months. It has aged sufficiently when drops of liquid, the so-called *lacrime*, appear when a slice is pressed with a finger.

MONTE PORO PECORINO

Monte Poro, in the province of Catanzaro, offers abundant pasture rich in aromatic grasses and herbs. Sheep have always been raised here in the natural state. The excellent pecorino made with their milk is granular, with irregular "eyes." Its color varies from milk to snow white. The body is rich, with a flavor of mint, wildflowers, hedgerow, and hay. In the mouth, it is mellow with agreeable hazelnut nuances and a relatively piquant finish.

MOSCATO DI SARACENA

This sweet wine has been produced in the town of Saracena since the sixteenth century using an unusual combination of local Muscat (*Moscato*) grapes, together with Grenache, Malvasia, and Odoacra grapes. To make this passito wine, the Muscat grapes are dried for fifteen to twenty days, then pressed and combined with the boiled must of the other three grapes. The resulting wine offers resinous and aromatic notes, along with a refined scent of dried figs and tropical fruit, almonds, and honey, and a pleasantly bitter note that makes this wine a particularly suitable accompaniment for sweet biscuits.

Sicily

BELÌCE VASTEDDA

Vastedda is the only *pasta filata*, or kneaded curd, sheep's milk cheese in Italy. In the past, dairymen produced it in the Belìce valley during the summer as a way of recycling damaged sheep cheeses by recooking and reworking the curd. The name *vastedda* probably comes from the dialect word *vasta*, meaning damaged or gone off. Today, it is made from the fresh milk of Belìce sheep. Wonderfully fragrant and intense on the palate, the cheese should be eaten very fresh.

BRONTE PISTACHIO

This variety grows only in the hilly, volcanic soil of Bronte. Emerald green in color with an intense, unctuous, and resiny aroma, Bronte pistachios are harvested by hand in small quantities. Though superior in quality, this pistachio is struggling to withstand competition from less flavorful and less expensive nuts from Iran, Turkey, and America.

CASTELVETRANO BLACK BREAD

The round loaves of Castelvetrano black bread have hard, coffee-colored crusts sprinkled with sesame seeds and a soft, wheat-yellow interior. The dough is kneaded with two flours: Sicilian white flour and a local flour made from an ancient corn variety. It is the corn-based flour that gives Castelvetrano bread its dark color, softness, and distinctive "toasted" flavor. The other ingredients are water, salt, and natural yeast. This bread is baked only in woodburning ovens.

CIACULLI LATE-WINTER MANDARIN

Long ago, the Conca d'Oro plain that surrounds Palermo welcomed weary travelers to rest in its verdant orchards. Today, the Conca d'Oro is shrinking: in the last fifty years, it has lost 80 percent of its growing area due to urban expansion. In the villages of Ciaculli and Croceverde Giardina—areas that have remained intact—a natural variation of the

Avana mandarin orange that arose in 1940 produced a new variety that matures from January through March (much later than usual). This remarkably sweet and juicy mandarin has few seeds and a thin skin.

DELIA CUDDRIREDDRA

Taking its name from the Greek *kollura* (usually ring-shaped, toasted bread), this bread is coiled into an intricate crown shape and is said to have been created in homage to the ruling gentry that lived in Delia during the Sicilian Vespers war. Made with hard wheat flour, eggs, sugar, a little lard, red wine, cinnamon, and orange zest, Delia Cuddrireddra was originally baked at home during Carnevale, where it obtained the characteristic ridges made by a special comb, a tool borrowed from weavers that can no longer be found.

ETNA TABACCHIERA PEACH

Peach cultivation on Etna began after the end of World War II. Here, the well-drained soil, abundant water, and considerable changes in temperature ensure fine-quality produce. Many varieties have been introduced. One of the finest is the Tabacchiera, unmistakable for its flat shape (*tabacchiera* means "snuffbox"). Peaches have soft, sweet white or yellow flesh and are beautifully scented.

FAVIGNANA *BOTTARGA*

The Sicilian tuna catch, the *mattanza*, is an age-old tradition. Today, however, the *mattanza*, as well as the traditional practice of locally processing and preserving the catch, are at risk of disappearing because of the dwindling tuna population and because Favignana fishermen now look for the fish in other waters. One lone fisherman from the Florio clan continues to produce the local speciality of tuna *bottarga*, or preserved tuna roe, but he finds it increasingly difficult to locate raw materials. Until the end of the 1950s, the Florio family produced many local tuna specialties, employing many Favignana locals in the process.

GIARRATANA ONION

Giarratana, located in the Iblei Mountains, is famous for its large, incredibly sweet onions. The bulbs have a light brown skin, white, savory flesh, a slightly flattened shape, and can weigh up to 2 kilograms. They are delicious when eaten raw, in a salad, or when dressed with oil and salt. Given their size, the onions are often used as a "spoon" to hold fava beans from the plateau of Modica.

GIRGENTANA GOAT

This goat, whose name comes from Girgenti (modern-day Agrigento), has distinctive long, spiralled horns and resembles Asian breeds. Some experts trace its origins to Tibetan goats. Medium-size with long, thick, white and occasionally dappled fleece, this goat has a short beard and a thick shock of hair hanging over its eyes. The Presidium endeavors to establish a high-quality Girgentana cheese. The aim is to raise the profile of these breeders and make their livelihoods more viable by increasing the numbers of their herds.

INTERDONATO LEMON

The Interdonato lemon is an old cultivar obtained at the end of the nineteenth century, when Giovanni Interdonato crossed a citron with the *ariddaru*, a local lemon variety. Medium-large in size, with a delicate, slightly acidulated flavor, the lemon has a finely textured skin, for which it is also called *frutto fino*. At the end of World War II, these lemons were primarily sold in England, where they were a favored accompaniment for tea. After the citrus crisis of 1980, cultivation of this variety was reduced by half, and today the many orchards have since been abandoned.

LATE-HARVEST LEONFORTE PEACH

Leonforte peaches ripen in September and October and even as late as November. They are wrapped in paper bags to protect them from the wind and parasites and are harvested only when perfectly ripe. Protected inside the bags, they ripen late and take on a bright yellow color with red streaks. Wonderfully scented, the peach boasts yellow, firm flesh that is sweet with a distinctive, slightly caramelized flavor.

LEONFORTE BROAD BEAN

Delicious Leonforte broad beans are described as *cucivole*, a word that describes how these beans cook easily and do not require much soaking. This fava variety was once very common and was cultivated in rotation with grain to enrich the soil. Once picked, the beans are seasoned with salt and eaten with pecorino cheese. When dry, they are used in the traditional Sicilian pasta dish, *pasta ccu' i favi a du' munni', frascatula'* (polenta of toasted broad beans and chickpeas with baby wild fennel bulbs), as well as many other dishes.

MADONIE MANNA

Manna, a natural sweetener with a very low glucose and fructose content, is produced from the bluish, resinous substance extracted from the bark of the ash trees of Castelbuono and Pollina in the Madonie Mountains. When exposed to the sun, this substance solidifies into manna. The extraction technique for collection is very ancient indeed and has survived only in this small corner of the Mediterranean. The high-quality Presidium product is made only from the purest *manna eletta*, which forms "stalactites" down the sides of the tree without touching the bark.

MADONIE *PROVOLA*

This exceptional cheese is produced in one of Italy's most biologically diverse areas: the Madonie Mountains in the Madonie Regional Park. A typical kneaded-curd cow's milk cheese similar to its cousin from the Nebrodi, this *provola* is shaped like a wine flask and has a fine straw-yellow rind. The artisan dairymen of the Presidium still make this cheese with raw cow's and sheep's milk. Madonie *provola* is also available lightly smoked.

MAGGHIA MASCULINA ANCHOVY

The Gulf of Catania is dotted with small fishing boats along the horizon: from Capo Mulini in the north, with its string of the Cyclops Islands, to Capo Santa Croce in the south, the fishermen set out their drift nets at night and catch the *masculini* fish just as fishermen did in the times of Homer. Also called *anciuvazzu* and *anciuvurineddu*, there are many names for these small, wriggling anchovies. The small heads of the fish get caught in the net, creating a natural bleeding, which produces a tastier and more highly valued fish.

MAIORCHINO

Maiorchino is one of the greatest pecorino cheeses in Italy in terms of both size and quality. Suitable for long aging, maiorchino is produced (in good years) from February until mid-to-late June. The cheese is made in small quantities from raw sheep's and goat's milk, and the animals live in the wild pastures of the Peloritani Mountains. The production technique is highly complex and involves the long, patient job of *bucatura*—repeated piercing with a long needle to extract the excess whey from the center of the cheese.

MINUTA OLIVE

This rare and ancient Sicilian olive cultivar is hardy and resistant to extreme climates. It grows on the highest hillsides of Monti Nebrodi. The Minuta olive, with its high concentrations of polyphenols and vitamin E, offers notable nutritional qualities. The medium-small fruit are hand-harvested from mid-October through mid-December. The oil from these olives is delicate in flavor, well-balanced between bitter and spicy, and rich in fruity aroma, with floral notes. This oil is unusual for Sicily as it has a very delicate flavor and therefore is suited to very refined dishes.

MODICANA COW

Long a part of Sicilian agriculture, this breed of cow has a red coat shaded with black. Grazed outdoors all year round, they are brought under cover only for milking. Like all such naturally raised cows, they only produce milk when suckling calves. Their wonderful milk provides the raw material for one of Sicily's most prized cheeses: Ragusano. The fact that these cows are raised completely outdoors also guarantees excellent-quality, highly flavorful meat.

NEBRODI BLACK PIG

Raised in the beech and oak forests of the Nebrodi Mountains, this pig breed is small and black. Though frugal and hardy, this breed has diminished considerably in number in recent years. To encourage the cultivation of Nebrodi black pigs, it is vital to promote its excellent meat. Products made from the meat of Nebrodi black pigs include Salame di

Sant'Angelo in Brolo, cured hams, Nebrodi sausage, and cured meats such as *capocollo* and pancetta.

NEBRODI PROVOLA

This *provola* is a traditional *caciocavallo* cheese produced by the dairymen of the Monti Nebrodi. Size varies according to the area of production: from 1 kilo in the northwestern Nebrodi Mountains to 1.5 kilos or more in the central Nebrodi, to 5 kilos in the eastern Nebrodi. The cheese has the typical oval *caciocavallo* shape and is covered in a smooth, glossy, amber-yellow outer rind. With aging, the flavor varies from sweet to spicy.

NOTO ALMONDS

Three varieties of Noto almonds are cultivated here: Romana, Pizzuta d'Avola, and Fascionello. The first has the best flavor, intense and aromatic, but is the least appreciated by the market on account of its chunky, irregular shape. The almond is the queen of Sicilian confectionery and is used to make *pasta reale* (marzipan), *martorana* (marzipan fruit and vegetables), almond milk, nougat, *mustazzuoli* biscuits, amaretti, and *cassata*, the baroque pudding par excellence.

NÙBIA RED GARLIC

The name given to this garlic variety derives both from a small hamlet near Paceco and from its deep red color. The bulb normally has around twelve cloves and is white outside and bright red and intensely flavored inside. Traditionally woven into large plaits of one hundred bulbs and hung from balconies or stored in cellars and warehouses, this garlic is integral to the cuisine of Trapani, particularly in dishes such as *pasta con il pesto alla trapanese* and fish couscous.

POLIZZI BADDA BEAN

The bicolored Polizzi badda bean has been grown in the Polizzi Generosa gardens in the Madonie Regional Park for two centuries. Round and medium-small, the bean's name, *badda*, a term from the local dialect, refers to its ball-like shape. The bean is ivory-colored with pink or orange markings on a violet background, so dark it verges on black. The badda bean can be cooked fresh or dried in traditional Polizzana dishes.

RAGUSAN DONKEY

Until thirty to forty years ago, the donkey played an important role in the countryside of the south of Italy. Today Sicily's native breeds, including the Ragusan, are in danger of extinction. The Ragusan donkey has a dark bay coat, a grey muzzle, a black mane and tail, large eyes circled with white, straight, medium-long ears, a broad girth, and robust limbs. The properties of donkey's milk are very similar to those of human milk and may be used to feed babies with digestion problems.

RAGUSANO

This cheese, known as "the treasure of the Iblei Mountains," has a rich, golden rind. To make this rare cheese, the cheesemaker must be strong and, at the same time, possess the finesse of a fine craftsman. This cheese is produced from November through May when the local pastures offer over one hundred different varieties of herbs. Made with raw milk from cows, primarily the Modicana breed, the best Ragusano is aged from eight months to two years.

RIBERA STRAWBERRY

The diminutive strawberries that are still grown around Agrigento are thought to derive from plants that were brought to Sicily by World War II veterans. A few Sicilian soldiers gathered these wild strawberries from underbrush up in the Alps and introduced them to the hardy Sicilian terrain, where they adapated and flourished in this very different environment. This delicate, highly fragrant strawberry is bright red in color, and must be eaten within one or two days of harvesting.

SALINA CAPER

On the island of Salina, the caper bush is part of the landscape. Until the advent of tourism, the caper was the crux of the island's economy, but is now in crisis due to competition from cheaper North African produce. The capers are picked one by one and stored in wooden barrels in layers alternated with rough marine salt and are ready to be eaten after a couple of months. Salina capers stand out for their firmness, perfume, and uniformity. They can be stored for up to three years.

TRAPANI ARTISAN SEA SALT

This unrefined artisan sea salt is produced by evaporating sea water in huge, shallow pools near the seashore. On the coast near Trapani, against a scenic backdrop of water, windmills, and white pyramids that turn pink with the sunset, craftsmen work the piles of salt in the traditional way. Trapani artisan sea salt seems saltier than commercial table salt, as the large flat flakes dissolve more quickly on the tongue, imparting a salty sensation faster than normal square crystals. This salt is actually saltier than table salt, as it contains more potassium and magnesium and less sodium chloride.

USTICA LENTIL

Italy's smallest lentils grow on the southern island of Ustica. Sown in volcanic, fertile soil, the lentils are cultivated almost entirely by hand. Brown in color, tender, and flavorful, they do not need to be soaked and cook in three-quarters of an hour. The two classic uses for these lentils are in traditional basil- or wild fennel-scented vegetable soup or in *pasta e lenticchie*, which is made with broken spaghetti.

WINTER MELONS

Melon is among the oldest and most important product of Trapani agriculture. The Purceddu Alcamo winter melon is oval in shape with a rough green skin; it has white, juicy flesh and becomes better and sweeter with time, which accounts for its designation as a "winter" melon. An excellent table fruit, it is also used for ice cream and traditional Sicilian granita. Best from Christmas onward, the Cartucciaro winter melon also ripens well after it is picked. Traditionally after harvest, melons are left on terraces or hung from balconies of homes. Paceco Cartucciaro is one of the most treasured varieties, and it has an elongated shape, yellow rind, and juicy, white pulp.

Sardinia
CASIZOLU

Montiferru is home to a truly unusual cheese called Casizolu. The existence of this ancient, pear-shaped cow's milk cheese is especially surprising given that Montiferru is right at the heart of an area known for goat and sheep cheeses. Most Casizolu cheesemakers are women who work the fresh milk and knead the fresh curd under hot water to give it its classic shape. Casizolu is produced from the milk of Sardinian Modican cows, or with Brown Swiss-Sardinian crosses. These rustic animals are raised free in woodland pastures, hence their wonderful herby, woody, and leaf-scented milk.

FIORE SARDO SHEPHERDS' CHEESE

Traditionally this cheese is made exclusively from freshly drawn, raw ewe's milk. Native Sardinian sheep are believed to be descended directly from the wild mountain sheep that today still inhabit the most inaccessible parts of the island, and the origins of this cheese go back possibly even to the Bronze Age. Production is authorized throughout the whole region but traditionally *fiore Sardo* is made by mountain shepherds in the huts, known as *pinnette*, whose central open fires give the authentic version its characteristically smoky overtones. A Slow Food Presidium will soon be launched to keep the shepherds' traditional cheesemaking technique alive.

MARCEDDÌ ARSELLE CLAM

In Sardinia's Arborea lagoons, clams are still harvested one by one with a mirror and a knife. From May until August, fishermen gather these valuable mollusks from the sand beds, packaging them in net sacks to be sold all over Sardinia and elsewhere on the mainland. This traditional harvesting system is completely sustainable and highly selective. This technique avoids the use of rakes and shovels, which can damage sand beds. Fishermen here wish to ensure that these local clams are identified in the marketplace. Stores and restaurants make numerous false claims of authenticity despite the mollusks' distinguishing features. The Presidium aims to secure the future of local fishing by setting up a shop near the fishing lagoon where the clams can be sold and served by the fishermen themselves.

OSILO PECORINO

One of the smallest of the classic Sardinian pecorinos (narrower in diameter but taller than the classic Sardinian product), Osilo pecorino has a fine, delicate consistency due to a heavy pressing during production. Its aromas are typical of rustic pecorino; but the flavor is unusually buttery, with notes of toasted hazelnuts. It is also critical to protect the production system for this unusual cheese, as hundreds of shepherds rely on it for their livelihoods. They also produce the unusual byproduct *mustia*, a smoked ricotta.

OZIERI *COPULETA*

Ozieri is in the center of northern Sardinia—equidistant from both the island's coasts—far off the common tourist routes. Today, this area is known for sweets that are celebrated and sold throughout the nation. Ozieri *copuleta* is evidence of the refinement of this ancient popular culinary tradition. It is a bar of the thinnest pastry, placed on oval or round shapes that are filled with *pan di spagna*, almond paste, a bit of lemon, and, according to the particular recipe, perhaps a dash of liqueur.

POMPÌA

This tree, originally from the Baronia coast, is similar to the orange but has thorny branches. Its bright yellow fruit is comparable in size to grapefruit, with thick, warty skin and very acidic juice. Only the skin of this citrus fruit is consumed. It is used to make liqueurs, and the pith is candied to make *aranzata*, a cake made of chopped *pompìeca* (a citrus fruit), almonds, wildflower honey, and candied nuts.

SAN GAVINO MONREALE SAFFRON

Crocus flowers are hand-picked at dawn when they are still closed or only slightly open. The petals are then opened by hand and separated from the stigmas which, when dried, are known as saffron. Then they are hand-rubbed with extra-virgin olive oil and left to dry. Every cultivated hectare yields 9 to 10 kilos of dried saffron. San Gavino Monreale saffron is bright red in color with a heady aroma and a strong flavor.

SARDINIAN MODICAN COW

This wild red-coated breed lives year-round on the pastures of Montiferru. The Sardinian Modican cow produces excellent milk and delicious meat. In Montiferru, this beef is either boiled (*petza in brou*) or spit-roasted (*petza arrustida*). It is also traditionally prepared in stew (*ghisadu*) and meatballs (*bombas*) and is either fried or boiled in stock as a classic feast-day soup.

Multiregional
HIGH MOUNTAIN HONEYS

There are three high-altitude Alpine honeys, all strictly whole, virgin, and produced exclusively from nectar collected at an altitude of 1,200 meters above sea level: resin honey, rhododendron, and wildflower. The honey made from the "honeydew" resin residue of the fir tree is very dark—almost black—in appearance. The resinous aroma is reminiscent of burnt wood and caramelized sugar. This honey is less sweet than nectar honey, with hints of malt and balsam flavors. The rhododendron and wildflower honeys are pale in color, fresh, and delicate in flavor.

INTERNATIONAL PRESIDIA

To find contact information for the individuals coordinating Slow Food's efforts at preserving these endangered tastes, go to SlowFood.com

Argentina
ANDEAN CORN (*Santa Maria and San José, Catamarca Province*)

Corn originated in the center of South America thousands of years ago and is one of the most widely consumed grains in the world today. In the Argentinian province of Catamarca, many ancient varieties still exist. The abandonment of rural areas, the lack of ready access to water, and the appeal of hybrid varieties have put Andean corn varieties in real danger, and this Presidium is working to counteract these trends. Each variety of native corn has a role in the local cuisine and festivities, three of which are the focus of the Presidium's work—Amarillo Socorro, Capia, and Blanco Criollo—each chosen for their taste and agricultural qualities.

QUEBRADA DE HUMAHUACA ANDEAN POTATOES (*Tumbaya, Tilcara, and Humahuaca, Quebrada de Humahuaca, Jujuy Province*)

The first signs of the cultivation of potatoes in the Quebrada de Humahuaca date back four thousand years. A great part of the potato varieties once cultivated here has been lost: the seventy varieties registered here forty years ago have been reduced by more than half. The varieties of Andean potatoes that have survived are distinguished by their flavor, color, and high protein content. In 2002, the Cauqueva Cooperative received the Slow Food Award for Biodiversity, and the Presidium was founded at the beginning of 2004 to recognize the cooperative's exceptional work.

YACÓN *(Quebrada de Humahuaca, San Salvador de Jujuy)*
The origin of this ancient Andean melon-flavored root is lost in Argentina's pre-Hispanic past. Yacón has a great potential for development because of its superb flavor, versatility, and potential use for those who suffer from diabetes. Slow Food will work to assist the producers of Yacón to promote their product and to find new markets in cooperation with the local association Fundandes (Foundation for the Environmental Development of Local Products). The thirty farmers from Quebrada involved in this Presidium cultivate land that was previously abandoned or neglected, and continue to prepare Yacón according to traditional recipes.

Armenia

MOTAL *(Aragatson and Ararat)*
The Armenian regions named after the country's highest mountains are home to shepherds who make *motal*, an age-old Armenian raw-milk goat cheese. *Motal* producers maintain small herds and work in extreme conditions with scarce financial resources at their disposal. Their cheeses are generally sold directly to consumers or through middlemen after they have just been taken from the brine: often they do not have enough time and resources to preserve the cheeses for longer in terracotta as traditional technique requires. The Presidium was created to allow producers to work together to improve cheesemaking techniques and to obtain the sanitary authorization for the sale of the product on national and international levels.

Bolivia

PANDO BRAZIL NUT *(Pando, Amazonian Region)*
The indigenous tribes of the Pando Altopiano, a Bolivian region bordering Brazil, depend on harvesting Brazil nuts for their livelihood. The

Brazil nut tree, Bertholletia *excelsa*, is a magnificent native species of the Amazon forest that can only grow in the primary forest, where an indigenous species of bee has evolved to pollinate the flowers on the highest branches. Brazil nuts are eaten raw, but are also used as a base for traditional, local products. The Presidium will be setting up a project to safeguard and promote the Pando Brazil nut and to ensure the postharvesting drying, packing, and transport stages do not compromise the quality of the product.

POTOSÍ LLAMA *(Potosí Region)*
The Incas were the first to domesticate the llama: they developed an economy based almost entirely on its meat, wool, and leather. Two llama breeds have been selected and developed in the Andean highlands: the Thampulli, selected for meat production, and the K'ara, which is best for wool. To create a wider market for llama products, it is necessary to introduce methods of animal husbandry, veterinary care, animal shelter systems, and to teach new techniques for preparing wool and meat. This Presidium will work to safeguard the millennial tradition of llama husbandry and thus protect an important part of Bolivia's culinary heritage.

Bosnia-Herzegovina
POZEGACA PLUM *SLATKO* *(Drina River Valley, Goradze)*
Slatko is the name for a handmade preserve of sweet, firm plums packed in dense sugar syrup made throughout Bosnia, Serbia, and Croatia. In the Upper Drina Valley, local Pozegaca plums are used for making *slatko* and *slivovitz*, a popular eau de vie. Once preserved, the plums have a wonderful light, creamy texture and a sweet flavor reminiscent of Turkish rose jam that pairs well with young cheeses. Recently, the local producers have joined to form an association to market *slatko* in Sarajevo markets and abroad.

Brazil
CANAPU COWPEA *(Piauí)*
The Canapu cowpea can be eaten fresh or dried, and it is an ingredient in a range of local dishes, including *mugunzá*, a dish made from corn, pork,

and beans eaten on feast days. Locals have refused to substitute this indigenous variety with more productive cowpea strains because of its excellent taste. Canapu cowpeas are particularly interesting for their sustainable and natural production system and their strong links to the identity of the local culture. The Presidia's objectives include the organization of a nucleus of producers, the creation of a production protocol, and the promotion of the Canapu cowpea to a broader market.

JUÇARA PALM HEART
(San Paolo State, Guaraní Reserves of Silveira and Boa Vista)
The most traditional and flavorful variety of *palmito*—or palm heart—comes from the Juçara (*Eutherpes edulis*), which grows naturally in the heart of the remaining portion of the Atlantic forest in southern Brazil. The Juçara requires little sunlight and no fertilizers or other treatment, and is also the variety most at risk. The Juçara palm heart is traditionally eaten raw with honey, but can also be boiled, roasted over an open fire, or fried. The Presidia's first steps are designed to identify ways to cultivate and harvest the palms and educate local families in the hope of reinvigorating the Rio Silveira Reserve.

MELIPONA HONEY
This Presidium was started to protect the Melipona honey, which is produced during the season of the flowering of the guarana plant by the Sateré Mawé Indians. The Melipona type of bees, which are small in size and do not sting, carry out a fundamental role in the ecosystem of the Amazonian forest by pollinating many different plants. The honey they produce is particularly fluid, aromatic, and delicious.

SATERÉ MAWÉ NATIVE GUARANÁ
(Amazonas and Pará States, Andirá-Marau Tribal Land)
Guaraná has been grown and harvested for thousands of years by the Sateré Mawé Indians. The Mawé do not "farm" per se: seeds that fall from Guaraná trees in the forest are collected and planted in clearings, watered by the rain, and tended minimally. The fruit extract is used to make a variety of syrups and drinks such as soda guaraná (Brazil's national drink). Guaraná is also important in Mawé religious culture, where it has a symbolic role similar to that of wine in the Catholic

liturgy. In addition to conserving native Guaraná, the Presidium will assist in developing and producing Guaraná syrups and other products for sale internationally.

UMBU *(Bahia State, Sertão Bahiano Municipalities)*
Umbu grows in the wild chaparral scrub across dry lands of the Sertão, and is an important resource for one of the poorest regions of Brazil. Umbu fruit can be as small as cherries or as large as lemons, and can be eaten fresh or made into jams or other sweetened preserves like fruit cheese. The fresh pulp is mixed with milk and sugar to make *umbuzada*, a rich beverage that is a common substitute for a full meal. The Presidium will draw up a production protocol that ensures the artisan quality of the products made from these fruits and raises the profile of the products on the national and international markets.

Canada
RED FIFE WHEAT *(Central Ontario, Alberta, Saskatchewan, and Manitoba)*
Red Fife wheat was first grown in the Otonabee region of what is now central Ontario in the 1840s. The unique properties of Red Fife and its adaptation to the Canadian climate have made it the genetic parent to virtually all Canadian wheat grown on the prairies. Today, Red Fife has survived only due to the work of a handful of organic heritage farmers who have been faithfully growing the wheat to keep it from extinction. Canada's first Presidium seeks to bring Red Fife wheat back into commercial circulation for use in artisan bread baking.

Chile
"BLUE EGG" CHICKEN *(Bio Bio and Araucania Regions)*
The Araucana is unique for a genetic trait that turns the bird's white eggs blue and its brown eggs green. It is unclear whether this is an indigenous breed or a descendant of the chickens first brought from Spain by the conquistadores. These chickens must be kept outside in order to produce eggs. In Chile, where agriculture is rapidly intensifying, the blue eggs are a uniquely valuable "self-identifying" product: the eggshells themselves are a sign of free-range quality and one that cannot be coun-

terfeited. The Presidium will support the research and selection of the historic Araucana breed.

CALBUCO BLACK-BORDERED OYSTER *(Calbuco Archipelago)*

On the island of Chiduapi, the tradition of catching wild oysters during the twice-daily low tides has been passed down for at least four generations. Calbuco black-bordered oysters are smaller than those found in other parts of the world—where they are cultivated in clusters suspended in the water—but offer better taste and texture and can easily be distinguished by their distinctive black fringe when opened. This Presidium's goal is to preserve a traditional and sustainable fishing practice, as well as to secure a distinct market for an excellent product. Currently, wild and cultivated oysters are sold at the same price in Chile.

MERKEN *(Municipality of Temuco)*

Merken is a spice mixture made primarily of a long, pointed chili pepper called *aji*. The dried chilies are smoked for half an hour, dried in the sun, and finely ground, first with a stone mortar, then in an automatic grinder. Lightly smoked coriander seeds and sea salt are added to the *aji* powder. *Merken* is always made with at least 70 percent chili powder and never more than 20 percent salt. The spice is used to flavor soups, meats, omelets, and salads and was once always found on the table in Chilean homes. The Presidium will promote the production of *merken* in traditional areas according to the authentic recipe, to encourage native farmers and spice-makers to cultivate and use local ingredients.

PURÉN WHITE STRAWBERRY *(Municipality of Purén)*

This strangely colorless fruit gave rise to all the world's strawberries, after European growers crossed it with other Native American varieties in the 1600s. The Chilean white strawberry is rotund with a small point and pale flesh, sometimes just barely tinged pink, but more often ivory with points of rose or red. It is eaten at Christmas and New Year's the way mandarin oranges are in Europe and North America. The Presidium was formed in collaboration with the city of Purén to spread knowledge and appreciation for this fruit, and the production protocol will ensure that the origins of this fruit are documented.

ROBINSON CRUSOE ISLAND SEAFOOD *(Juan Fernandez Archipelago, Robinson Crusoe Island)*

Eighty-three percent of animal and plant species on this island are indigenous, including native species of seaweed, birds, mammals, fish, and shellfish. The most celebrated catch, which dates back to at least 1700, is the local rock lobster, found only here and in the waters of the Desventuradas Islands to the north. Many other species of interesting fish, mollusks, and shellfish can be found, such as the red crab, the black sea urchin, and the sea bream. This Presidium was established to protect a unique ecosystem and an exceptional example of exclusively artisan fishing, to make the island's fish resources more widely known, and to ban industrial fishing vessels from entering these waters.

China

TIBETAN PLATEAU YAK CHEESE *(Maqin County, Golok Prefecture, Qinghai Province)*

At a small dairy located in a magnificent valley near Golok, Tibetan and Nepalese cheesemakers make a range of Tibetan and European-style cheeses from fresh yak's milk that showcase the excellent pasture of the region. This milk is skimmed for cheesemaking and retains a splendid flavor similar to that of springtime sheep's milk. The cheese can taste like a rough pecorino, and the aged forms develop strong grassy scents tempered by the milk's natural richness. The Presidium was set up with the aim of improving and promoting production at this small cheese-making plant on the Tibetan Plateau.

Croatia

GIANT ISTRIAN OX *(Istria)*

The Istrian ox, also known as Boscarin, is reared for milk, meat, and farm labor. Its massive frame and great strength made the breed an asset to any small farm until the advent of the tractor. Once numbering over fifty thousand, only two hundred exist today in Istria. To save this ancient breed, the Presidium will work with the Istrian Regional Authority to provide economic assistance to interested breeders. Later, when the oxen population increases, the development of a gastronomic niche will become the priority.

Cyprus
TSAMARELLA

Tsamarella is a traditional meat product that has been produced on the island for centuries. It was favored among sailors as long as two hundred years ago for its taste and keeping qualities. *Tsamarella* is made exclusively from goat breeds that are native to the island. The meat is covered with sea salt and dried in the sun. Then the salt is washed away and replaced by a coating of dried oregano, which imparts a deep red to brown color and a special savor to the goat meat.

Denmark
ARTISANAL SALTED BUTTER (*Jutland Peninsula*)

In all of Denmark, there now are only twenty local dairies producing artisanal salted butter. The butter's shape, variegated hay-yellow color, and sweet fragrance distinguish it from industrial products. One industrial brand now dominates the entire market, and resources for artisan producers are becoming scarce. Slow Food created this Presidium to address this problem, and to protect the centuries-old tradition of quality butter production. The first objective of this project is to bring new attention to the quality of this product among local consumers.

Ecuador
NACIONAL CACAO (*Quichua villages around the Municipality of Tena, Napo Province*)

The plantations of "Gran Cacao"—especially those in Venezuela and Ecuador—were the chief exporters of cacao to Europe for some three hundred years. In the early nineteenth century, Ecuador produced over 30 percent of the world's cacao with almost sixty million planted trees. Almost all were of the Nacional variety, a descendant of the cacao trees first developed and cultivated by the Mayans, and an exceptionally flavorful and delicate type found only in Ecuador. The Nacional Cacao Presidium's aim is to assist the indigenous cacao farming communities in the fermentation and drying of their cacao beans and help them obtain better prices, in turn providing enormous benefits in terms of the environmental conservation of the region.

France

BIGORRE GASCONY BLACK PIG *(Haute-Garonne and Haute-Pyrénées)*

The Bigorre Gascony black pig, though the most ancient breed of pig known in France, is unsuited for intensive high-yield farming. Local breeders began producing salame, bacon, cured sausages, and prosciutto, and most notably a cured whole ham, called Noir de Bigorre. Noir de Bigorre has a product certification (CCP), which correlates with a production protocol that outlines rigid rules for production and animal husbandry. The objective of this Presidium is to continue to promote and conserve the exceptional quality of this noble breed through products such as these.

PARDAILHAN BLACK TURNIP *(Languedoc-Roussillon, Hérault Province, Pardailhan)*

The quality of the Pardailhan black turnip has been celebrated for centuries, and at the end of the nineteenth century, it was sold at high prices at international fairs. After World War II, however, local agriculture slumped and the cultivation of these tubers declined. Pardailhan black turnips are beautifully tender with a subtle, sweet flavor considered unique thanks to the region's climate and soil. The Presidium will encourage more producers to cultivate this local variety (around 30 to 40 tons are grown annually), to help rebuild the region's agriculture.

RANCIO WINES OF ROUSSILLON *(Languedoc-Roussillon, Pyrénées-Orientales)*

Roussillon, nestled in the Pyrenees, is famous for the sweet wines Banyuls, Maury, and Rivesaltes. Made from Grenache and Maccabeu grapes, fermented dry, and aged in open barrels to promote oxidation—a process that gives the wines their characteristic rancio, or maderized, flavor—these wines are a unique part of the region's local winemaking history. Their intense flavors of licorice, walnuts, and vanilla are best enjoyed as an aperitif accompanying tapas. The Presidium was created to bring attention to this wine and to educate consumers interested in oxidized wines.

RENNES COUCOU CHICKEN *(Brittany and Pays-de-Loire)*

The gradual decline of the Rennes Coucou began in 1950 and is linked to the industrialization of Brittany and to the development of more competitive meat-producing breeds. In 1989, the ecological museum of Rennes brought together a group of farmers and enthusiasts, dedicated to keeping the animal a rustic farmyard variety and raising it free-range with natural and foraged food, to try to revive the breed. The Presidium's objective is to support the association in preserving and promoting the high quality of their birds.

SAINT-FLOUR PLANÈZE GOLDEN LENTIL (Auvergne, Cantal)
The quality of the golden lentil depends on the soil in which it is grown. The preparation of the terrain, the harvest, and the threshing of the lentil plants are key phases of production and are thus very important to coordinate to ensure an excellent product. The goal of the Presidium is to slowly increase the number of towns where the product is commercialized without compromising product quality. Given that the product is well known at a local level, the producers will work to expand beyond Saint-Flour into other areas of the Auvergne.

Great Britain
COLCHESTER NATIVE OYSTER (Essex)
Colchester native oysters are harvested from September through May in the shallow creeks off Mersea Island in Essex and north of the River Thames. The shell is flat and the flesh firm and often tinged with green. The distinctive creamy and salty taste comes from the marsh-fringed environment and the fact that the Blackwater is the second most salty river in the country. Stocks have suffered in recent years from pesticide run-off from farmland, but oystermen believe that global warming and the rising temperatures of the creek beds may turn out to be the greatest threat yet.

CORNISH PILCHARD (Cornish Coast)
Cornish salt pilchards taste similar to salted sardines, although they are meatier and left whole. Today, one plant, the Pilchard Works, continues the ancient tradition of salting pilchards using methods and equipment that date back almost a century. It has been designated a "working museum" by the British government, and is thus allowed to continue using its antique equipment. The Cornish salt pilchard Presidium was

created to recognize one of the British Isles' most historic foods, which dates back to the 1500s, yet is almost nonexistent today.

GLOUCESTER CHEESE *(Gloucestershire County)*

The county of Gloucestershire, comprising both the Cotswolds and the low-lying Severn Valley, has been a center of British cheese production for centuries. Traditionally, Gloucester cheese was produced with milk from the local Old Gloucester cattle breed. Sadly, as the production of Gloucester cheeses boomed, the use of traditional Old Gloucester cow's milk was phased out. The Presidium will encourage farmers in Gloucestershire and bordering counties to take up and maintain the ancient art of traditional raw milk Single and Double Gloucester cheesemaking to the highest standards using milk from Old Gloucester cows.

OLD GLOUCESTER BEEF *(Gloucestershire County)*

The Old Gloucester was already well known in the thirteenth century, when it was used for beef, milk, and draft work on Gloucestershire farms. Though it thrives with little care and produces fine-quality meat that improves with the animal's age, by 1972 only one viable herd remained. Local farmers have brought it back from the verge of disappearance over the past thirty years. The Gloucester Cattle Society encourages breeders across the United Kingdom, though the long-term goal of the Presidium is to revive the breed fully in its home territory.

THREE COUNTIES PERRY

(Counties of Herefordshire, Worcestershire, and Gloucestershire)

Perry is a little-known traditional English drink made from the fermented juice of Perry pears. The ancient Perry orchard is a classic part of the British landscape and its tall, majestic trees provide the basis for an important ecosystem, considered a unique habitat by British naturalists. Most British perry comes from the "three-counties" area of Herefordshire, Worcestershire, and Gloucestershire, and is consumed almost exclusively in the region of production. The Presidium works to establish guidelines to stabilize production quality, while retaining the natural variety of a product made from various Perry pear varieties.

Greece
MAVROTRAGANO (*Eastern Santorini Island*)
Unlike most European grapes, Santorini's Mavrotragano has never been grafted onto New World rootstock and is harvested entirely by hand. Typical of southern wines, it is clear violet in color with an opulent and fruity aroma redolent of some of the wines of the southern Rhône Valley. The excellent quality of the red Mavrotragano has attracted renewed attention from wine lovers in Greece and farther afield. This Presidium will support the activity of two extant producers to encourage new plantings, increase output, and set production guidelines to guarantee the quality of the product.

NIOTIKO (*Ios Island*)
Some four thousand goats roam the tranquil interior of Ios, but only twenty goatherds on Ios continue to produce the island's rustic, raw milk cheese, *niotiko*. The animals are kept on pasture and fed only natural products. *Niotiko*'s flavors recall the aromatic herbs of the Mediterranean scrub: wild sage, thyme, and pine. The Presidium will endeavor to join the shepherds into a cooperative to establish the best aging procedures, so ensuring a market for this ancient product. In this way pastoral farming can survive and Ios' rural culture may have a future.

Guatemala
HUEHUETENANGO HIGHLAND COFFEE
(*Western Altipiano of Huehuetenango, Municipalities of San Pedro Necta, La Libertad, Cuilco, La Democracia, and Todos Santos Cuchumatanes*)
Huehuetenango, at the foot of the Cuchumatanes, is one of the best regions in Guatemala for coffee production. The indigenous inhabitants of Huehuetenango are among the poorest in Central America as a result of their historic isolation from the Guatemalan population. Adding to that, the recent collapse in coffee prices has caused a similar collapse in the local economy. The only means of escaping this vicious circle is through developing high-end niche-market coffees. The next step of the Presidium will be the constitution of coffee-roasting facilities in Guatemala, in order to allow the producers to promote their coffee on the American market.

Hungary

MANGALICA SAUSAGE *(Kiskunsag Region)*
The producers who still make sausages from the meat of Mangalica pigs are a small, dedicated, and well-organized group, all of whom are certified organic. They are located in the Kiskunsag region just south of Budapest at the center of one of the most important national parks in the country. These farmers raise the pigs, produce sausages and hams in-house, and even produce their own paprika to season their sausages. The Presidium is working to help this group promote their product by gradually increasing the number of animals raised and intends to bring together other groups of Hungarians who are trying to save this breed.

India

DEHRADUN BASMATI RICE
(Uttar Pradesh State, Saharanpur [Punjab Basmati, Desi Basmati], Uttaranchal State [Kasturi Basmati, Dehradun])
Basmati rice varieties were developed over centuries in the agricultural lands carved out of the foothills of the Himalayas. The first written reference to Basmati rice dates back to the beginning of the eighteenth century, and since then, farmers have developed hundreds of types. Dehradun Basmati rice is cultivated without pesticides and can range in color from clear yellow to deep, dark brown, and is prized for its fragrance, with scents as diverse as jasmine and sandalwood. The Presidium is working to promote Dehradun Basmati rice varieties both nationally and internationally through events, publications, and dinners.

MUSTARD SEED OIL *(Chanadn Hari, Uttar Pradesh)*
India is one of the world's primary producers of oil seeds, and mustard in particular. Small producers plant mustard because it guarantees a high yield with low production costs. The harvested seeds are pressed in *ghani*, or small mills. Mustard is a symbol of springtime and rebirth and plays a fundamental role in both Indian culture and Indian cuisine. Mustard seed oil is also important to traditional Ayurvedic medicine, where it is used for massages and to cure muscular pains. The primary objective of the Presidium is to improve the collection, selection, con-

servation, and distribution of various mustard varieties, as well as conversion to organic agriculture.

Ireland
IRISH RAW COW'S MILK CHEESE

Driven by a mixture of idealism and the need to make a living from their farms, a new generation of artisan producers and cheesemakers drew upon skills and knowledge from all over the world to reintroduce cheesemaking to rural Ireland. Using the same raw materials that served the island's ancient cheesemakers, they made a diverse array of new cheeses from local, fresh raw milk. The Presidium will celebrate the distinctive merits of these cheeses and, by working to protect them for future enjoyment, continue the revival of artisan cheesemaking traditions.

Lebanon
DARFIYEH *(Bcharré, Ehden, Inata)*

Darfiyeh is an ancient cheese made with raw goat's milk, produced in the Mount Lebanon range, aged and packaged in cleaned goatskins. The Presidium was founded to protect the traditional production of an ancient cheese at risk of extinction. Over time, the project hopes to include all producers of this cheese. Among its goals, the Presidium hopes to resolve the problem of pasturing the goats, which must be regulated but not fenced in. The Souk El Tayeh, the first farmers' market in Beirut where small-scale producers can sell their products directly, is an important outlet for this Presidium.

Madagascar
ANDASIBE RED RICE
(Municipalities of Ambatavola, Beforona, and Andasibe, Tamatave Province)

In Madagascar, all varieties of locally grown rice fetch the same price at market, but there is one variety, a dusty red grain, that sells out before the others. Called *vary mena* in local dialect, this red rice is considered Madagascar's indigenous variety and is thought to be more nutritious than white rice. The Andasibe red rice Presidium combines an innovative agricultural approach with the promotion of five indigenous red rice varieties. This technique gives high yields with minimum impact on the environment and, most importantly, is an economically viable alternative to slash-and-burn cultivation.

MANANARA VANILLA *(Ten villages in the Mananara-Nord Biosphere Reserve)*
Madagascar produces over two-thirds of the world's vanilla, all of which is cultivated in the island's humid northern regions. Larger plantations are slowly replacing the traditional style of cultivation, in which vines are planted at the base of large trees in the rainforest. This Presidium is working to improve cultivation techniques and to develop autonomy among farmers in the sale and marketing of this valuable spice. By forming a cooperative and setting up a structure for direct purchase, the Presidium will guarantee that a higher percentage of profits from production of one of the world's most precious spices is reinvested in the community.

Malaysia
BARIO RICE *(Island of Borneo, Sarawak State, Kelabit High Plains)*
The terrain in Sarawak, on the island of Borneo, has been transformed into rice paddies through centuries of labor; buffalo live on the fallow fields, eating the weeds and fertilizing the soil. Bario rice has tiny, opaque white grains. It is a favorite among Malaysian chefs and ideal for desserts like rice pudding. The Presidium has been developed to give concrete assistance to local growers and thus help them reach a more remunerative market. In the long term, the Presidium will work to develop seed farms that will aid the conservation of diverse strains of Bario rice and perpetuate the purest versions of this extraordinary variety.

Mexico
CHINANTLA VANILLA *(Oaxaca)*
The hot and humid forest of Chinantla is both the only region in the world where vanilla grows wild and the area with the species' greatest genetic diversity. Vanilla farming fell into neglect in the nineteenth century and was only revived in the 1990s as an alternative to coffee farm-

ing. Chinantla vanilla is finely scented and the beans are soft and flexible with a deep brown coffee color. The Presidium is working to identify the various varieties of vanilla, and to improve its production with a small group of farmers dedicated to improving quality and reducing agricultural impact on the forest.

TEHUACÁN AMARANTH (Tehuacán Valley, Puebla)

Amaranth has been almost completely abandoned, despite being fundamental to the diet of pre-Hispanic peoples from Mexico down to Peru. Rich in protein and higher in iron than spinach, it could enrich the poor diet of many in Central and South America. The Presidium will work to promote a traditional sweet food based on amaranth (alegría), develop experimental amaranth-based products to be used in gluten-free diets, and set up a center for exhibiting, growing, and selling amaranth in a "Water Museum." The museum will also host other Mexican Presidia and thus become an important focal point where people can learn about biodiversity and pre-Hispanic traditions.

Morocco

ARGAN OIL (Essaouira, Taroudant, and Chtouka Ait Baha Provinces)

Argan oil is a deep golden yellow in color, and the flavor is clean-cut and intense, with notes of hazelnut and toast. A few drops added to a freshly cooked pot of couscous or to a fish or meat tagine gives an additional depth of flavor. Mixed with almonds and honey, Argan oil is used for amlou beldi, the traditional creamy spread that is served with bread and mint tea as a sign of welcome. This new industry provides an important income for women in this area, who often have few opportunities for work. This Presidium supports the work of the cooperatives by seeking new outlets for the sale of Argan oil.

The Netherlands

AGED ARTISAN GOUDA (Green Hart Region)

Some three hundred farmers in the Netherlands still produce raw-milk farmstead cheese. Aged artisan gouda, called Boeren-Goudse Oplegkaas in Dutch, is made from raw milk only during summer, when cows graze on the open pastures of peat meadows, and is peerless in taste. Its sweet mild flavor blooms in the mouth with a well-structured aftertaste, light acidity, and the warm caramel taste that characterizes most gouda. Urban expansion, increased production costs, hygiene restrictions, and cheap pasteurized imitations all endanger traditional cheesemaking. This Presidia promotes Boeren-Goudse Oplegkaas directly to consumers.

CHAAM CAPON *(Chaam village)*

This indigenous European chicken breed belongs to the species of the so-called "peeled" chicken found from northern France to northern Germany. The most visible characteristics are the black spots (peels) on the silver-white feathers. They have blue-greyish legs, white earlobes, and white eggs. Historically the meat was prized by well-to-do Dutch families and was served often at gala dinners in the Royal Palace. A few years ago some hobby breeders succeeded in back-crossing to produce the original Chaam capon, which had been officially considered extinct. Slow Food is connecting producers to colleagues who raise the famous Poulet de Bresse in France and the Morozzo capon in Italy.

EASTERN SCHELDT EUROPEAN LOBSTER *(Eastern Scheldt, Zeeland)*

Homarus gammarus lives hidden among the rocks and stones of the dams and dikes along the Eastern Scheldt. To prevent overfishing and the depletion of this unique variety of lobster, fishing is carried out on small-scale terms and strictly regulated. Fishermen carefully return small lobsters and females with eggs back into the water to provide the basis of lobster fishing for years to come. The Eastern Scheldt European lobster Presidium recognizes a sustainable low-impact fishing system and a uniquely well-organized and responsible group of small artisan producers.

TEXEL SHEEP CHEESE *(Texel Island)*

After World War II, the production of artisan Texel cheese was drastically reduced, and with it five centuries of local history is disappearing. This rustic cheese, made from raw sheep's milk, has a lingering elemental flavor of the sea. Many endangered farms can be saved, along with the island's rural economy, by the added income from traditional cheese production. Sheep play an important role in preserving the island's ecosystem by grazing salt-resistant vegetation. The Presidium aims to help

Texel cheese regain its reputation for quality and to encourage additional farmers to adopt quality standards.

Norway

ARTISAN SOGNEFJORD *GEITOST* (Sognefjord, Undredal)

The villages scattered along the Sognefjord, Norway's longest and deepest fjord, have an ancient tradition of fresh raw-milk goat cheese, centered in the village of Undredal. The village's sweet, caramelized "brown" cheese—*geitost*—is made with an unusual technique found only in Norway and Sweden. In 1991, local authorities demanded that Undredal's cheesemakers use pasteurized milk. In response, small regional cheesemakers founded Norsk Gardsost to defend traditional production methods and raw milk cheeses. The Presidium promotes both farmers' rights and the quality foods produced in the remote ecosystem of the Sognefjord.

CURED AND SMOKED HERRING (Sunnmøre)

Herring have been an essential part of the Norwegian diet for thousands of years. As early as the thirteenth century, the country was already enforcing laws regulating herring fisheries. A series of unfavorable fishing seasons in the 1950s compelled most small processing companies to shut down. Competition with mass food production has gradually estranged Norwegians from consuming artisan herring. The Presidium is working to educate consumers about this product, to revive traditional production techniques at risk of extinction, and to support small-scale sustainable fishing.

STOCKFISH FROM THE ISLE OF SØRØYA (Finnmark, Isle of Sørøya)

The isle of Sørøya has long been known for *tørrfisk*, or stockfish, made by local fishermen and artisans. The cod used in making stockfish are fished mainly with a *juksa*, or a hook, and line, which allows the artisan to attain a more prized product than that caught in nets. The Presidium aims to promote this traditional product, made from cod caught with sustainable fishing techniques. Sørøya is one of only two areas of the world where cod shoals are in good health.

Peru

ANDEAN FRUIT *(Cajamarca, San Marcos, Chota, and Baños del Inca Provinces)*
The Cajamarca region at the foot of the Andes boasts an extraordinary variety of domesticated plants, particularly fruit, attributable both to this region's wealth of natural resources and the pre-Columbian Incas' belief that all forms of life—men, animals, vegetables, as well as wind, streams, and land—are intimately connected. The Presidium has worked to identify the traditional region of production for three selected fruit varieties, the tomatillo, poro poro, and pushgay, and has assembled a group of eight interested producers. The objective of the project is to define a protocol outlining both the cultivation of the fruit and the production of jams, juices, and other fruit-based products.

ANDEAN SWEET POTATOES *(Calca Province, Cusco Region)*
Compared to Europe and North America, where one species of potato dominates cultivation, in the Andes there are nine species, traditionally selected for color, shape, and flavor, now diversified into over nine hundred varieties. The Presidium has selected the five most interesting varieties from an agricultural and gastronomic perspective—the Locka, Ococuri, Ccompis, Pitiquiña, and Mactillo—and has begun work with eight farmers who will improve the quality of the seed stock and dedicate more land to growing potatoes for seed potato selection. The next objective is to define a production protocol for each variety that guarantees the traceability of the potatoes, prohibits the use of pesticides and fertilizers, and ensures the quality of the final product.

KAÑIHUA FROM THE ANDES *(Municipalities of Ayaviri, Cupi, and Santa Rosa)*
Kañihua is a unique indigenous grass most often used to make a fine brown flour, called *kañihuaco,* for oven-dried *kispiño,* cakes, refreshments, soups, and even hot drinks. The pre-Columbian people domesticated it well before 1000 BC, as a good substitute (if only partially) for animal by-products, such as milk, that can be difficult to obtain high in the Andes. Over time, many farmers have chosen to grow more profitable crops like oats and medicinal herbs. The Kañihua Presidium intends to pursue a variety of objectives with the main goal of preserving the identity of this local cultivation and exploring new uses and economic outlets.

TRADITIONAL *CHUÑO BLANCO* (*Puno*)

The processing of potatoes into *chuño* is a technique with ancient origins. It is a complex procedure that alternates drastic hot and cold temperatures, taking advantage of the frigid waters of the rivers in the Andean plateau and the baking midday sun there. The end product is a very light, white potato (essentially dehydrated and then frozen) that resembles a piece of chalk and can last a very long time when processed well. The Presidium wants to protect this ancient method of processing and using only bitter potatoes (otherwise inedible), utilizing the best local varieties.

Poland

OSCYPEK (*Tatra Mountains*)

Oscypek, a smoked, hard cheese made from the milk of Zackel sheep, has been produced in the Tatra Mountains since the fourteenth century. The cheese is compact with a pale straw-yellow color, offering a clean, lightly toasted aroma with pleasant mineral notes and a chestnut flavor. *Oscypek* is usually served in thin slices accompanied by wine, vodka, or beer, and is also excellent grilled. The project's primary objective is to promote this product within the region, particularly to the best restaurants of Krakow and Warsaw. *Oscypek* could also become an important agricultural export.

POLISH MEAD (*Warsaw*)

Mead, along with vodka, was once prepared in all Polish homes. Today, few producers remain, and only one mead maker in all Poland still uses the traditional recipe, which begins by boiling honey and water mixed with local herbs. The mixture is then fermented and aged in large stainless steel barrels. Some varieties are traditionally flavored with raspberry, apple, or grape juice. The Presidium will promote and develop authentic Polish mead to guarantee that it's sold at a fair price on the market. Only then will producers overcome their fear of the initial investment and revive this ancient product.

Portugal

MIRANDESA SAUSAGE *(Trás-os-Montes Region, Miranda do Douro)*

Among Portuguese cow breeds, the Mirandesa is an important source of identity in and around Miranda do Duoro and is considered one of the most valuable. Mirandesa sausage, or *chouriço*, is made according to a centuries-old, traditional recipe. It's cooked over a wood fire, left to dry, and smoked for three to four days. Once it is completely dry, it can be enjoyed raw, grilled, or boiled. Those who raise the Mirandesa are passionate about keeping this hardy breed alive, and the Presidium was created to raise the profile of Mirandesa sausage.

Romania

BRÂNZÁ DE BURDUF *(Brasov County)*

Using sheep's and goat's milk, Transylvanian shepherds make *kas*, the basis for Brânzá de Burduf, the most valuable among Romanian cheeses and the most suitable for long conservation. According to ancient tradition, Brânzá de Burduf must be aged wrapped in a thin sheet of pine tree bark, its flavor becoming increasingly spicy with the length of aging. Much must be done to establish consistent quality among the various artisan producers. A production protocol will be drafted, defining the feed of the animals and the production and aging processes, vouching for the final product's traceability and high quality.

Spain

EUSKAL TXERRIA PIG *(Basque Territories)*

Euskal Txerria pigs are raised naturally on acorns, chestnuts, hazelnuts, and grass. Their diet is regulated only during the two months leading up to slaughter, when corn, fava beans, and bran are introduced. The sole Presidium producer cures the meat to make chorizo (aged seven months), *lomo* (aged five months), and *salchichón*, which is eaten fresh, and is now experimenting with prosciutto. This project was created to bring attention to the cured meats made from these pigs and to motivate ranchers and local butchers to adhere to methods that will guarantee the quality and traceability of the product.

GAMONEDO *(Eastern Asturias, Municipalities of Cangas de Onís and Onís)*

Asturias is famous for Cabrales, one of the spiciest blue cheeses in Europe, as well as *gamonedo*, a cheese made from the mixed milks of goats, cows, and sheep. Lightly smoked in oak embers and aged in stone-lined caves for up to five months, *gamonedo* is creamy with a slight peppery flavor. Its bluish veins usually extend throughout the cheese and grow spontaneously, unlike the blue molds in Roquefort or Gorgonzola. The Presidium will work to restructure some of the remote aging caves and make them available to shepherds and valley cheesemakers alike.

GANXET BEANS *(Vallès)*

Recent studies in genetics have established that this variety has ties to Mexican species. It was brougth to Catalonia in the nineteenth century following the frequent migrations of Catalans to Central and South America. The bean is easily recognizable for the flattened hook shape of its seeds, which is maintained even after cooking. Its very thin skin, buttery texture, and delicate taste make it a particularly versatile product. Because of its low but high-valued yield, it is sold at high prices at market. This has led to the proliferation of look-alike hybrids with lesser taste, which threaten to replace the original bean if it is not protected.

JILOCA SAFFRON *(Teruel Province, Jiloca)*

Brought to the Iberian Peninsula more than a thousand years ago by North African Arabs, saffron became an indispensable component in various traditional dishes. Jiloca has always been known for its saffron, locally known as *oro de los pobres*, or "poor man's gold." Harvesting the crocus stigmas and preparing the saffron involve two or three weeks of heavy work and contribute to the spice's notable expense on the market. The Presidium will work to connect communication about this product with guided tastings and comparative samplings of various types of saffron, including those made from lesser spices and added aromas.

SITGES MALVASIA *(Sitges, Catalonia)*

The present survival of Sitges Malvasia is due to the farsightedness of Catalan diplomat Manuel Llopis de Casades, who bequeathed his properties in Sitges to the Hospital de Saint Juan Bautista de Sitges on the condition that they continue production of Sitges Malvasia from 2.5 hectacres of vines on the land. The resulting wine is a strong sweet passito granted the *Denominación d'Origen Penedès* in 1991. The Presidium aims to share the compelling, romantic story behind this wine, to help preserve these vineyards from land speculation, and perhaps to support other enterprising producers wishing to plant Malvasia in neighboring areas.

TOLOSA BLACK BEANS *(Basque Territories, Oria River Valley)*
Tolosa beans were already known at the beginning of the ninth century, and have been cultivated on small plots in the Oria River Valley for at least a millennium. Dense and aromatic, simply boiled they become a delicious and velvety soup. The dried bean is unusual in not requiring soaking before cooking. The Presidium works to help the producers of tolosa beans defend the integrity of their product and educate consumers and restaurateurs to allow them to distinguish authentic tolosa beans from the inferior varieties sold under the same name.

Sweden
REINDEER *SUOVAS* *(Swedish Sápmi)*
Reindeer meat is the traditional food of the Sámi people, a native European tribe that live in an area called Sápmi, which spreads across the north of Sweden, Norway, Finland, and Russia. Presidium *suovas* is made from semi-wild reindeer that feed entirely on natural forage and never receive any antibiotics or man-made feeds; it is prepared throughout the year with the most traditional techniques of salting, smoking, and curing. The Presidium works to raise awareness of this ancient cured meat and to encourage the use of reindeer meat, instead of introducing high-input domesticated animals that tax this Arctic region's delicate ecosystem.

Switzerland
LOCARNO VALLEYS *CICITT*
(Vallemaggia and Valle Verzasca of the Canton Ticino)
This ancient, traditional sausage is made with the less-valued parts of the goat and its fat. To these are added the blanched stomach and heart, spiced with salt, finely chopped garlic, pepper, cinnamon, nut-

meg, cloves, and red and white wine. *Cicitt* can be found from the end of October through December; during the summer, the goats are out to pasture.

MUGGIO VALLEY *ZINCARLIN* *(Muggio Valley)*
Zincarlin is a raw milk cheese seasoned with black pepper, usually made from cow's milk, sometimes with small quantities of goat's milk. One of its distinctive features is that the curds are never broken but left to drain for a day and a night through a cloth, then pressed for six hours. The Presidium has managed to recover the traditional version of the cheese, aged for at least two months, and treated with white wine during the first fifteen days of aging. In 2004, the first draft of a production protocol was written, suitable premises for aging were found, and an association was created with the aim of collecting, developing, and marketing the cheese.

United States
AMERICAN RAW MILK CHEESES
(California, Connecticut, Indiana, New Jersey, North Carolina, Oregon, Vermont, Virginia, and Wisconsin)
Throughout the past twenty-five years, American cheesemakers have developed extraordinary handcrafted raw milk cheeses that highlight the unique flavors of the land, soil, and climate where they originate, as well as reflecting the uniqueness of the individual producers. The cheeses included in this Presidium are made with raw milk from either the cheesemaker's or a local farm, and created with a powerful commitment to sustainable agriculture and artisan production. A group of tasters select the best American raw milk cheeses each year from among participating producers. These cheeses become the ambassadors of the project, representing the Presidium and serving as an example of high quality for American producers.

ANISHINAABEG MANOOMIN *(Minnesota State, Anishinaabeg Tribal Lands)*
Genetically more similar to corn than rice, Manoomin is actually an aquatic grass and predates the first indigenous population by at least a millennium. The fresh grains—all colors of green, tan, and brown—are

husked and then parched in a wide shallow drum. Manoomin tastes richly complex with notes of mushrooms, forest undergrowth, and wood smoke. Several threats face this traditional indigenous North American product. Key among them are proliferation of genetically modified rice, which will devastate natural diversity of the crops and the destruction of the natural ecosystems of the Minnesota lakes. The Presidium works with the White Earth Land Recovery Project to promote the identification (labeling) and consumption of traditionally harvested and prepared wild rice.

CAPE MAY SALT OYSTER *(New Jersey, Delaware Bay, and Cape May)*
Once abundant but now endangered by overfishing, pollution, parasitic diseases, and damage done to the Delaware Bay, the Cape May salt oyster Slow Food Presidium supports harvesters as they maintain a low environmental-impact system of cultivation, such as that tried and tested in France. A state of the art "Rack and Bag" technique produces oyster spat in hatcheries that are then placed on nets hanging from racks stretching across shallows exposed to the tide. The oysters, "planted" in the sea, feed naturally by filtering ocean water and are not given any artificial feed or antibiotics.

HERITAGE TURKEY BREEDS
Nearly all of the 270 million turkeys raised now in the United States are one variety, Large White, introduced in the 1950s and subsequently bred for industrial production, rather than the wild, indigenous breeds, which are the ancestors of all modern turkeys. Raised free-range on pasture and forage, "heritage" turkeys develop much stronger legs, thighs, and breasts than industrially produced birds, and their meat is very firm and dark in color, as well as succulent, rich, and flavorful. The Presidium has encouraged farmers to raise the eight traditional varieties, and has been the single most successful agricultural conservation project in the United States.

UNITED STATES ARK OF TASTE

BEVERAGES
American Artisanal Cider
Traditional American Root Beer
Shrub
Greenthread Tea

CEREALS/GRAINS
Chapalote Corn
Chicos (dried corn)
New Orleans French Bread
Anishinaabeg Manoomin
(Anishinaabeg Wild Rice)
Tuscarora White Corn

CHEESES
Creole Cream Cheese
Dry Monterey Jack Cheese

FRUITS
American Heirloom Apples
Capital Reef Apple
Gravenstein Apple of Sonoma
County

Blenheim Apricot

Bronx Grapes
Charbono Grape of California

Napa Gamau/Valdiguie Grape of
California
Norton Grape

Meyer Lemon of California's
Central Coast

Crane Melon

Pawpaw

Baby Crawford Peach
Fay Elberta Peach
Oldmixon Free Peach
Rio Oso Gem Peach
Silver Logan Peach
Sun Crest Peach

American Heirloom Pears

Beaver Dam Pepper
Chiltepin Chile
Fish Pepper
Jimmy Nardello's Sweet Italian
Frying Pepper
New Mexico Native Chiles
Sheepnose Pimiento
Wenk's Yellow Hot Pepper

American Persimmon
Japanese Massaged Dried
    Persimmon

Elephant Heart Plum
Inca Plum
Laroda Plum
Mariposa Plum
Padre Plum
Wild Plum

Southern Louisiana Satsuma
    (Brown's Select and Owari)

Amish Pie Squash
Boston Marrow Squash
Sibley Squash

Louisiana Heritage Strawberry
Native American Strawberry

Pixie Tangerine of Ojai Valley

Amish Paste Tomato
Aunt Molly's Husk Tomato (aka
    Ground Cherry)
Aunt Ruby's German Green
    Tomato
Burbank Tomato
Cherokee Purple Tomato
German Pink Tomato
Orange Oxheart Tomato
Sudduth Strain Brandywine
    Tomato

Yellow-Meated Watermelon

HERBS & SPICES
Desert/Mexican Oregano
Traditional Sea Salt from Hawai'i

MEAT & POULTRY
Corriente Cattle
Florida Cracker Cattle
Milking Devon Cattle
Pineywoods Cattle

Black Jersey Giant Chicken
Delaware Chicken
Dominique Chicken
New Hampshire Chicken
Plymouth Rock Chicken
White Jersey Giant Chicken
Wyandotte Chicken

American Buff Goose
American Pilgrim Goose

Ossibaw Island Hog
Mulefoot Hog

American Rabbit
American Chinchilla Rabbit
Giant Chinchilla Rabbit
Silver Fox Rabbit

Navajo-Churro Sheep

American Bronze Turkey
Bourbon Red Turkey
Jersey Buff Turkey
Naragansett Turkey

MEAT PRODUCTS
New Orleans Daube Glacé
Southern Louisiana Hogshead
    Cheese
Southern Louisiana Ponce
Southern Louisiana Traditional
    Tasso

NUTS
American Butternut
American Chestnut
American Native Pecan
Emory Oak "Bellota" Acorn
Nevada Single Leaf Pinyon
(pine nut)
Shagbark Hickory Nut

PULSES
Arikara Yellow Bean
Bolito Beans
Brown Tepary Bean
Cherokee Trail of Tears Bean
Christmas Lima Bean
Crowder Cowpeas (Mississippi
Silver Hull Bean)
Four Corners Gold Bean
Hidatsa Red Bean
Hidatsa Shield Figure Bean
Hutterite Soup Bean
Marrowfat Bean
Mayflower Bean
Mesquite Flour Bean
O'odham Pink Bean
Petaluma Gold Rush Bean
Rio Zape Bean
Santa Maria Pinquito Bean
Southern Field Peas
True Red Cranberry Bean
White Tepary Bean
Yellow Indian Woman Bean

SHELLFISH & FISH
Bay Scallop
Delaware Bay Oyster

Goeyduck
Louisiana Oyster
Olympia Oyster
Wild Catfish
Wild Gulf Coast Shrimp

VEGETABLES
Inchelium Red Garlic
Lorz Italian Garlic

Amish Deer Tongue Lettuce
Grandpa Admire's Lettuce
Speckled Lettuce
Tennis Ball Lettuce (black seeded)

I'itoi Onion

Green Mountain Potato
Ivis White Cream Sweet Potato
Ozette Potato

Gilfeather Turnip

WINES & VINEGARS
Wine Vinegar

PREPARED FOODS
American Artisanal Sauerkraut
Kalo Poi Taro from Hawai'i
Roman Taffy Candy

OTHER
Alaskan Birch Syrup
Traditional Cane Syrup
Traditional Sorghum Syrup

HOW TO CONTACT SLOW FOOD

SLOW FOOD USA
20 Jay Street, Suite 313
Brooklyn, NY 11201
Tel: 718-260-8000
Fax: 718-260-8068
info@slowfoodusa.org
www.slowfoodusa.org

**SLOW FOOD INTERNATIONAL
AND SLOW FOOD ITALY**
Via della Mendicità Istruita 8
12042 Bra (Cuneo)
Tel: 39-0172-419-611
Fax: 39-0172-421-293
info@slowfood.it
international@slowfood.com

SLOW FOOD FRANCE
Agro Montpellier
Bâtiment 12
34060 Montpellier
Tel: 33-4-99-61-30-45
Toll-free: 0800-90-71-64
Fax: 33-4-99-61-30-14
france@slowfood.fr
www.slowfood.fr

SLOW FOOD GERMANY
Hasseler Weg 3
27232 Sulingen
Tel: 49-4271-951165
Fax: 49-4271-951166
info@slowfood.de
www.slowfood.de

SLOW FOOD JAPAN
Wellcom21, Tohoku-Fukushi-Univ.
6-149-1, Kunimigaoka, Aoba-ku,
Sendai
989-3201 Japan
Tel: 81 022-727-2347
Fax: 81 022-727-2281
slowfood@tfu-ac.net
www.slowfoodjapan.net

SLOW FOOD SWITZERLAND
Case postale, 8034 Zurich
Tel: 800-56-28-98
Fax: 41-1-380-2990
info@slowfood.ch
www.slowfood.ch

TOLL-FREE NUMBERS AND WEBSITES

Australia	1800-00-96-84	www.safoodcentre.com
Austria	0800-28-11-41	www.slowfoodaustria.at
Belgium	0800-79-329	
Canada	1 8662-66-66-61	
Ireland	1800-55-39-30	www.slowfoodireland.com
The Netherlands	0800-022-77-94	www.slowfood.nl
Poland		www.slowfood.pl
Singapore		www.slowfood.org.sg
Spain	9009-86-946	
Taiwan		www.slowfood.com.tw
UK	0800-901-71-232	

INTERNET SITES OF SLOW FOOD INSTITUTIONS WITHIN ITALY:
Agenzia di Pollenzo: www.agenziadipollenzo.com
Foundation for Biodiversity: www.fondazioneslowfood.it;
    www.slowfoodfoundation.org
Terra Madre: www.terramadre2006.org
University of Gastronomic Sciences: www.unisg.it
Wine Bank: www.bancadelvino.it

CHRONOLOGY
OF THE MOVEMENT

1949: Carlo Petrini is born to Maria and Giuseppe Petrini on June 22.

1966: At age seventeen, Petrini becomes president of the local branch of the Society of St. Vincent de Paul in Bra.

1971: Petrini and his friends found the Circolo Leonardo Cocito, based in the historic center of Bra.

1974: The first issue of *In Campo Rosso* is published.

1975: The Spaccio di Unità Popolare store opens, and on June 17, Radio Bra Onde Rosse makes its first transmission. The pirate radio station remains on the air until 1978.

1976: Petrini becomes a member of the Bra city council representing the PDUP (Democratic Party for Proletarian Unity) and in June participates in the founding of the Cooperativa Libraria la Torre, a bookstore.

1978: The "Trio from Bra," made up of Petrini, Azio Citi, and Giovanni Ravinale, debuts at the Club Tenco in Sanremo.

1979: The first international Canté i'euv festival is held in Piedmont from April 5 to 8; the festival is repeated in 1980 and 1981.

1980: Petrini is reelected a member of the Bra city council for the PDUP. In May, he meets the Nete twins in Monforte.

1981: The Osteria dell'Unione in Treviso opens on May 1. In November, the first meeting of the Free and Meritorious Association of the Friends of Barolo is held.

1982: The Cooperativa I Tarocchi is founded in Bra on April 16. In October, the first issue of the cultural magazine *La Gola* appears.

1983: In June, Petrini begins his career as a journalist with contributions to *La Gola*, among other publications.

1984: The l'Osteria del Boccondivino opens in December, located at number 12 Via Mendicità Istruita, Bra.

1986: The I Tarocchi co-op opens the Osteria dell'Arco in Alba in March. Arci Gola (later to become "Arcigola") is founded in a series of meetings held on July 26 and 27 in Barolo and at the Fontanafredda estate in Serralunga d'Alba. Petrini is unanimously elected president. The first issue of *Gambero Rosso*, then an eight-page insert in the newspaper *Il Manifesto*, appears on December 16.

1987: The first issue of *A/R* (*Andata e Ritorno*), a magazine devoted to leisure and gastronomy, appears as a supplement to the April 23 issue of the newspaper *L'Unità*, with contributions by Petrini; *A/R* remains in circulation until 1988. On November 3, the Slow Food Manifesto, written by Folco Portinari, appears in *Gambero Rosso*. The first edition of *Vini d'Italia* is published in Florence in December.

1988: Arcigola's first national congress is held in San Gimignano, Montalcino, and Siena from November 10 to 13.

1989: The inaugural meeting of the International Slow Food Movement is held at the Opéra Comique in Paris from December 8 to 10, attended by delegates from around the world.

1990: The first edition of *Osterie d'Italia* marks the debut of Slow Food Editore. The first international convention on the wines of Piedmont is held November 15 to 18. The first Slow Food international congress meets in Venice in November–December.

1991: At its second international congress, held June 13 to 16, Arcigola adopts the name of Arcigola Slow Food. In the autumn, the first international convention devoted to Tuscan wines takes place.

1992: Arcigola Slow Food edits the daily *Vinitaly News* during the Vinitaly wine fair in Verona and presents a wide selection of foods and wines at its stand. Slow Food Germany is launched.

1994: The Taste Workshops debut at the Vinitaly fair in Verona, as part of Arcigola Slow Food's "Grand Menu" presentation.

1995: Slow Food France is launched.

1996: The first issue of *Slow* appears in April. From November 29 to December 2, the first Salone del Gusto is held in Turin.

1997: The mission statement of the "Ark of Taste" is published on June 29, during a conference at the Fontanafredda estate. The biennial trade fair Cheese: Milk in All Its Shapes and Forms is launched in Bra from September 19 to 22. The second international congress of the Slow Food movement meets in Orvieto from October 16 to 19.

1998: On June 27, the Agenzia di Pollenzo foundation is formed, with the goal of raising funds for a Slow Food campus on the former royal estate. Petrini begins writing for *La Stampa*. The second Salone del Gusto is held from November 5 to 9. Slow Food Japan is launched.

1999: Città Slow is founded, with the cities of Bra, Orvieto, Positano, and Greve in Chianti as founding members. The Scientific Commission of the Ark is founded.

2000: The first Slow Food Awards for the Defense of Biodiversity are awarded in Bologna in October. On October 30, Petrini is named "Communicator of the Year" at the International Wine and Spirit Competition. Slow Food USA is founded in New York with a thousand members and twenty Convivia.

2001: The web site slowfood.com is launched. In Porto, Portugal, the second presentation of Biodiversity Awards is made.

2002: The fifth national congress is held in Riva del Garda. The association has a new name: Slow Food Italia. The international Presidia are launched at the fourth Salone del Gusto in Turin, and the third Biodiversity Award recipients are named. On November 8, European Commissioner Romano Prodi awards Petrini the Sicco Mansholt Prize for 2002, in recognition of his innovations in the field of agriculture.

2003: The Slow Food Foundation for Biodiversity is founded. During the International Convention on the Future of Food in Tuscany, Petrini collaborates on the Manifesto on the Future of Food with numerous leaders of the antiglobalization movement. On July 10, the Suor Orsola Benincasa Institute in Naples confers an honorary degree in anthropology on Petrini. Petrini is again named president at the fourth international congress of Slow Food on November 6 to 9. The first edition of "Aux Origines du Goût" is held.

2004: The Agenzia di Pollenzo, home to the University of Gastronomic Sciences and the Wine Bank, opens on April 30. The first students arrive at the university for the 2004–2005 academic year. The Slow Fish trade fair opens in Genoa in June. In early October, *Time* magazine names Petrini European Hero of the Year. The first Terra Madre assembly meets at the Palazzo del Lavoro in Turin on October 20 to 23. The fifth Salone del Gusto is held at the Lingotto in Turin. Slow Food Japan is born.

2005: On January 1, the Italian president names Petrini "Grande Ufficiale" of the Republic of Italy. The Slow Food master's program in Colorno is inaugurated in March. Slow Food UK is born. Slow Food now counts roughly eighty-three thousand members around the world.

GLOSSARY

AGENZIA DI POLLENZO: an agricultural complex in Pollenzo, near Bra, once owned by Italy's former royal family, the House of Savoy; now the campus for Slow Food's University of Gastronomic Sciences and Wine Bank.

ARCI (*ASSOCIAZIONE RICREATIVA CULTURALE ITALIANA*): a national cultural association traditionally supported by the Italian Left. The many local chapters of the Arci (pronounced "AR-chee") organize cultural activities such as festivals, debates, and sporting events. In 1983, Arci was restructured to provide greater independence to the different groups under its tutelage.

ARCI GOLA: a nationwide oeno-gastronomical league started in Bra in 1983 by Petrini and his associates. Officially established in 1986, Arci Gola (later known simply as Arcigola) was the forerunner to Slow Food, emphasizing the pleasures of conviviality and gastronomic knowledge, together with the preservation of vanishing food products.

ARCI LANGHE: the local Arci branch which Petrini and his colleagues joined in the late 1970s and used as an early platform for their activities. Their activities in Arci Langhe led to the formation of Arci Gola.

THE ARK OF TASTE: a compendium of endangered food products. Launched by Slow Food in 1997, the Ark documents disappearing local and regional specalities and animal breeds worldwide and seeks to preserve them in the face of a rising flood of mass-produced food products. See Presidia.

BAROLO: an intense red wine made from Nebbiolo grapes grown in the Langhe region of Piedmont, awarded Italy's top wine status, DOCG (*Denominazione di Origine Controllata e Garantita*), in 1980. Prominent producers include: Elio Altare, Massimo Martinelli, Bartolo Mascarello, Renato Ratti, Giovanni Battista Rinaldi, and Luciano Sandrone.

BRA: a small town in Piedmont, birthplace of Carlo Petrini and head-quarters for the Slow Food movement.

CANTÉ I'EUV (*"Singing for eggs" in Piedmontese dialect*): a traditional spring celebration in Piedmont, in which singers serenade farmers in exchange for food and wine. In 1979, the Arci Langhe launched an international Canté i'euv festival, with concerts in towns throughout the Langhe.

CIRCOLO LEONARDO COCITO: a cultural club founded by Petrini and his friends in 1971, named after a hero of the local resistance to Fascism.

CITTÀ SLOW (SLOW CITY ASSOCIATION): a movement launched in 1999 to promote the concept of "urban sustainability." Member cities commit to pursue environmental and urban preservation and the promotion of artisanal food production, among other goals.

CONVIVIA (*known as "Condotte" in Italy*): the local chapters of the Slow Food movement. Convivia organize food-related events, often working in conjunction with schools and local producers.

COOPERATIVA I TAROCCHI (*Cooperative of the tarots*): a management company for the various wine and food initiatives launched by Petrini and Arci Gola, founded in 1982.

FESTE DELL'UNITÀ: a massive annual summer cookout held in towns throughout Italy, organized by the PCI to raise funds for the party's newspaper, *L'Unità*.

GAMBERO ROSSO EDIZIONI: a media company born out of the gastro-nomic monthly, *Gambero Rosso,* originally launched by Stefano Bonilli and Arci Gola in 1986. In addition to the publishing firm, Bonilli's group now owns a satellite television channel devoted to gastronomy and a center for cooking classes, wine tastings, and other events.

IL MANIFESTO: a radical leftist newspaper launched in 1971, together with a small political party that debuted in the 1972 elections.

IN CAMPO ROSSO ("In Red Domain"): a radical leftist political journal in Bra published monthly by Petrini and the Circolo Cocito from 1974 until 1985.

L'UNITÀ: the official newspaper of the PCI.

LA GOLA: a monthly magazine devoted to food and food culture, launched by Gianni Sassi. The journal appeared from 1982 until 1988 and featured articles by writers, poets, and artists.

LIBERA E BENEMERITA ASSOCIAZIONE DEGLI AMICI DEL BAROLO (Free and meritorious association of the friends of Barolo): a loosely con-structed group with ties to Arci Langhe, founded in 1981 by Petrini with the goal of promoting the wines of Barolo.

OSTERIA ("tavern"): typically a simple, unpretentious restaurant offer-ing home-cooked food and regional specialties. Restaurants like Pina Bongiovanni's Osteria dell'Unione, and Maria Pagliasso's Boccondivino, located in the courtyard of the Slow Food offices in Bra, have played an important role in Slow Food's development.

PCI *(Partito comunista italiano):* the Italian Communist Party. In the 1970s, the PCI, led by Enrico Berlinguer, was the strongest Communist party in Europe. Berlinguer was the first to propose the idea of a grand coalition between the Communists and Italy's more conservative ruling party, the Christian Democrats.

PDUP (*Partito democratico di unità proletaria*): democratic party for proletarian unity, an independent leftist political party active in the 1970s. In 1976, Petrini was elected to the Bra city council as a member of the PDUP.

PRESIDIA: small-scale projects devoted to the preservation of a specific food product. The Presidia help artisan producers promote their foods, develop markets, and preserve their traditional production techniques. The Presidia are the working arm of the Ark of Taste.

RADIO BRA ONDE ROSSE (*Radio Bra Red Waves*): a pirate radio station launched by Petrini and his associates that was in operation from 1975 until 1978.

SALONE DEL GUSTO: a biennial trade fair devoted to artisanal food products held in Turin in October. Launched by Slow Food in 1996, the fair also features the products of the Presidia and numerous Taste Workshops (see below) on foods and wines.

SLOW FOOD EDITORE: the publishing arm of the Slow Food movement, founded in 1990. It produces the quarterly magazine, *Slow,* as well as the popular guidebook, *Osterie d'Italia.*

SLOW FOOD FOUNDATION FOR BIODIVERSITY: a nonprofit organization founded in 2003 and devoted to the defense of agricultural biodiversity around the world. The foundation dispenses the Slow Food Award for the Defense of Biodiversity.

SPACCIO DI UNITÀ POPOLARE (*"store of popular unity"*): a cooperative grocery store in Bra selling products from small local producers at reasonable prices, launched by Petrini and his associates in 1975.

TASTE WORKSHOP: a straightfoward educational event in which participants can taste food products while they are discussed and explained by the producers. A workshop might focus on a single product, or compare two or more similar products.

TENCO FESTIVAL: a three-day gathering of Italian and international singer-songwriters launched by the Tenco Club in Sanremo, which was founded in 1972 by Amilcare Rambaldi.

TERRA MADRE: Slow Food's "world meeting of food communities," first held in 2004. Terra Madre brings together farmers and food producers from around the world, with the goal of creating international networks of sustainable artisanal food production and distribution.

UNIVERSITY OF GASTRONOMIC SCIENCES: a fully accredited university launched by Slow Food in 2004. Located on two separate campuses, the university offers several undergraduate and graduate degrees in gastronomy, using an interdisciplinary curriculum with courses in history, literature, science, and economics.

VIA MENDICITÀ ISTRUITA: a small street in the town of Bra where Petrini and his associates had their first office. Slow Food International still has its main address there, and the name is often used to refer to the Slow Food headquarters.

VINITALY: Italy's largest wine trade fair, held in Verona in April. Starting in 1991, Slow Food experimented with presentations of regional food products during the fair, culminating in the "Grand Menu" presentation of 1994, a forerunner to the Salone del Gusto.

SELECTED BIBLIOGRAPHY

Ariès, P. *I figli di McDonald's. La globalizzazione dell'hamburger.* Bari: Dedalo, 2000.

Asor Rosa, A., ed. *La letteratura italiana Einaudi.* Milan: Einaudi-Mondadori Informatica, 2000.

Barbery, M. *Una golosità.* Milan: Garzanti, 2001.

Berry, W. *What Are People For?* New York: North Point Press, 1990.

Boccaccio, G. *Il Decameron.* Ed. Carlo Salinari. Bari: Laterza, 1969.

Borgna, G. *Storia della canzone italiana.* Milan: Mondadori, 1992.

Brackett, S., Moore, S., and Downing, W. *The Slow Food Guide to San Francisco.* White River Junction, Vermont: Chelsea Green, 2005.

Caracciolo, L., ed. "Il cibo e l'impegno." *Micromega* 1, 2 (2004).

Cassano, F. *Modernizzare stanca.* Bologna: Il Mulino, 2001.

Ceccarelli, F. *Lo stomaco della Repubblica.* Milan: Longanesi, 2000.

Codeluppi, V. *Il potere della marca: Disney, McDonald's, Nike e le altre.* Turin: Bollati Boringhieri, 2001.

Collodi, C. *Pinocchio*, translated by M. A. Murray, New York: Penguin, 1996.

Conte, P. *Le parole.* Turin: Umberto Allemandi, 1993.

Del Piano, M. *La Sagra di San Francesco di Lula.* Cagliari: Ettore Gasperini, 1972.

Eldredge, N., ed. *La vita sulla terra.* Turin: Codice, 2004.

Fernald, A., Milano, S., and Sardo, P., eds. *I Presìdi nel mondo. Cibi, culture, comunità.* Bra: Slow Food, 2004.

Gambera, A., ed. *Ricette delle osterie di Langa.* Bra: Slow Food, 1992.

Gho, P., ed. *Osterie d'Italia.* Bra: Arcigola Slow Food, 1990.

——, ed. *Osterie d'Italia 2005*. Bra: Slow Food, 2004.

Gionco, E. "La laguna di Orbetello: la pesca, l'allevamento e i prodotti trasformati." Laurea degree thesis, University of Milan, 2004.

Godard, M. *Il gusto dell'agro*. Bra: Slow Food, 1994.

Grandinetti, M. *I quotidiani in Italia 1943–1991*. Milan: Franco Angeli, 1992.

Grasso, A., ed. *Enciclopedia della televisione*. Milan: Garzanti, 1996.

Honoré, C. *In Praise of Slowness*. New York: HarperCollins, 2004.

Jaillette, J. C. *Les dossiers noirs de la Malbouffe*. Paris: Albin Michel, 2000.

Kiple, K. F., and Coneè Ornelas, K. *The Cambridge World History of Food*. Cambridge: Cambridge University Press, 2000.

Kuoljok, S., and Utsi, J. E. *The Sami: People of the Sun and Wind*. Lulea: Grafiska Huset, 1993.

Kummer, C. *The Pleasures of Slow Food*. San Francisco: Chronicle, 2002.

Lagorio, G. *Tra le mura stellate*. Milan: Mondadori, 1991.

Lancerini, E. "Territori lenti." Doctoral dissertation, Iuav University of Venice, 2004.

Lanchester, J. *Gola*. Parma: Guanda, 2002.

Lévi-Strauss, C. *Il crudo e il cotto*. Milan: Net Saggiatore, 2004.

Martins, P,. and Watson, B. *The Slow Food Guide to New York City: Restaurants, Markets, Bars*. White River Junction, Vermont: Chelsea Green, 2003.

Mereghetti, P. *Il Mereghetti: Dizionario dei film 2004*. Milan: Baldini Castoldi Dalai, 2003.

Milano, S., Ponzio, R., and Sardo, P. *L'Italia dei Presidi*. Bra: Slow Food, 2004.

Miravalle, S., and Vallinotto, M. *L'Insieme*. Piobesi d'Alba: Sorì, 2004.

Montalbán, M. V. *Millennio*. Milan: Feltrinelli, 2004.

Montanari, M. *Il cibo come cultura*. Bari: Laterza, 2004.

Negro, M. V., ed. *Terra Madre. Comunità del Cibo del mondo*. Bra: Slow Food, 2004.

Petrini, C., ed. *Guida ai Vini del Mondo*. Bra: Slow Food, 1992.

——. *Slow Food le ragioni del gusto*. Bari: Laterza, 2001.

Ratti, R. *Manuale del bevitore saggio*. Rome: Scalpi, 1974.

Revelli, N. *Il mondo dei vinti*. Turin: Einaudi, 1977.

Robinson, J. *Guida ai vitigni del mondo*. Bra: Slow Food, 1996.

Ruffa, G., and Monchiero, A., eds. *Il dizionario di Slow Food*. Bra: Slow Food, 2002.

Sardo, P., ed. *Il buon paese,* Bra: Slow Food, 1994 (and following years).

Scaramucci, B., and Ferretti, C. *RicordeRai 1924/1954/2004*. Rome: Rai Eri, 2003.

Schlosser, E. *Fast Food Nation*. New York: Houghton Mifflin, 2001.

Schneider, E. "La comunicazione della *corporate social responsibility* in una organizzazione *non profit*: il caso Slow Food." Laurea degree thesis, Bocconi University, 2004.

Scotellaro, G. "Radio Bra Onde Rosse: precursori senza discendenza?" Doctoral dissertation, University of Turin, 2004.

Segre, C., and Ossola, C. *Antologia della poesia italiana*. Turin: Einaudi, 1997.

Shiva, V. *Terra madre. Sopravvivere allo sviluppo*. Turin: Utet, 2004.

Stout, A. *The Old Gloucester. The Story of a Cattle Breed*. Gloucester: The Gloucester Cattle Society, 1993.

Tamani, E., ed. *Gli anni d'oro della cucina parmigiana*. Parma: Gazzetta di Parma, 2005.

Veronelli, L. *Alla ricerca dei cibi perduti*. Rome: Derive/Approdi, 2004.

ACKNOWLEDGMENTS

This book is the result of a collaboration between Carlo Petrini, the founder of Slow Food, and a journalist who appreciates the themes and commitments of the movement, yet is not one of its members.

I have to thank Carlin first, because he has agreed to tell this story. An honest, enthusiastic, and willing companion in many adventures, he was never reticent when asked questions.

A warm thanks goes to Clara, my wife, who believed in this book and, consummate editor that she is, helped me with her ideas and corrections; and to my daughter Alice, who has transcribed and translated the interviews from the Terra Madre assembly.

I am grateful to Rizzoli RCS Libri, and to Diego Pavesi for his attentive editing, as well as to Rizzoli International Publications, Inc. and its president and CEO, Marco Ausenda, whose fundamental and enthusiastic support has allowed me to overcome any obstacles in the way of this edition. Thanks also to those who helped put together this edition: Francesca Santovetti, translator; Anne O'Connor, copy editor; and Christopher Steighner, editor.

A special thanks goes to all the people—there were more than eighty—whom I interviewed, and to the entire Slow Food "galaxy," which has provided me with information, contacts, and suggestions. I would like to thank first the director of the press office, Valter Musso, along with Alessandra Abbona and Paola Nano. Thanks to Serena Milano and Raffaella Ponzio at the Slow Food Foundation for Biodiversity, for their help with the appendix of Presidia, and to Erika Lesser at Slow Food USA. Thanks also to the entire staff of Carlin's office in Bra:

Laura Bonino, Emanuele Enria, Marcello Marengo, and Carlo Bogliotti; and Fabio Bailo, Roberto Checchetto, Carla Coccolo, Luca Fabbri, Carlo Fanti, Anya Fernald, Anna Ferrero, Paola Gho, Simona Luparia, Raffaella Ponzio, Giovanni Ruffa, Anna Sulis, Robert LaValva, Ugo Vallauri, Sarah Weiner, Galdino Zara, and Bruna Sibile, who made it possible for me to look through the precious back issues of *La Gola*, *In Campo Rosso*, and *Slow Food* magazines.

I have gathered information also through the documentation center of *La Stampa*; the press office of the region of Tuscany (Paolo Ciampi and Daniele Pugliese); the press office of the University of Gastronomic Sciences in Pollenzo (Paolo Enria); the press office of the town of Bra (Raffaele Grillo); the Coop Italia (Sergio Soavi); and Alessandro Regoli and Irene Chiari of the "Winenews" web site.

A final thanks also to Lisetta Burlotto, Andrea Grignaffini, Laura Lajolo, Maria Teresa Mascarello, Sergio Miravalle, Beppe Rinaldi, Terenzio Vergnano, and to Salvatore Polo of the local action group of Montiferru Barigadu Sinis in the province of Oristano, Sardinia.

— Gigi Padovani, Turin, June 2006